Stabilization and Adjustment in Egypt

To my Mother and the memory of my Father

Stabilization and Adjustment in Egypt

Reform or De-Industrialization?

Gouda Abdel-Khalek

Faculty of Economics, Cairo University, Egypt

With a foreword by Ibrahim Shihata

Edward Elgar

Cheltenham, UK • Northampton, MA, USA

Published by
Edward Elgar Publishing Limited
Glensanda House
Montpellier Parade
Cheltenham
Glos GL50 1UA
UK

Edward Elgar Publishing, Inc.
136 West Street
Suite 202
Northampton
Massachusetts 01060
USA

A catalogue record for this book
is available from the British Library

Library of Congress Cataloguing in Publication Data
'Abd al-Khaliq, Judah.
Stabilization and adjustment in Egypt: reform or de-industrialization / Gouda Abdel-Khalek.
p. cm.
Includes bibliographical references and index.
1. Egypt–Economic policy. 2. Economic stabilization–Egypt. 3. Structural adjustment (Economics)–Egypt. 4. Industrialization–Egypt. I. Title

HC830 .A5254 2001
339.962–dc21

00.069502

ISBN 1 84064 620 9

Typeset by Manton Typesetters, Louth, Lincolnshire, UK.
Printed and bound in Great Britain by MPG Books Ltd, Bodmin, Cornwall.

Contents

List of tables vi
Acknowledgements ix
About the author xi
Foreword xii
Introduction xiv

1. Stabilization experience before the 1990s 1
2. Economic 'reform' in the 1990s 42
3. The macroeconomic effects of ERSAP: structural reform or Dutch disease? 57
4. The main features of the manufacturing sector 91
5. The microeconomic effects of ERSAP: 1. The aluminium industry 112
6. The microeconomic effects of ERSAP: 2. The iron and steel industry 132
7. ERSAP and industrialization: concluding remarks 155

Annexes 167
Bibliography 181
Index 189

Tables

1.1	Resource balance at current prices, 1974–1983/84	4
1.2	Oil exports, total exports and resource gap excluding oil exports, 1974–1983/84	5
1.3	Development of private sector's deposits with banks	7
1.4	Remittances and invisible receipts, 1975–1984/85	8
1.5	Structure of interest rates	10
1.6	Selected monetary indicators	11
1.7	Credit guidelines in the 1979–81 stabilization agreement	14
1.8	Selected fiscal indicators	16
1.9	Ratio of farm-gate prices to unit costs, constant-value prices and international prices of government-marketed agricultural crops, 1974–83	20
1.10	GDP sectoral shares and growth rates, 1969/70–1984/85	21
1.11	Balance of payment on capital account, 1974–1983/84	23
1.12	Financing current account deficit, 1974–1981/82	24
1.13	Long-term debt and debt burden	26
1.14	Relative magnitude of public sector, 1975–79	33
1.15	Inflation trends, 1965/66–1985	35
1A.1	Price formation during the 1970s and 1980s	40
2.1	Selected economic indicators, 1985/86–1991/92	43
2.2	Fiscal variables under ERSAP	45
2.3	Exchange rate for tariff purposes	47
2.4	Comparison of old and new public enterprise laws	48
2.5	Domestic production coverage of NTBs	50
2A.1	Trade liberalization measures under ERSAP, 1991–98	55
3.1	Trade balance, 1985/86–1995/96	59
3.2	Selected economic indicators, 1987/88–1995/96	60
3.3	Trade balance, implicit exchange rates and export/import ratios, 1978–1991/92	63
3.4	Direct and total intermediate import requirements, 1989/90	65
3.5	Real effective exchange rate, 1973–96	69
3.6	Deposit interest rate on Egyptian pound and libor rate for US$	70
3.7	Treasury bills issues, interest rates and international reserves	72

3.8	Deposits in the banking system, 1989–93	76
3.9	Development of nominal tariff rates mean and dispersion	79
3.10	Nominal and effective protection, 1986–96	80
4.1	GDP growth and structure, 1981/82–1995/96 in constant 1981/82 prices	93
4.2	Contribution of manufacturing to the economy, 1960/61–1995/96	96
4.3	Pattern of ownership in the manufacturing sector, 1975–1995/96	99
4.4	Relative importance of various manufacturing activities 1975–1995/96	102
4.5	Annual compound growth rates of the capital/labour ratio, total factor productivitity and average labour productivity, 1970–1986/87	105
4.6	Capital intensity in manufacturing, 1987/88–1995/96	106
4A.1	Development of manufacturing exports, 1981/82–1991/92 and targets for 1992/93–1996/97 at current prices	110
4A.2	The divergence between economic and financial profitability: single year estimates, FY 1980/81	111
5.1	Likely effects of ERSAP on EGYPTALUM	115
5.2	Electricity energy sold by EEA, 1992/93–1997/98	117
5.3	Development of sale price of electricity supplied to EGYPTALUM (ultra-high voltage), 1976–98	118
5.4	Standard and EGYPTALUM performance data	120
5.5	Cost vector for hot aluminium	121
5.6	Electricity consumption per tonne of aluminium	122
5.7	Export revenue of EGYPTALUM, 1984/85–1997/98	126
5.8	Sale prices of aluminium, 1986/87–1997/98	127
5.9	Development of product mix, 1983/84–1997/98	130
5A.1	Various phases of EGYPTALUM, design capacity expansion	131
6.1	Output, domestic sales and exports, 1984/85–1997/98	135
6.2	Labour, capital and factor intensity in HADISOLB	136
6.3	Equity, debt and leverage, 1984/85–1997/98	138
6.4	Output, electricity consumption and cost, 1987/88–1997/98	139
6.5	Electricity requirement per tonne of finished steel products	142
6.6	Energy input prices, 1973–97	144
6.7	Steel output, costs and prices of electricity, 1987/88–1997/98	146
6.8	Output quantity, value and price per tonne of steel, 1984/85–1997/98	149
6.9	Interest payments, wages, rent and value added, 1988/98–1997/98	151
6.10	Stock of finished steel at HADISOLB, 1990/91–1997/98	152

AI.1	Development of the exchange rate system and exchange rates, 1945–97	167
AII.1	Exchange rate 1973–97	168
AIII.1	Depletion rate of petroleum	173
AIV.1	Development of domestic energy prices under ERSAP	175

Acknowledgements

Many institutions and individuals have contributed to make the present work possible. The Central Agency for Public Mobilization and Statistics facilitated the fieldwork on which part of this research (the two industry case studies) is based.

Eng. Zaki Bassyouni, Chairman of the Aluminium Company of Egypt (EGYPTALUM) and the staff of the company, were supportive to the endeavour. The late Soliman Reda, former Chairman of EGYPTALUM and ex-minister of Industry and Mineral Wealth, was extremely helpful throughout the field work.

Eng. Ali Helmy, Chairman of the Egyptian Iron and Steel Company (HADISOLB) and staff of the company did their best to answer the author's queries, expressed their views, and provided valuable information. All this was vital for the completion of the work.

The Fondazione Eni Enrico Mattei (FEEM) gave financial support both for carrying out the research and for discussion of preliminary results in conferences in Cairo and Milan. Special acknowledgement is due to Dr. Giacomo Luciani, ENI's Deputy Director for International Strategies for his unfailing support throughout the various stages of the present work.

The author also acknowledges the help he received from individuals in various capacities. They are indeed too many to mention individually. But he would like to acknowledge helpful suggestions by participants of conferences and seminars both in Cairo and Milan in which various parts of the work were discussed.

In particular, special debt is owed to Ismail-Sabri Abdalla, Chairman, Third World Forum (Cairo Office); Ibrahim El-Issawy, INP, Cairo; Said El-Naggar, Society for New Appeal; Eng. Mohamed Abdel-Wahab, former Minister of Industry and Mineral Wealth; Karima Korayem, al-Azhar University; Monji Boughzala, University of Tunis; Chang-Po Yang, Senior World Bank Resident Economist in Egypt; Ibrahim Shihata, Vice-President and Legal Counselor, World Bank; Arvind Subramanian, former IMF Resident Representative in Cairo; Steven Yeo, Centre for Economic Policy Research, London; and Ahmed Galal, Director, Egyptian Center for Economic Research (ECES), Cairo.

To all these individuals and institutions, I express my appreciation and gratitude. But none is to be held responsible for the views and any errors of omission or commission except the author.

Last but not least, a word of special gratitude to Karima Korayem – a special colleague, sincere friend and dear wife. I am really so much indebted to her support and encouragement for getting the job done.

About the Author

Gouda Abdel-Khalek is Professor of Economics in the Faculty of Economics and Political Science at Cairo University, and holds a Ph.D. from McMaster University (Canada). He was advisor to various organizations, including Egypt's Energy Planning Agency and the National Bank of Egypt. As consultant, he served with the UN (ECA, ESCWA, UNU), the Population Council, and the International Development Research Centre (IDRC). He was senior Fulbright visiting scholar at Johns Hopkins University, visiting professor at UCLA, and also served as senior expert in the World Bank.

His publications include: *The Political Economy of Income Distribution in Egypt, Stabilization and Adjustment Policies and Programmes*, plus articles in *Cairo Papers in the Social Sciences*, *L'Egypte Contemporaine*, *Energy Economics*, and *Social Problems*.

In this vital and timely study, the author analyses the impact of Egypt's Economic Reform and Structural Adjustment Programme (ERSAP), at two distinct levels: macro and micro. At the macro level, he analyses the effects of ERSAP on variables including interest and exchange rates, domestic public debt, trade balance, budget deficit and inflation. According to the author, wrong sequencing and absence of an industrial-policy component are reasons for concern that ERSAP may lead to de-industrialization. His predictions of a widening trade deficit coupled with pressure on the pound and mounting domestic debt seem to be supported by latest developments and policy debates in Egypt.

This book will interest and inform practitioners, policy makers and scholars of economics, industrial economics, energy economics, development economics and development and area studies. The IMF and the World Bank may also benefit from the findings of this study in designing future reform packages.

Foreword

The author of this book is a well-known Egyptian economist who belongs to a highly respected opposition party with strong leftist leanings. His study does not however necessarily argue against Egypt's last Reform and Structural Adjustment Programme (ERSAP) that was supported by the IMF and the World Bank. It only attempts to show that some of the adverse effects attributed to that programme could have been avoided or minimized. Trade liberalization, lowering credit limits as well as raising interest rates and adjusting energy prices could have been better sequenced, the exchange rate regime could have been reworked to avoid the effective appreciation of the dollar-pegged Egyptian pound, fiscal retrenchment could have been modestly relaxed and capital mobility should have remained subject to some controls. The author's arguments are well presented, even though they run counter to a widely-held view that Egypt's ERSAP greatly improved its macro-economic conditions and would have even fared better if its implementation had gone faster, especially when it came to privatization and wage and price rationalization.

The author admits that the effect of ERSAP on the public sector-dominated Egyptian industry has been mixed. He argues, however, that deeper restructuring of major industries should have preceded or accompanied the introduction of reform measures. By way of example, he points to the iron and steel factory in Helwan (HADIDSOLB). It is doubtful however, that any restructuring could have saved that overstaffed enterprise and it continues to inflict huge losses on the economy. The author's ideological orientation seems to have prevented him from considering measures that, despite their socially undesirable effects in the short term, may present the only cure for a heavily subsidized and highly inefficient industry.

The author is right in pointing out to the misalignment of some fundamentals in the Egyptian economy after ERSAP – a local currency that kept appreciating (until recently), a rapidly rising domestic debt that is being serviced at the expense of vital social expenditures, a widening trade gap, and low saving and investment rates. One need not share the author's ideology to agree with this conclusion. Although the Egyptian economy after ERSAP seems, on the whole, to be in a much better shape, it still has a long way to go on the road of reform.

There are many lessons to be drawn by Egypt and other developing countries from the author's analysis of what went wrong in the implementation of Egypt's economic reform. The staff of the IMF and the World Bank may also have a hard look at the findings of this well-written study to make sure that similar pitfalls may be tackled in a timely manner in future reform programs.

Ibrahim Shihata
Former Senior Vice President and General Counsel
World Bank

Introduction

Egypt's economic reform and structural adjustment programme (known as ERSAP) has been under way since 1991. Coming after stabilization episodes in the 1970s and 1980s, it has already generated a great deal of interest on the part of the government, business, international organizations and the academic community. Naturally, different views of the programme have been expressed. Some are totally backing it, on the grounds that it represents a success story. In fact, the World Bank and the IMF consider ERSAP, in many ways, an example for other countries to follow. On the other hand, some are fiercely opposed to the programme. They resent its tendency to downsize the government, and fear that it may eventually have negative effects on growth and development. In addition, the negative social effects of ERSAP have also been a cause for concern. Occasionally, they may go even further to suggest alternative measures.

As the title indicates, the focus of the present study is on the impact of ERSAP on the industrialization of Egypt. The analysis of the effects of ERSAP is conducted at two distinct levels; the macro and the micro. At the macro level, we investigate the actual and/or likely effects of ERSAP on such variables as interest rate, exchange rate, domestic public debt, trade balance, budget deficit, inflation, saving, investment, growth and structure of GDP. At the micro level, two industry case studies are conducted in detail, since the focus of the study is on industrialization. The first case study is the aluminium industry and the second is the iron and steel industry. The reasons for the choice of these two industries should be explicitly declared from the beginning. Both are energy-intensive industries which are affected specifically and directly by one of ERSAP's main components: raising energy prices towards eventual parity with world prices. They are also usually considered essential to any serious industrialization effort. The two case studies are based partly on guided interviews with the help of a questionnaire and field visits to the Aluminium Company of Egypt (EGYPTALUM) and the Egyptian Iron and Steel Company (HADISOLB). EGYPTALUM is the only aluminium smelter and HADISOLB is the oldest integrated steel mill in Egypt. Both are among the largest industrial enterprises in the country. Although the two firms are in the public sector, they appear to have been affected differently by ERSAP. This indicates that the effects of ERSAP may depend more on the nature of the activity or industry than on the type of enterprise (public or private sector). It seems that the major difference here is that HADISOLB is an import-substituting firm, while EGYPTALUM has been conceived from the outset as an export project.

The study consists of seven chapters. Chapter 1 deals with the stabilization experiences in the 1970s and 1980s as precursors to ERSAP. Chapter 2 is concerned with the main components/measures of ERSAP. The focus here is on the essentials without getting bogged down in tiny details. Specifically, we deal with the following elements: macroeconomic reform, public enterprise reform, domestic price liberalization, foreign trade liberalization, private sector reform, and the Social Fund for Development.

The assessment of the effects of ERSAP is undertaken in Chapters 3, 5 and 6.

In Chapter 3, we deal with some of the macroeconomic effects. The analysis is conducted taking into account the external shocks to which the Egyptian economy was exposed, particularly in the late 1980s. Such external shocks manifest themselves in the gyrations of the main foreign-exchange sources: oil revenues, workers' remittances, Suez canal dues and tourism revenue. The assessment of ERSAP is also based on certain guiding principles, which serve as criteria for judging success. Such principles include growth, equity and employment generation – these being the most pressing tasks for Egypt in our view. Also as a basis for the assessment, the performance of the Egyptian economy since 1987/88 (the period immediately preceding ERSAP) is examined.

The assessment focusses on the two elements most closely related to industrialization: foreign-exchange reform and trade liberalization. Attention is given to the sequencing of these macroeconomic measures and its implications for the sustainability of reform. Foreign-exchange reform occupies a central place as a component of ERSAP. The changes in the foreign-exchange regime are thoroughly documented and the real exchange rate under ERSAP is estimated. Despite the devaluation of the Egyptian pound as part of the ERSAP package, there has been significant real appreciation. The implications of this development for the competitiveness of Egyptian industry and the prospects of industrialization are self-evident.

Several measures of trade liberalization have been implemented during the various phases of ERSAP. They involved both bringing down the average tariff height (through a series of tariff cuts), tariffication of non-tariff barriers, and reduction of tariff dispersion. The Harmonized Tariff System was also adopted. Chapter 3 contains a comparative analysis of Egypt's trade liberalization effort under ERSAP in terms of design, speed and sequencing. Clear distinction between trade liberalization and import liberalization is maintained throughout. The chapter also discusses the liberalization of capital transactions in the balance of payments. Issues of sequencing and sustainability are considered in detail here as well. The analysis demonstrates quite clearly that the so-called reform has actually generated clear Dutch disease symptoms.

In Chapter 4 we deal with the main features of the manufacturing sector within the broader context of the Egyptian economy prior to ERSAP. This involves first examining some sector indicators of manufacturing: growth and structural change, contribution to total value added, and share in total investment and exports. The issue of factor proportions and the related question of comparative advantage are also examined in this chapter. Available evidence suggests that Egypt may have been witnessing a process of de-industrialization prior to ERSAP. A relevant question therefore is whether ERSAP will sustain this trend or will reverse it.

From the macroeconomic analysis of Chapter 3 we move to the microeconomic analysis in Chapters 5 and 6. The analysis is conducted against the background of the development of the main features of the manufacturing sector in Chapter 4. Thus, Chapters 5 and 6 include two case studies for assessing the effects of ERSAP at the micro level: one study on the aluminium industry and the other on the iron and steel industry. These two studies are based on field work, organized around a questionnaire and discussions with officials of the two companies.

The case of the aluminium industry, where only one firm is involved, is examined in Chapter 5. Aluminium smelting is by far the most energy-intensive industry in Egypt. Energy in the form of electricity represents some 35 per cent of unit cost, and the activity uses 6–7 per cent of total annual electricity sales. ERSAP is likely to impact on aluminium smelting in a number of different ways: some of which are positive, the others negative. For example, raising energy prices is decisively the most important factor on the negative side. Devaluation may be the most significant factor on the positive side. Liberalizing input and output prices, trade liberalization, liberalizing interest rates, and abolition of credit ceilings also push in various directions. But overall, one may say that ERSAP will have a benign effect on aluminium smelting.

The question of the shadow price of electricity and determination of the long-run marginal cost (LRMC) of electricity is discussed at length in this chapter. This issue is central to any serious discussion of the prospects of the aluminium industry in the context of ERSAP. The analysis shows that the future of aluminium smelting may not be bleak, provided EGYPTALUM takes the necessary measures. Such measures fall within two distinct categories: measures necessary to cut cost through raising X-efficiency, and measures necessary to increase value added. Foremost in the first category are measures to reduce the specific energy consumption. Among measures of the second category, increasing the proportion of fabricated/semis to total production of aluminium and moving further downstream are the most important.

In Chapter 6 we take up the other case study in this volume: that of the iron and steel industry. To examine the likely effect of ERSAP on such basic industry, we have chosen to focus on the Egyptian Iron and Steel Company (HADISOLB). Established in the 1950s, this is the oldest integrated steel works in Egypt. As in the case of the aluminium industry, albeit to a lesser extent, steel production is an energy intensive activity. Coke is the most important input. The steel industry is also a highly capital intensive activity. HADISOLB is an ideal prototype of an import-substituting public sector enterprise which has been operating significantly below capacity in a non-competitive environment until recently. The company is also one of the largest in the industrial sector in Egypt in terms of employment; its work force is more than 20 000 strong. With regard to the likely effects of ERSAP on HADISOLB, the following measures are particularly relevant: raising energy prices, liberalizing interest rates, trade liberalization, aggregate demand deflation, and devaluation. These factors, as they impinge on HADISOLB, are discussed in detail in this chapter. The results of the questionnaire and field interviews regarding the views of HADISLOB's management on ERSAP are also reported in this chapter.

Chapter 7 is the concluding chapter. This chapter puts in perspective the relation between economic reform and industrialization. What are the prospects of industrialization under ERSAP? Will ERSAP lead eventually to industrialization or de-industrialization? Such questions constitute the heart of this chapter. It draws on the main findings of all the previous chapters.

POSTSCRIPT

Since the manuscript of this book was sent to the publisher, most recent developments seem to provide support to its main conclusions. There is now growing evidence that ERSAP has resulted in the de-industrialization of Egypt, as private investment in manufacturing failed to fill the vacuum resulting from the downsizing of the public sector. Although external debt was maintained at about US$ 28 billion, domestic public debt continued to mount, approaching LE 250 billion by end of June 2000 (representing 87 per cent of GDP). Pressures in the foreign-exchange market are increasingly felt as the trade deficit has increased, and the pound was recently devalued by about 15 per cent. There are public suggestions of imposing some discipline on imports to avoid the continued drawing down of international reserves of the country.

G.A.-K.

1. Stabilization experience before the 1990s

Our main emphasis in this volume is on the stabilization and structural adjustment experience in Egypt during the 1990s. However, it is useful, in the way of a background, to make a brief digression on the experience in the 1970s and 1980s. Discussion of such experience has to take into consideration that earlier programmes between Egypt and the IMF were either aborted or only partly implemented.

Although Egypt is a founding member of both the IMF and the World Bank, its relations with the two Bretton Woods institutions, particularly the Bank, was turbulent throughout the 1950s and much of the 1960s. The High Dam episode and later socialist transformation both constrained the relation between Egypt and the two institutions. During 1961–62 the country faced a foreign exchange crisis as a result of a number of unfavourable developments. There was a cotton crop failure and a fall in rice output which resulted in a significant drop in export proceeds. As a result, between 1960 and 1962 cotton exports fell by 38 per cent and total merchandise exports fell by 20 per cent. At the same time, Egypt had unavoidable standing commitments on capital account. Faced with a foreign exchange crisis, Egypt signed a stabilization agreement with the IMF in May 1962.

But the May 1962 stand-by agreement proved short-lived; it collapsed soon after it was signed. That was to be Egypt's only stand-by agreement with the Fund until the late 1970s. The shift in Egypt's policy orientation away from central planning and Arab socialism towards a market economy and *infitah* in the mid 1970s paved the road for more intensive relations with the IMF and the World Bank.

We examine the stabilization experience in the 1970s and 1980s in sequence.

STABILIZATION EXPERIENCE IN THE 1970s

As already mentioned, the adoption of the open-door policy (*infitah*) in the mid-1970s paved the way for more active relations between Egypt and the Bretton Woods institutions. Thus, two letters of intent were submitted by the

Egyptian government to the Fund in March 1977 and in June 1978. The first furnished the basis of a one-year stand-by arrangement, whereby Egypt was to receive SDR 125 million. The second laid the foundation for an Extended Fund Facility (EFF) in the amount of SDR 600 million, to be purchased by Egypt over a three-year period starting 1979. The 1979–81 EFF may indeed be considered a continuation of the 1977 stand-by arrangement. Therefore, the combined elements of both packages will be summarized under the following headings: structural reform measures; fiscal policy; monetary and credit policies; and exchange rate, trade and debt policies.

The Main Components

The *structural reform* involved planned changes in the organizational structure of the public sector, reducing direct control by government organs and placing the operations of public-sector enterprises on a sounder commercial basis, redefining cost/price relations to eliminate distortions, putting more emphasis on agriculture, and encouraging foreign investment. A number of elements were in line with the basic institutional and structural changes envisaged under the open-door economic policy, *infitah* (Abdel-Khalek, 1982).

The *fiscal policy* component of the package included measures aimed at reducing the ratio of the fiscal deficit to GDP, cutting subsidies – particularly for food, energy, and government services – and changing the basis of valuation of customs duties from the official to the commercial exchange rate.

In the field of *monetary and credit policies*, measures involved reducing the rate of credit creation and raising interest rates. Such measures were conceived as means of combating inflation, encouraging domestic saving through the financial system and encouraging asset substitution by shifting from foreign exchange balances into Egyptian pound balances.

The main measures in the field of *exchange rate and external trade and debt policy* were: devaluation-cum-unification of the exchange rate supported by managed floating, terminating bilateral trade-and-payments agreements, liberalizing imports, freeing external transactions and reducing reliance on short-term credit facilities. While the 1977–78 package stipulated also the gradual elimination of arrears on current payments, the 1979–81 package did not have a similar component, thanks to the long-term loan of the Gulf Organization for Development in Egypt (GODE). By virtue of this loan Egypt's short-term debt was converted into longer maturities.

The basic features of the above stabilization packages were similar to those concluded between the IMF and other developing countries (Killick, 1985; Williamson, 1982), perhaps with some variations reflecting the specificity of the Egyptian case in particular areas (such as the then dominant role of the public sector in the economy).

The Macroeconomic Effects

We now discuss the effect of the stabilization policies in the 1970s, focussing on a selected list of the measures adopted: devaluation, raising domestic interest rates, credit ceilings, fiscal measures, and structural reform.

Devaluation

The development of the exchange-rate system since 1945 and the values of the various nominal rates over the period 1973–97 are given in Annexes I and II. The devaluation of the 1970s started in effect in 1973 with the establishment of the parallel-market exchange rate. But the major step was taken during 1977–78, when a significant part of convertible currency transactions was shifted from the official rate of LE 0.39 to the US dollar to the then parallel rate of LE 0.70 per dollar.

However, some foreign exchange transactions continued unofficially (in the black market) carrying a premium of about 90 per cent above the official rate. The premium was cut down to less than 10 per cent with the devaluation of 1979. At the beginning of that year, all transactions were formally subjected to the new rate, actually implying a maxi devaluation of almost 80 per cent plus a number of mini devaluations.

In theory, real devaluation improves the trade balance if the export and import elasticities are such that the Marshall–Lerner condition is satisfied, *ceteris paribus*. Against this background, we test the hypothesis that the 1979 devaluation improved the trade balance. Our starting point is to establish whether the *nominal* devaluation indicated above has actually translated into lasting *real* devaluation. We thus examine the real exchange rate.

Available evidence shows very clearly that Egypt has maintained an inflation rate significantly above its main trading partners. During the period 1979–84, the rise in the general price level in Egypt (measured by CPI) outpaced the rise in the price level in its major trading partners by about 47 per cent.[1] Adopting a purchasing power parity approach, the real exchange rate index (1991=100) declined from 94.9 in 1979 (the devaluation year) to 51.3 in 1984 (Table 3.8). We thus conclude that despite the maxi devaluation of the official exchange rate from LE 0.391 to LE 0.70 per US dollar in 1979 and the devaluation of the declared rate in the authorized banks' pool from LE 0.70 to LE 0.832 per US dollar in 1981 (see Annex II), the pound appreciated significantly in the early 1980s. Nominal devaluation did not stick; it has not actually translated into lasting real depreciation.

For evidence on the effects of devaluation we examine the response of exports and imports. Table 1.1 shows that in the period 1974 to 1983/84 the current account deficit as a proportion of GDP peaked in 1979, reaching 19 per cent. The average for the two years 1978 and 1979 (the period during which devaluation actually took place) was 17 per cent. The data in Table 1.1 show that the relative magnitude of the current account deficit had declined after 1979, but it was still above the pre-devaluation average. At the same time the deficit rose in absolute terms after devaluation.

Table 1.1 Resource balance at current prices, 1974–1983/84

				C		I		
	GDP	M	X	CP	CG	IP	IG	Domestic absorption
1974	1.00	0.37	0.21	0.74	0.21	0.05	0.17	1.17
1975	1.00	0.41	0.20	0.63	0.25	0.12	0.22	1.22
1976	1.00	0.34	0.22	0.59	0.25	0.10	0.19	1.13
1977	1.00	0.33	0.22	0.62	0.20	0.07	0.22	1.11
1978	1.00	0.37	0.22	0.63	0.21	0.06	0.25	1.15
1979	1.00	0.48	0.30	0.69	0.17	0.08	0.25	1.19
1980/81	1.00	0.49	0.33	0.67	0.19	0.09	0.21	1.16
1981/82	1.00	0.47	0.32	0.64	0.21	0.09	0.21	1.15
1982/83	1.00	0.43	0.29	0.59	0.24	0.09	0.22	1.14
1983/84	1.00	0.45	0.29	0.63	0.25	0.09	0.19	1.16

Notes:
GDP = Gross Domestic Product
M = Imports of goods and non-factor services
X = Exports of goods and non-factor services
C = Total consumption
CP = Private consumption
CG = Government consumption
I = Total investment
IP = Private investment
IG = Government investment

Source: Based on data from Ministry of Planning, the Central Bank of Egypt and IBRD estimates as reported in World Bank, *Arab Republic of Egypt: Current Economic Situation and Medium-Term Prospects* (March 18, 1985), Table 2.3.

The observed decline in the ratio of the current account deficit to GDP noted above had very little to do with devaluation. It was exclusively due to the rise in the value of oil exports over the period. The weighted-average export price of Egypt's oil rose from $12.41 a barrel in January 1979 to a peak of $38.15 in January 1981. The value of oil exports jumped from $1261 million in 1978 to $2825 million in 1979 and to $4489 million in 1980/81 (World Bank, 1985). Table 1.2 shows that when oil exports are excluded, the resource gap as a proportion of GDP was much larger after devaluation than

Table 1.2 Oil exports, total exports and resource gap excluding oil exports, 1974–1983/84 (US$ million)

Year	Oil exports	Exports of goods and nfs excluding oil	Resource gap excluding oil exports: value	Resource gap excluding oil exports: as % of GDP
1974	98	792	824	19
1975	185	868	1286	25
1976	324	1174	1113	17
1977	400	1476	1294	16
1978	490	1640	1986	20
1979	1978	1799	4342	34
1980/81	3142	2638	5809	34
1981/82	3268	3195	6273	31
1982/83	2916	3832	6089	26
1983/84	3177	4725	7510	27

Source: Same as Table 1.1.

before. In fact the value of Egypt's non-oil exports fell steadily during the 1970s – both before and after devaluation.

On the other hand, imports continued to rise. As a proportion of GDP, they jumped from about one-third during 1976–77 to about 45 per cent during 1979–1981/82. Little information is available on the price responsiveness of demand for imports in Egypt for this period (El-Sheikh, 1980). But it cannot be concluded on the basis of the circumstantial evidence provided by the behaviour of the ratio of imports to GDP alone, that such responsiveness is nil. We suggest that, concurrently with devaluation, there was an upward shift in the import function caused by a number of factors: import liberalization, phasing out trade-and-payments agreements, increased remittances, broadening the scope of the own-import system, and increased capital inflows. These measures actually started under the stand-by agreement of 1977. Thus, out of 25 bilateral trade-and-payments agreements outstanding, only 12 remained by June 1978. By September 1981, the number was down to only four such agreements, two of which were with IMF members (the Sudan and the Peoples' Republic of China) and two with non-IMF members (the Soviet Union and North Korea).

But we conjecture that devaluation in and of itself was not to bring about a lasting improvement in the balance of payments. This was partly because the most important tradable commodities in Egypt were subject to the fix-price rule during this period. Administered, centrally determined prices, coupled with the system of government procurement of basic agricultural commodities, effectively divorced prices in local currency from foreign currency prices. In such a setting, the exchange rate adjustment, even if it were real, was bound to fail in providing an incentive for increasing the supply of exportables, particularly basic agricultural commodities. In fact, thanks to this institutional peculiarity, devaluation has failed to produce the requisite shift in the internal terms of trade in favour of tradables. Furthermore, it is most probable that devaluation has jeopardized the objective of encouraging the shift of resources to non-agricultural exportables by raising production costs, and hence reducing the competitiveness of exportables. This is especially true in view both of the high import content of the Egyptian non-agricultural output and devaluation-induced inflation.

Devaluation proved inflationary for a number of reasons. First, it produced an increase in the pound cost of imported inputs – both intermediate and capital goods. Second, it contributed to increasing the budget deficit and the resort to inflationary finance, at least in a first-round sense. Total budget deficit rose from LE 2097.7 million in 1978 to LE 2680.1 million in 1979, mainly because of devaluation. Bank finance of the deficit jumped from 16.7 per cent to 44.7 per cent (CBE, 1979, p. 4). This is clear evidence of the lack of fiscal discipline needed to support devaluation in producing the required expenditure-switching effects. Third, in view of the significant dollarization (tendency of residents to hold significant foreign currency deposits over the entire period – see Table 1.3) devaluation was a source of increasing domestic liquidity. The rationale is that revalued foreign currency deposits provided expanding collateral for bank credit.[2] As is clear from Table1.3, the pound value of private sector foreign currency deposits rose at a much higher rate after 1979; the average annual growth rate of these deposits rose from 38.5 per cent during 1977–79 to 60.7 per cent during 1979–1981/82. Actually, from its level in 1979, the pound value of foreign currency deposits doubled in 1980/81 and 1981/82. In addition to this, the wealth effect of devaluation appears to have been reflected in increased aggregate demand, some of which was naturally directed to imports. However, this runs counter to the theory of devaluation which assumes that the domestic hoarding schedule is unaffected by devaluation, and hence domestic monetary stock equilibrium would continue to prevail (Dornbusch, 1973). In Egypt's experience in the 1970s, dollarization partially stifled the expenditure-reducing effect of devaluation. Lack of data precludes estimating the exact magnitude of the wealth effect of devaluation in the 1970s. But as we shall see in the next section, the wealth effect in 1985/86 amounted to a significant 10 per cent of GDP.

The nature of the foreign exchange market during that period engendered exchange rate volatility. Despite several attempts throughout the various

Table 1.3 Development of private sector's deposits with banks (LE million)

End of period	1977	1978	1979	June 1980	1980/81	1981/82	1982/83	1983/84
Private Sector Deposits	1435	1931	2554	3185	4664	7356	9411	11472
1. demand deposits	782	945	855	995	1251	1513	1912	2061
2. time and savings (non-demand)	653	983	1699	2190	3413	5843	7499	9411
a. local currency deposits	237	365	907	1054	1679	2441	3484	5097
b. F/C deposits	416	618	792	1136	1734	3402	4015	4314
Shares of:								
non-demand to total	46	51	66	69	73	79	80	82
local currency deposits to non-demand	36	37	53	48	49	42	46	54

Notes: Foreign currency (F/C) deposits include foreign currency deposits of banks with the Central Bank of Egypt.
It is assumed that all foreign currency deposits are non-demand, which approximates reality, although it may not be absolutely correct. In 1983/84 foreign currency demand deposits represented only 10 per cent of total foreign currency deposits. There is no separate data on each of the two types of deposits before 1981/82.

Source: Central Bank of Egypt.

stabilization experiences at exchange rate unification, the 'law of one price' was far from applicable to the foreign exchange transactions during much of the 1970s and 1980s. In fact as the situation stood in the early 1980s, there were at least three markets with three main rates (see Annex I). But the black market rate constantly pushed the other rates up, engendering currency speculation and foreign exchange trading outside authorized banks (illegal during this period), continued to expand. The result was a growing preference for expatriate Egyptians to remit through the own-import system (see Table 1.4) – further depressing the value of the pound. This eventually led to the mini-devaluations which have brought down the 'declared parallel rate' from

Table 1.4 Remittances and invisible receipts, 1975–1984/85 (LE million)

	Remittances						
Year	Monetary (1)	IN	Own-imports (2)	IN	Total[4] (3)	Invisible Receipts (4)	(3) as % of (4) (5)
1975[1]	171.8	100	51.8	100	223.6	635.2	35.2
1976[1]	238.1	139	155.7	301	393.8	1317.9	29.9
1977[1]	358.2	208	267.2	516	625.4	1784.7	35.0
1978[1]	661.6	385	610.0	1178	1271.6	2410.0	52.8
1979/80[1]	792.6	461	1247.2	2408	2039.8	3459.5	59.0
1980/81[1]	854.4	497	1250.8	2415	2105.2	3834.9	54.9
1981/82[2]	532.7	310	842.7	1637	1375.4	3288.7	41.8
1982/83[2]	846.7	493	1312.0	2533	2158.7	5209.8	41.4
1983/84[2]	1057.0	615	1899.2	3666	2956.2	5873.1	50.3
1984/85[2]	724.3	422	2111.4[3]	4076	2835.7	5839.1	48.6

Notes:
IN Index Number
1 According to parallel-market exchange rate.
2 According to rates declared by the Central Bank as of August 1981.
3 Excludes resources for own imports provided by commercial banks (LE 25.9 million for 1984/85).
4 Monetary remittances are those foreign currency transfers by Egyptians working abroad exchanged for Egyptian pounds through the banking system according to the parallel exchange rate (prior to 1/8/1981) or the rate declared by the Central Bank (starting 1/8/1981). On the other hand, foreign currency deposited by those Egyptians in banks in Egypt are not included in remittances.
The total given in the table therefore is grossly underestimated on this account.

Sources: Remittances: The period 1975–1982/83, Shoura Council (1984), pp. 123 and 129. The period 1983/84–1984/85, Central Bank of Egypt, *Annual Report 1984/85*. Invisible Receipts: The period 1975–1981/82, Shoura Council (1984), p. 196, but applying parallel exchange rate. The period 1982/83–1984/85, Central Bank of Egypt, *Annual Report 1984/85*.

LE 0.70/US$ in 1979 to LE 1.33/US$ by the end of 1985 (see Annex II). In addition the easy use of foreign exchange, particularly the American dollar, both as a store of value and as a means of payment, has put the monetary system of the country virtually on a dual-currency basis. This has fostered further monetary instability.

Increasing domestic interest rates

As already mentioned, the rationale for this measure was twofold: to increase private saving through the financial institutions (financial deepening), and to encourage the conversion of dollar deposits to pound deposits (de-dollarization). Table 1.5 contains data on the development and structure of interest rate during 1976–83. It shows that nominal interest rates on time and savings deposits more than quadrupled between January 1976 and July 1982. The *effective* interest return was raised further by the removal of the 40 per cent withholding tax on interest income from deposits. Parallel to this, lending rates were raised. Despite such increases in nominal interest rates, the real interest rates continued to be negative throughout the period, with the possible exception of 1979 (see Table 1.5). Nevertheless, taking the consumer price index as given, the data in Table 1.5 show that there was an improvement in the real return on holding deposits, thanks to the increase in the nominal interest rate. This important development contributed to what McKinnon calls 'financial growth'.[3] This is confirmed by the data in Table 1.6, which indicate a dramatic rise in the ratio of time and savings deposits to money supply (M_1) from about 25 per cent in 1976–77 to 95 per cent in 1981–82.

But the response of time deposits to interest rate increases was not uniform across various maturities. According to one study, only time deposits with a maturity of one year or more have an interest elasticity significantly larger than one (NBE, 1985). The Central Bank of Egypt also attributed most of the increase in the private sector's time deposits to the administered increase in interest rates (CBE, 1985, p. 5). The share of one-year-or-more time deposits rose from almost nil in 1976 to one-fifth of non-government time deposits by the end of 1983 (NBE, 1985, p. 26).

More broadly, there has been a manifest change in the division of total private-sector bank deposits between demand and other deposits. The latter (which we shall call non-demand deposits for short) include deposits at cooperative and specialized banks, but apparently exclude Postal Saving deposits. The share of non-demand to total private sector deposits rose consistently and significantly over the period. From only 46 per cent at the end of 1977, it reached two-thirds by the end of 1979 and 83 per cent by the end of 1983/84 (see Table 1.3).

Raising domestic interest rates has also resulted in asset substitution in the form of a redistribution of private deposits between local currency and

Table 1.5 Structure of interest rates (percentages)

Effective from Rate (annualized)	Jan.1 1976	Mar.1 1977	Jun.1 1978	Jan.1 1979	Apr.1 1980	Jan.1 1980	Jan.1 1982	Aug.1 1981	Jul.1 1982	Dec.1 1983
Central Bank: discount rate	6.0	7.0	8.0	9.0	10.0	11.0	12.0	12.0	13.0	13.0
Commercial banks										
Time and savings deposits										
3 months	2.4	4.0	5.5	6.0	7.0	7.5	8.5	8.5	8.5	8.5
6 months	2.7	4.5	6.0	6.5	7.5	8.0	9.0	9.5	9.5	9.5
1 year	3.0	5.0	6.5	7.0	8.0	9.0	9.5	10.0	11.0	11.0
2 years	3.0	5.0	7.0	7.5	8.5	9.5	10.5	10.5	12.0	12.0
3 years	3.0	5.0	7.0	9.0	9.0	10.0	11.0	11.0	12.5	12.5
5 years	3.0	5.0	7.0	8.5	9.5	10.5	10.5	11.5	13.0	13.0
Savings	2.4	5.0	5.0	6.0	7.0	8.0	8.5	8.5	10.0	10.0
Lending rates										
minimum	7.0	8.0	9.0	10.0	11.0	12.0	13.0	13.0	13–15[1]	–
maximum	8.0	9.0	11.0	12.0	13.0	14.0	15.0	15.0	16.0[2]	–
Cotton or export related										
minimum	6.75	7.75	8.5	9.5	10.0	11.0	11.0	11.0	11.0	11.0
maximum	6.75	6.75	8.5	9.5	11.0	12.0	13.0	13.0	13.0	13.0
Real interest rate for										
3–5 year time deposit	–8.1	–6.1	–5.5	0.4	–14.2	–13.2	–1.1	–1.1	–1.8	–1.8

Notes:
1. Industrial sector maximum 13 per cent and service sector 13–15 per cent.
2. Commercial sector 16 per cent with no maximum.

Real interest rate: is calculated as the excess of the nominal interest for 3–5 year time deposits over official estimate of inflation rate measured by the consumer price index.

Source: Nominal interest rate: Central Bank of Egypt.

Table 1.6 *Selected monetary indicators (in millions of Egyptian pounds)*

	1976	1977	1978	1979	1980/81	1981/82	1982/83
Domestic credit	4565	5422	8673	11419	15192	20859	24022
Claims on government[1]	2896	3382	5955	7627	8303	11031	12485
Claims on private sector	441	647	818	1433	3329	5579	6903
Money and quasi-money	*2411*	*3185*	*4114*	*5211*	*8342*	*12044*	*15432*
Currency	1388	1750	2183	2657	3678	4688	6021
Private sector deposits	1023	1435	1931	2554	4664	7356	9411
a. demand deposits	540	782	948	855	1251	1513	1912
b. other deposits[2]	483	653	983	1699	3413	5843	7499
Private foreign currency[3]	–	416	618	792	1734	3402	4015
Public sector deposits	931	1331	1794	3026	4349	4973	5574

Notes:
1. Includes central and local governments only, and this excludes public sector enterprises and public authorities.
2. Includes cooperative and specialized banks.
3. Includes earmarked deposits.

Source: Central Bank of Egypt.

foreign currencies. The ratio of private local currency deposits to total private non-demand deposits rose from 36 per cent in 1977 to 53 per cent in 1979. Despite some decline in the ratio in 1980/81 and 1981/82, it climbed up again to 54 per cent in 1983/84.

But the increase in interest rates on bank deposits depressed the market value of government bonds (CBE, 1981, p. 30). A structural characteristic of the capital market in Egypt during this period, was that government securities were the most predominant type of bonds available. Thus, raising interest rates as part of the stabilization package has negatively affected private savings through the capital market (in the form of government bonds). Financial intermediation was therefore weakened rather than strengthened. In addition, it put the banking system in a better position to commit itself to financing longer-term projects than before. But the potential made possible by the increased availability of loanable funds appears to have been largely wasted because of the banking system's traditional aversion to less liquid but often more socially productive lending. Thus, while in 1979 bank loans to industry amounted to more than half of commercial banks' lending, the ratio was less than one-third in 1985. According to the Central Bank, corresponding ratios for trade and services combined were 40.5 per cent and 55.7 per cent for the two years respectively (see CBE, 1979 and 1985). This pattern seems to run counter to the one hypothesized by McKinnon, who argued that an increase in the real interest rate will encourage more productive investment (McKinnon, 1973).

On the other side of the ledger, raising interest rates should drive up the cost of production, on account of working capital. One can only conjecture here, since hard data are lacking. Such an ensuing rise in production costs will have different implications depending on the organizational form of the enterprise. Private sector enterprises will try to pass the higher costs on to final consumers. Ultimately, this will result in inflationary tendencies to the extent that interest payment is a significant element of cost. In this case, raising interest rates may actually defeat one of the basic purposes of the stabilization package – reducing the rate of inflation. As to public sector enterprises, where product prices were administered by the government during that period (see Appendix 1.1), the rise in interest rate will weaken their financial position. It eventually may lead either to heightened demand for subsidy support or increased pressure to raise output prices to avoid the risk of shutdown. The risk of shutdown should in effect be expected to increase for enterprises unable to adjust, thanks to yet another element of the stabilization package, namely, import liberalization.

In addition, raising interest rates in an economic environment where the government budget deficit is a permanent feature and where the deficit is partly bank-financed can only compound the problem of fiscal deficit. For example, in 1979 total net bank requirements from the government amounted to LE 7298 million (CBE, 1980, p. 14). The one-percentage-point increase in the lending interest rate such as that taking place effective January 1 1979 immediately means increased interest payments of more than LE 70 million. This consideration reveals the dangers involved in the partial implementation of the stabilization package.

In conclusion, several lessons can be drawn with respect to Egypt's experience with raising interest rates as a component of the stabilization package. First, care should be taken in the design of monetary and fiscal policies to ensure that measures will not result mainly in substituting one financial asset for another, when the intention is to increase total financial assets. Second, the essence of interest rate measures should be to increase financial intermediation. The crucial factor here is not the high nominal interest rate, but rather the real return on financial assets. This could be achieved by reducing the rate of inflation. We argue that, in McKinnon's terms, Egypt during the 1970s was on the verge of breaking out of financial repression and accomplishing financial growth. But the success eventually faltered because of the failure to bridge the fiscal gap (budget deficit). The objective of raising the real rate of return on financial assets is important, but in view of the institutional characteristics of the Egyptian economy (large bank-financed budget deficit), it should be achieved via reducing the rate of inflation rather than raising the nominal interest rate. The Egyptian experience provides yet another example of the dangers of a piecemeal approach.

Credit ceilings

Establishing credit ceilings was perhaps the most critical element of the IMF stabilization package. The theoretical basis for it is provided by the monetarist model of internal and external balance. In practical terms, the IMF stabilization packages invariably set specific guidelines for domestic credit expansion. Implementation of such guidelines is instrumental in the Fund's decision to authorize continuation of withdrawal of resources under the agreement.

Against the background of a rapid expansion of domestic credit at an annual rate averaging some 25 per cent during the period 1974–78, the letter of intent of June 10 1978 stipulated specific credit guidelines as shown in Table 1.7. Such guidelines limited the annual rate of overall credit expansion to about 15 per cent, with differential higher rate to the private sector.[4] But the actual growth rate of the domestic assets of commercial banks was 21.8 per cent in 1979 (see CBE, 1979, p. 131). This was two and a half times the real annual rate of growth of GDP of about 8 per cent. Aside from any monetarist paradigm, such a high growth rate of liquidity threatens to undermine macroeconomic stability. Experience in other countries under various

Table 1.7 Credit guidelines in the 1979–81 stabilization agreement

Ceiling on Date	Net domestic assets of banking system (1)	Net bank credit to the public sector (2)	(2) as % of (1) (3)
March 31, 1979	4173.7	3729.9	89
Sept. 30, 1978	4493.7	3789.9	84
Dec. 31, 1978	4808.7	4009.9	83
March 31, 1979	4723.7	3999.9	85
June 30, 1979	4978.7	4114.9	83

Source: Based on terms in the letter of intent dated June 10, 1978.

socio-political regimes has shown the dangers involved in disregarding monetary restraint.[5]

Irrespective of the justification for these credit and monetary policy measures, they must have had an impact on macro-variables of interest for our study. *Ceteris paribus*, such measures should moderate the growth of aggregate demand and the rate of inflation. But it is rather hard to single out their own effect because other factors have been at work simultaneously.

Let us consider the effect of enforcing differential credit ceilings in the manner shown above on efficiency and equity. Clearly, the stipulated credit ceilings would make it easier for the private sector to expand faster than the public sector. From an efficiency standpoint, the shift of resources toward the private sector could be a positive development only if private sector enterprises were more efficient. Its impact on equity may be easier to infer, although much depends on the nature of government policy and the type of private sector. In Egypt, where a tradition exists of the public sector providing basic goods and services, a shift of resources away from the government and the public sector would probably be less egalitarian.

Fiscal measures

Various fiscal measures were included in the Extended Fund Facility (EFF) of 1979–81, including modifying the tax structure to increase the elasticity of the tax system, raising service charges of the government and the public sector, and so on. Such measures were aimed to bring down the fiscal deficit from 27 per cent of GDP in 1978 to 16 per cent in 1981.[6]

The goal of reducing the budget deficit may be defended on several grounds. First, it may help to reduce foreign indebtedness, since the budget deficit is partly foreign-financed. Second, it may promote price stability, since part of the deficit is bank-financed. During 1976–78, gross public sector deficit was 40 per cent foreign-financed and 35 per cent bank-financed. This clearly underlined the need for budget restraint, and may provide the rationale for the differential ceiling on net bank credit to the public sector. But it should be noted that inflation in Egypt cannot be exclusively viewed as a demand-pull phenomenon; it is also partly cost-push. In the dynamic context of devaluation-cum-foreign finance, monetary expansion may also be an *effect* as well as a *cause* of ensuing inflation. Under passive monetary policy, money supply may rise in order to accommodate the increased transactions demand for money caused by devaluation and foreign finance. But such a monetary stance may defeat the ultimate purpose of devaluation.

The fiscal deficit in Egypt during the stabilization episodes in the 1970s and 1980s included the position of public-sector entities in addition to that of the government in the narrow sense. Thus, on the revenue side, it included transferred profits and investment self-financing by public-sector enterprises.[7] On the expenditure side, it includes the current deficit and investment expenditure of public economic authorities. In this context, a process of reducing the proportion of public-sector deficit should be carefully designed, phased, and implemented such as to avoid either endangering social equity or undermining the growth prospects of the economy. Against this background, one can discuss the specifics of the fiscal measures embodied in the EFF of 1979–81, and their implications for macro-variables.

According to the letter of intent of 1978, the Egyptian government expressed the commitment that during the programme years subsidy expenditure growth would be at a rate significantly below that of overall public expenditure. Subsidy expenditure did not actually represent an excessively large proportion of overall public expenditure in late 1970s early 1980s; for the three years immediately preceding the programme period, it averaged only 14 per cent of total public expenditure (see Table 1.8). Nevertheless, considering that Egypt imported about 60 per cent of its food consumption, subsidy expenditure was very significant from a balance-of-payments point of view.

Moreover, food subsidies accounted for a significant proportion of the expenditure of low-income groups. For example, according to the results of the Household Budget Survey for 1974/75, 60 per cent of the urban population in Egypt was spending one-fifth to one-half of their total budget on the main subsidized food items (Korayem, 1982). In 1981/82, transfers through the subsidy system contributed about 13 per cent and 18 per cent of the expenditure of the poorest quartile in urban and rural areas, respectively (Alderman and von Braun, 1984). As a result, they have contributed to a more egalitarian income distribution (El-Edel, 1982; Korayem, 1982). Hence, subsidy expenditure was also important from a social-equity viewpoint.

Table 1.8 Selected fiscal indicators (LE million)

Year	1976	1977	1978	1979	1980/81	1981/82	1982/83
Total public revenue	*2015.3*	*2755.4*	*3306.3*	*3683.8*	*7372.8*	*8230.6*	*10160.1*
Government current expenditure	1670.0	1701.0	2037.0	2494.7	3691.0	4893.5	6374.2
Public economic authorities' current deficit	42.0	55.0	58.0	60.0	67.3	100.4	127.6
Subsidies	434.0	650.0	710.0	1352.0	2166.4	2192.1	2053.6
Net capital expenditure [1]	154.0	214.0	443.0	643.0	864.9	1030.0	1170.7
Investment expenditure	980.0	1549.0	2311.0	2547.0	3675.6	4671.0	5007.0
Total public expenditure	*3280.0*	*4169.0*	*5559.0*	*7098.7*	*10555.2*	*12887.2*	*14733.1*
Overall public-sector deficit	1264.7	1413.6	2252.7	3412.9	3182.4	4656.5	4573.0
External financing	488.0	602.0	882.0	1135.3	1101.9	1212.4	1361.5
Domestic financing	*776.7*	*805.6*	*1370.7*	*2277.6*	*2080.5*	*3444.1*	*3211.5*
non-bank	339.7	334.6	453.7	695.0	1206.4	1261.4	1997.6
bank	437.0	471.0	827.0	1582.6	874.1	2182.7	1213.9
GDP at current market prices	6727.0	8344.0	9795.0	12705.0	17320.0	20221.0	23227.0
Public sector deficit as % of GDP	18.8	16.9	23.0	26.9	18.4	23.0	19.0
Subsidies as % of public expenditure	13.2	15.6	12.8	19.1	20.5	17.0	14.0

Notes: 1. Includes instalment on government debt (domestic plus foreign), net capital transfers to public economic authorities and public-sector companies, and miscellaneous.

Source: Ministry of Finance.

But irrespective of the rationale for reducing the proportion of subsidies to total public expenditure, the ratio was effectively cut. Although subsidy expenditure rose in absolute terms from LE 710 million in 1978 to LE 1352 million in 1979, and in relative terms from about 13 per cent to about 19 per cent of public spending between 1978 and 1979 (Table 1.8), such a rise was more apparent than real. The figures for the period starting 1978 are not comparable to pre-1978 ones. Starting in 1978, there was the *de facto* maxi devaluation of the pound by almost 80 per cent, which arithmetically meant a higher value for subsidies in Egyptian pounds. The increase in the pound value due to devaluation must have been particularly large in the case of food subsidy expenditure in view of its high import content. Whether correction for this devaluation-induced increase in subsidy expenditure would in itself result in a lower proportion of the latter to total government expenditure is open to question; the available data are too scanty to enable making the appropriate correction. But as subsidies stagnated even in nominal terms in 1981/82, and declined in 1982/83 (see Table 1.8), there clearly was a drop in the ratio of subsidies to government expenditure. Thus, the IMF line was *actually* followed despite the discontinuation of the EFF agreement.

Structural reform

The centrepiece of structural reform as conceived by the IMF is the removal of cost/price distortions. It is argued in numerous IMF and World Bank publications that such distortions have restrained output growth and hindered the process of reallocating resources to investment.

As is well known, the structure of relative prices can be manipulated to serve many purposes – economic and non-economic. The strong emphasis placed by the Fund on market forces as a determinant of allocative efficiency and hence the rationality of the price structure may seem unwarranted in view of the established literature on market failure,[8] and the structuralist debate in the 1950s and 1960s (Seers in Jansen, 1983). Consider the debate on energy prices. The IMF and the World Bank have strongly argued that energy is one of the most blatant examples of price distortions in the Egyptian economy. Their argument is that energy is significantly underpriced, in the sense that domestic sale prices of energy products in Egypt are much lower than world energy prices. Consequently, the Bretton Woods institutions have repeatedly maintained that energy prices should be raised towards the international level (World Bank, 1983, 1985; IMF, 1985).

As this prescription recurs in the Bank and Fund documents on Egypt, it should perhaps be discussed in somewhat greater detail. First, we should demystify the so-called 'international prices' of oil. No convincing justification has been given for adopting such prices as the norm. The fact that Egypt is a price taker on the world oil market does not justify the adoption of such prices as the measure of the domestic value of oil. It was argued elsewhere that the shadow price or scarcity value of oil for Egypt may perhaps be much higher than the world price (Abdel-Khalek, 1982; Dervis et al., 1984). We have proved this formally using a two-period model of oil extraction (see Annex III). This is based on the concept of scarcity premium for depletable resources – given the fact that the production/reserve ratio (the inverse of the rate of depletion) in Egypt is much higher compared to that of the world as a whole. The oil depletion rate in Egypt – given proven reserves and the rate of annual production – is almost 3–4 times that for the world. That should not mean of, of course, raising actual prices to the extent thus warranted on this basis, but rather using this shadow value for investment planning and resource allocation. Second, the domestic price of oil is a national parameter. It should mesh in with other parameters of the economy. For example, one cannot ignore the existence of significant *per capita* income differentials among countries; it may not be appropriate to fix the same price for energy in high-income and low-income countries.

Third, the argument for raising the domestic price of energy products could be put on a more solid basis. This is derived from the strong evidence that the real relative price of energy in Egypt exhibited a downward trend over the entire period from the late 1960s through to the early 1980s (Abdel-Khalek, 1988). A case may thus be made for putting real energy prices back in line with other prices in the economy. But it does not necessarily follow that raising it to the level of world prices is the appropriate course of policy. Considering that 85 per cent of the domestic consumption of oil is intermediate, raising domestic energy prices given these structural characteristics may result in a significant reduction in effective protection. Furthermore, due to the 'excise-tax' effect, raising domestic energy prices is bound to reduce aggregate demand, thanks to its negative effect on real incomes.

In this regard, it is significant that the World Bank has advocated a policy package involving both an exchange rate devaluation and a domestic oil price increase simultaneously. The devaluation component of the package is to be designed so as to compensate for the increase in domestic costs due to the higher energy prices (World Bank, 1983, p. 79). Such spillover effects would be significant in view of the low price elasticity of energy consumption in Egypt (Abdel-Khalek, 1988). In the context, therefore, of this price rigidity of energy consumption, the negative effects of the package on aggregate economic activity, on resource allocation to industry and on equity, must be weighed against any possible balance-of-payment benefits.

The upshot is that the domestic price/world price differential for energy is not always very meaningful as an indication of price distortion. Adopting IMF and World Bank suggestions in this regard may actually be destabilizing. It would result in increased vulnerability through tying the Egyptian economy to the gyrations of the world oil market. It would also endanger the standard of living of the poor. But our argument against pegging the domestic sale price of energy to world prices should not rule out the need for corrective measures to remove genuine cost/price distortions in the energy sector. Perhaps the more important aspect of energy pricing is the need to safeguard intergenerational equity and to ensure sustainability. That necessitates recognition of the fact that energy resources in Egypt are finite. More attention should be given to resource depletion and the optimal rate of oil production. Following the world price norm ignores these fundamentals, as we demonstrate rigorously with the help of the model in Annex III.

In addition to energy, two main areas stood out as priority areas for correcting cost/price distortions during this period, namely, basic agricultural products and public-sector products. In these areas, considerations of revenue generation and consumer subsidization are closely linked. The price determination rules applying to various factor and commodity markets during the period through the early 1980s are given in Appendix 1.1. As to agricultural products, private profitability of the basic agricultural products sustained a substantial decline over the decade 1974–83. Thus, the ratio of farm-gate price to unit production costs fell by 28 per cent for cotton, 21 per cent for wheat, 46 per cent for broad beans, and 50 per cent for sugar cane. Rice was the only case of a relatively small decline (see Table 1.9). Cotton, rice, and sugar cane were the most important summer crops marketed by the government during the period (in the late 1970s to the early 1980s); they accounted for nearly half the total cultivated area during 1977–83. Wheat and broad beans were the most important winter crops marketed by the government during the same period; they accounted for about one third of the cultivated area during 1977–83.

But the really crucial problem of pricing within the agricultural sector relates to the internal terms of trade between tradables and non-tradables. The most important tradables are the crops mentioned above (except sugar cane) in addition to maize. The most important non-tradables comprise Egyptian clover (*berseem*), which accounted for 55.3 per cent of the cultivated area of winter crops during the late 1970s–early 1980s. It is interesting to note that the devaluation of the 1970s failed to divert agricultural resources from the production of non-tradables to tradables (*berseem vs.* wheat in the case of winter crops). This may be attributed mainly to the rules of price formation applied in each case. While *berseem* prices were completely left to the free play of market forces, domestic wheat prices were highly controlled by the government and insulated from world prices in pursuit of social objectives (subsidization of urban consumers). Food aid helped bolster the effect of government policy of wheat subsidization to consumers. The problem was not necessarily with the objective (of subsidizing the poor), but rather with the means (administered prices coupled with compulsory delivery).

Table 1.9 Ratio of farm-gate prices to unit costs, constant-value prices and international prices of government-marketed agricultural crops, 1974–83

	1974			1979			1983		
Group	a	b	c	a	b	c	a	b	c
Cotton	152	98	39	185	117	52	109	81	88
Wheat	347	96	45	181	78	83	273	67	82
Broad beans	303	111	99	184	197	180	165	97	n.a.
Winter onions	177	110	26	123	155	32	139	132	33
Rice	137	88	18	133	99	66	131	94	48
Sugar cane	219	168	n.a.	188	199	n.a.	109	158	n.a.
Sesame	225	112	n.a.	166	186	n.a.	197	169	n.a.
Peanut	203	89	n.a.	203	124	n.a.	147	108	n.a.

Notes:
a = ratio of farm-gate prices to unit production costs.
b = ratio of farm-gate prices to national farm-gate prices ensuring constant value in terms of the rural cost of living index. This is in a sense a partial terms of trade.
c = ratio of farm-gate prices to international prices.

Source: Shoura Council (1985), Tables 31, 32 and 33.

Administrative procurement prices and compulsory delivery effectively amounted to an implicit tax on local wheat producers. The story was much the same for other main agricultural tradable crops, namely cotton and rice. The rate of the implicit tax exceeded 80 per cent for cotton and 50 per cent for rice during 1973/74–1975/76 (Korayem, in Abdel-Khalek and Tignor, 1982). Pricing policy appears to have thwarted the potential incentive effect of devaluation on the production of tradables. Available evidence shows that over the period 1980–93, the weighted average price of non-tradables rose by 230.8 per cent compared to only 189.9 per cent for tradables – taking 1986/87 as a base year. (El-Khawaga, 1996, p. 90). This generated an interesting and unfamiliar version of Dutch disease.

The EFF package dealing with structural reform emphasized the need to allocate more resources to agriculture. One cannot overestimate the need to strengthen the agricultural base of the Egyptian economy. Available evidence strongly suggests that agriculture has lagged behind the entire economy over the decade of the 1970s (Abdel-Khalek, 1982). Its GDP share has fallen from almost one-third to about one-fifth (see Table 1.10). During that period, the country imported about half of its food requirements and as much as 75 per

Table 1.10 GDP sectoral shares and growth rates, 1969/70–1984/85 (in 1975 prices)

Sector					Average growth		Annual rates
	1969/70	1977	1981/82	1984/85	1969/70 1977	1977 81/82	1981/82 84/83
Agriculture	31.1	22.7	17.3	16.6	2.0	2.6	2.9
Industry and mining	15.6	15.4	13.9	14.6	6.6	6.8	10.3
Petroleum and products	5.1	5.8	6.9	15.9	8.8	14.5	13.6
Electricity	1.0	1.3	1.1	0.7	10.8	5.4	10.7
Construction	6.2	4.9	5.4	4.5	3.0	12.8	6.7
Commodity sectors I[a]	53.9	44.3	37.7	36.4	3.7	5.4	6.3
Commodity sectors II[a]	59.0	50.1	44.6	52.3	4.2	6.6	7.6
Trans., comm. and storage	3.5	6.8	6.7	6.1	17.2	9.4	8.9
Suez Canal	0.0	2.5	4.1	2.6	–	24.0	0.4
Trade, finance and insur.	14.8	19.3	22.7	19.8	10.8	14.2	8.1
Hotels and restaurants	1.9	1.7	1.5	1.1	4.4	6.5	6.6
Productive services	20.2	30.3	35.0	29.6	13.1	13.8	7.4
Real estate	4.5	3.7	3.6	2.0	3.7	8.7	9.5
Public utilities	0.3	0.3	0.3	0.3	8.8	8.1	8.3
Social and personal serv.	5.5	4.2	4.2	4.2	2.8	9.6	8.3
Public services[b]	10.6	11.4	12.3	11.6	7.8	12.1	6.1
Social services	20.9	19.6	20.4	18.1	5.8	10.9	7.2
Total GDP	100.0	100.0	100.0	100.0	6.7	9.7	7.5

Notes:
a. I excludes petroleum and products, II includes them.
b. Public services include social insurance.

Sources: 1969/70–1981/82, MOP, *General Detailed Frame: Five-Year Plan for Economic and Social Development 1982/83 – 1986/87, Vol. I: Main Components*, Cairo: The Ministry, Nov. 1982, Tables 1 and 2.

cent of its wheat consumption. The poor performance of the sector may be explained partly by changing consumption patterns and labour migration, but also partly by the deterioration in the terms of trade of the agricultural sector (see Table 1.9); and Shoura Council, 1985, pp. 47–8).[9] Attracting more resources to agriculture, which is one aspect of the structural-reform component of the stabilization package, clearly requires *both* changing the incentive structure towards more favourable terms of trade for the sector as a whole, *and* giving better incentives to tradable agricultural products. But establishing the right incentive structure for agriculture necessitates price decontrol, a measure which was held back until the mid 1980s.

The manufacturing sector has also suffered the same fate as agriculture in the sense that it sustained serious cost/price distortions (Shoura Council,

1985; World Bank, 1983). As a result, manufacturing has been losing ground both in terms of its share in GDP (see Table 1.10) and its contribution to merchandise exports. The 1979–81 package did not have enough effective measures to address the problems besetting the manufacturing sector.

The basic structural problem of the Egyptian economy therefore has been that, aside from oil, the commodity-producing sectors have lagged behind. This has undermined the long-run growth potential of the economy, and has made the task of short-run management increasingly difficult. It is in this broader context that one should consider the selection of agriculture as a priority sector in the stabilization package of the 1970s. It may be argued that such priority should be extended to the other commodity sectors, notably manufacturing. In this context certain elements of the stabilization package, namely raising domestic energy prices to the level of world prices, raising interest rates and import liberalization, were inimical to manufacturing. If the intention of the package was to downsize this sector even further, then it was certainly well-designed. If, on the other hand, the intention was to encourage it, then the package suffered at the very least from internal inconsistency. Irrespective of the intention, however, manufacturing lost ground during the stabilization episode of the 1970s, and this decline cannot be divorced from certain elements of the stabilization package. The IMF package may have led to a process of de-industrialization.

STABILIZATION EXPERIENCE IN THE 1980s

As already mentioned, the 1977–78 and the 1979–81 stabilization packages were not fully implemented. Thanks to the large capital flows that Egypt received after 1979, she was able to cover its current account deficit without IMF official support. Annual net inflows for the period 1979–1981/82 averaged 119 per cent of the current account deficit (see Tables 1.11 and 1.12). Another booster was the second jump in oil prices in 1979–80. As a result, Egypt adopted an eclectic attitude towards stabilization. The government continued to implement certain elements of the EFF package such as devaluation (see Annex II), raising domestic interest rates (see Table 1.5) and reducing subsidies (see Table 1.8). With regard to devaluation, a partial and gradual approach was preferred to radical change. As shown in Annex II, during 1980/81–1986/87, the newly emerging Authorized Banks' Pool declared rate was devalued in 1981 by 19 per cent and another new declared rate was introduced in 1985 involving some 55 per cent devaluation. The latter was further devalued to LE 1.329/$ before it was replaced by the flexible rate (LE 1.362/$) in July 1986. The shift from the Authorized Banks' Pool exchange rate to the premium rate implied a nominal devaluation of

Table 1.11 *Balance of payment on capital account, 1974–1983/84 (million US dollars)*

	1974	1975	1976	1977	1978	1979	1980/81	1981/82	1982/83	1983/84
1. Current account balance	–1596	–2426	–1363	–1456	–1361	–1915	–2348	–3501	–2715	–3299
2. Autonomous capital flows	156	495	1091	1207	1528	2527	2280	2315	2512	2928
Direct investment	87	225	444	477	387	1275	836	885	966	897
Official loans (net)	–12	210	490	803	1028	890	1220	1385	1257	1762
Private loans (net)	90	59	157	–73	113	262	224	45	289	269
3. Balance on autonomous transactions	–1440	–1931	–272	–249	167	612	–68	–1186	–203	–371
4. Medium term BP financing	1261	1506	780	1601	809	72	–	–	–	–
Grants	1261	986	705	382	291	72	–	–	–	–
Loans	–	520	75	1219	518	–	–	–	–	–
5. Balance on non-monetary transactions	–179	–425	508	1352	976	684	–68	–1186	–203	–371

Notes: * Estimated

Sources: Central Bank of Egypt, IMF and World Bank staff estimates as quoted in World Bank (1985) Table 3.2. It should be noted that the World Bank gives another series for the current account balance different from that given above, significantly for some years. See World Bank (1983), Table B.8. The older data were disregarded.

Table 1.12 Financing current account deficit, 1974–1981/82 (LE million)

	Current account deficit		Net transfers		Net capital flows		Change in net foreign assets	
	Value	%	Value	%	Value	%	Value	%
At official rates								
1974	532.7	100	405.2	76.0	157.7	29.6	–30.2	–5.6
1975	968.6	100	421.3	43.5	695.3	71.8	–148.0	–15.3
1976	593.0	100	278.1	46.9	346.0	58.3	–31.1	–5.2
1977	493.0	100	174.2	35.3	388.0	78.7	–69.1	–14.0
1978	498.4	100	135.0	27.1	412.0	82.7	–48.6	–9.8
1974–78	3085.8	100	1413.8	45.8	1999.0	64.8	–327.0	–10.6
At incentive rates								
1979/80	561.2	100	65.3	11.6	1217.0	217.1	–721.1	–128.7
1980/81	1101.4	100	43.9	4.0	853.9	77.5	+203.6	+18.5
1981/82	1889.5	100	35.7	1.9	2163.9	114.5	–310.1	–16.4
1979/80–1981/82	3552.1	100	144.9	4.1	4234.8	119.2	–827.6	–23.3

Source: Shoura Council (1984), pp. 118–19.

62.4 per cent and resulted in an increase in domestic liquidity in 1985/86 by about 27 per cent, mainly due to the increase in quasi money by 37 per cent (CBE, *Annual Report 1985/86*, p. 26). This reversed the trend decline in the growth rate of domestic liquidity (M_2) since 1981/82. During 1985/86 foreign currency deposits expressed in Egyptian pound rose from LE 6.7 billion to 11.0 billion. This represents a rate of increase of about 64 per cent overall, and by 54 per cent due to devaluation. The conclusion is that devaluation in a dollarized economy is partly expansionary. Moreover, when we relate the increase in the value of foreign currency deposits due to devaluation (0.54 × LE 6.7 billion = LE 3.6 billion) to GDP for 1985/86 (= LE 36.4 billion), we obtain an estimate of the relative magnitude of the wealth effect of devaluation of about 10 per cent of GDP. That is quite substantial.

Other elements of stabilization, notably the budget deficit and credit ceilings, were not observed. On the whole, it may be said that Egypt continued to some extent along IMF-suggested policy lines without formal agreement (Korayem, 1986).

But the situation changed drastically in 1984/85. Old debt outstanding, particularly that owed to the Gulf Organization for Development in Egypt (GODE), fell due. At the same time long-term capital flows tapered off, and in 1981/82–1982/83 they fell short of debt repayment obligations, which approached two-thirds of merchandise exports (see Table 1.13). In addition to this, oil prices turned suddenly and drastically downward. For 1985/86, it was estimated that the drop in foreign exchange receipts in view of the deteriorating oil situation (both in terms of falling prices and reduced export volume) may reach some US$1200 million. In addition, oil fortunes in the case of Egypt also affect at least two of the country's major sources of foreign exchange; Suez Canal dues and workers' remittances.

This provides the background to the stabilization package in the 1980s, formally concluded in May 1987, after a long period of protracted negotiations. Under the terms of the stand-by agreement, the Fund was to support an economic and financial programme to be implemented by the Egyptian government, authorizing purchases of up to SDR 250 million (about US$327 million) through November 1988.

The Main Components

The broad objectives of the stand-by programme are: preparing the ground for sustained economic growth; reducing the rate of inflation; and stabilizing the current account deficit of the balance of payments.

To achieve these objectives, various measures were stipulated, covering exchange rate, monetary and fiscal policies. The most important measures are:

Table 1.13 Long-term debt and debt burden

					Debt burden	
	Current receipts	Merch. exports	Long-term loans	Debt repay't	% of Merch.	% of Rec't
OR						
1971	448.9	369.7	153.8	172.2	46.6	38.4
1973	562.7	396.3	136.5	213.9	54.0	38.0
1974	931.5	653.9	204.1	311.8	47.7	33.4
1975	1035.3	612.8	454.7	392.2	47.7	28.2
1976	1403.1	629.7	487.7	381.6	60.6	27.2
1977	1778.1	779.6	1071.9	422.0	54.1	23.7
1978	2124.5	776.2	779.8	472.5	60.9	22.2
UR						
1979/80	5829.4	2369.9	1144.6	996.9	42.1	17.1
1980/81	6544.1	2709.2	1408.4	1426.9	52.7	21.8
1981/82	6221.2	3692.6	1205.4	1637.1	60.8	26.2
1982/83	7226.3	2619.3	1386.8	1737.8	66.3	24.1

Notes:
OR = official rate ($2.556 per LE) applying to the period 1971–78.
UR = unified rate ($1.4286 per LE) applying to 1979/80–1982/83.

Source: Shoura Council Report of Committee on Financial and Economic Affairs (June 1985) Tables 55, 56 and 58.

a. Gradual simplification of the exchange rate structure, and setting the exchange rate according to market conditions. Thus, partial devaluation-cum-unification was the first step taken. Most of the transactions previously taking place at the adjustable commercial banks' rate (see Annex II) were shifted to the newly-established official free market for foreign exchange. This measure entailed a devaluation of the Egyptian pound on account of such transactions (about one third of current transactions) by 30 per cent (from LE 1.764 to LE 2.299 per US dollar at the start of the new system).
b. Increasing domestic energy prices gradually towards parity with international prices. A step was taken in this direction even before the signing of the stand-by agreement, when in April 1987 domestic prices of kerosene and gas oil were raised by 60 per cent. Prices of natural gas and fuel oil for industrial uses were also raised significantly.

c. Liberalization of compulsory delivery quotas and raising the procurement prices for agricultural crops.
d. Adjusting the public investment programme to match the availability of resources.
e. Reducing the budget deficit from a pre-programme level of over 20 per cent to 13 per cent of GDP for the fiscal year 1987/88.[10]
f. Increasing domestic interest rates towards 20 per cent. An initial step was the increase in debtor rates by up to 2 percentage points, and the introduction of a differential interest rate structure depending on the maturity of bank loans on top of the existing differential according to sector.[11] This naturally entailed corresponding increases in creditor interest rates.

During the earlier phase of the negotiation it was envisaged that the package will run for 36 months, and the IMF resources in support of the package would be in the range of $1000–1500 million (*MEED*, 21 December 1985; and *South*, April 1986). But the duration of the programme turned out to be much shorter and the IMF resources made available in support of it much less than what was originally contemplated. In fact, the Fund resources for the 1987–88 stand-by turned out to be only some 40 per cent of those for the EFF programme of 1979–81. The main reason for discontinuing the 1987–88 stand-by arrangement was the judgement by the IMF that the pace of economic reform was too slow. According to the Fund's officials, the Egyptian government adopted a lukewarm attitude and failed to meet performance criteria (IMF, 1991).

Assessment of the 1987 Stand-by Agreement

The concern with sustained economic growth expressed in the package was highly relevant in view of the strong deceleration of the growth of the Egyptian economy since the mid 1980s. Capital formation dropped in absolute terms by 21 per cent in 1986/87. Foreign exchange was the main factor constraining investment. As a result of foreign exchange shortages, imports as a whole fell by 23 per cent during 1986–87. Imports of fats and oils, mineral products and fuel dropped by a strong 34 per cent between 1984/85 and 1985/86. Manufacturing industry was running considerably below capacity due to the unavailability of imported intermediate goods. It was a situation of clear import strangulation.

As a result of these conditions, Egypt's economic growth took a real plunge. GDP growth rate went down from an average of 7.3 per cent per annum during 1980–85 to a modest 3 per cent per annum during 1986–87 (World Bank, *WDI 1998 CD-ROM*). The concern with growth expressed in the 1987–88 arrangement should therefore be seen against this background.

Also justified was the concern with curbing inflation, in view of the quantum jump in the inflation rate between 1984/85 and 1986/87.[12] The inflation rate jumped from 13 per cent in 1986 to 31 per cent in 1987 (World Bank, *WDI 1998 CD-ROM*). A number of measures were stipulated in the programme to deal with this problem. The most important single component is the reduction of the budget deficit. The target for the fiscal year 1987/88, as already mentioned, was to bring down the relative budget deficit to 13 per cent of GDP. This was a very ambitious undertaking, since it entailed almost halving the fiscal deficit in just one year. It is noteworthy that the budget deficit stood at a dangerously high rate of 27 per cent in 1985/86 (World Bank, 1992, p. 165), and may have been even higher for 1986/87.[13] At any rate, any reduction in the fiscal deficit would help cool off the economy and reduce inflationary pressures. However, the entire programme actually proved not to be viable because the government was unable to put its finances in order. This was due to the fact that the budget deficit target stumbled against sudden and unforeseen changes in Egypt's oil revenues. There was no clause in the agreement to deal with such unexpected external shocks as a strong deterioration in the terms of trade. This, in fact, is one of the major drawbacks of IMF stylized stabilization packages.

Assessment of the 1987–88 package is not really easy for a number of reasons. For one thing, the programme was not *fully* implemented, which raises the question of the likely inferiority of partial or piecemeal policies as implied by the theory of second best. For example, if devaluation is not supported by price liberalization in agriculture, it would be essentially a fiscal measure: a tax on producers of agricultural products. In addition, there would the *other* problem that measures do not deliver all their effects at once. Rather, some measures may result more readily in increasing production costs while their supply-inducing effect may take a little longer. This was probably the reason that some components of the stand-by programme may have had the unintended effect of raising the inflation rate. Most notable here are devaluation, raising interest rates, increasing domestic energy prices, and raising procurement prices of agricultural crops. It seems that conditions necessary for these measures to reduce domestic absorption were not met. For example, the expenditure-reducing effect of devaluation did not materialize because nominal devaluation did not translate into durable real devaluation (see Chapter 3, Table 3.5). Because of dollarization, devaluation created a wealth effect which seemed to stifle its expenditure-reducing effects. Increasing domestic energy prices helped reduce the budget deficit and hence lowered absorption. Their net effect on the balance of payments may have been negative, as the cost-push effects seem to have outweighed the absorption-reducing effects. In the short run, it seems that the inflationary effect of 'correcting prices' by eliminating the so-called cost/price distortions has outweighed the deflationary effect of reducing the rate of credit expansion. The net effect of all that was a rise in the inflation rate. Thus, according to official estimates of the Central Bank of Egypt the inflation rate doubled between 1984/85 and 1985/86, *despite the reduction of the rate of monetary expansion* from 15.3 per cent to 13.4 per cent between those two years (CBE, 1985/86).

Perhaps the most tangible result of the 1987–88 stand-by package was that it paved the way for rescheduling almost one-quarter of Egypt's foreign debt through the Paris Club. According to the terms of the rescheduling deal, about US$10 billion worth of Egypt's debt arrears through the end of 1986 were rescheduled over ten years, including a five-year grace period.

Such rescheduling definitely helped the country's short-run foreign exchange situation. But unless measures are taken to enhance the country's capacity to service its foreign debt, this may potentially introduce serious problems for the medium term when the rescheduled debt falls due. That was the hard lesson of the Egypt's rescheduling experience of the 1970s, through the Gulf Organization for Development in Egypt (GODE).

In order to complete the assessment of the 1987–88 stand-by package a number of additional remarks are pertinent in the present context.

1. The duration of the programme proved too short to allow for a reasonable increase in aggregate supply, thereby throwing the burden of attaining equilibrium on curtailing aggregate demand. This poses the danger of enforcing a recession. Given the nature of Egypt's economic problems as indicated below, it would have been more appropriate to design a reform package under the Fund's Structural Adjustment Facility.
2. It may be argued that the package was perhaps too contractionary. This is supported by the fact that efforts to reduce the budget deficit focused more on cutting government expenditure than on increasing government revenue. For example, there were reasonable economic and social grounds for imposing a capital gains tax on holders of foreign exchange assets to raise additional government revenue and to counteract the wealth effect resulting from devaluation. In addition, care should have been taken in imposing credit restraint.
3. This programme was not really very different from the 1979–81 EFF package in terms of content and overall orientation. Like that package, it has relied on too few policy instruments. But the emphasis in the new programme on raising producer prices for agricultural crops was definitely a good supply-side measure, if only it was placed within a longer-term perspective. The positive results of such a measure on aggregate supply will appear only in the medium term.
4. The package rested on the premise that Egypt's problems were *totally* of her own doing, thereby neglecting the adverse impact of the external

environment (deterioration of the oil market, the hike in the interest rate caused by the economic policies of industrialized countries, and the increase in protectionist tendencies). Any package that seriously attempts to tackle the basic problems of the Egyptian economy, and for that matter many LDCs, must take this factor into consideration.

It is our judgement, therefore, that the 1987 package, stressing as it did short-term stabilization rather than longer-term adjustment, turned out to be self-defeating. The most eminent danger was failure to meet the budget deficit criterion, leaving behind the legacy of a significatly depreciated pound and much higher interest rates. Inadvertently, the adverse distributional effects triggered compensatory measures to make things palatable. To alleviate the negative distribution effect, the government effected a 20 per cent increase in wages and salaries for workers in both the public and the private sectors. This may not have fully compensated for the increase in the cost of living due to implementing the programme, but it would also fuel inflationary expectations. Egypt was soon to find itself facing a crisis situation even more difficult than the one which led to the 1987 package. Such a situation necessitated the reform effort in the 1990s under the Economic Reform and Structural Adjustment Package (ERSAP). We shall discuss ERSAP in detail in the following chapters.

EFFECT OF STABILIZATION ATTEMPTS OF THE 1970s AND 1980s ON VARIOUS GROUPS

The Social Matrix: Whose Meat and Whose Poison?

Discussion of the political economy of a stabilization programme requires identification of the social forces affected, in various ways, by the programme. Measures taken often resemble a zero-sum game benefiting some socio-economic groups at the expense of others: one group's meat is another's poison. However, some measures may benefit or hurt all groups, though in differing degrees. The final outcome of any policy measure is conditioned by the nature of the various markets and institutions which shape production and distribution relations in society. The role played by the state assumes particular importance in this context. Not less important in determining the final outcome is the public response to the stabilization measures. In Egypt's case such a response strongly manifested itself in the violent mass riots and popular unrest in January 1977, which immediately forced the government to roll back certain unpopular measures. Studying the effect of stabilization effort of the 1970s and 1980s on the various socio-economic groups may provide some useful insights.

However, the identification of the socio-economic groups relevant to the discussion of the political economy of stabilization is usually difficult, and it is even hazardous in the case of the Egyptian economy during the 1970s and 1980s. This is because during that period such an economy may be characterized more as a constellation of sub-economies strung together, rather than as an integrated whole. The most important factors contributing to this complexity are the varied and changing pricing rules for factors and products (see Appendix 1.1), the pattern of ownership, the role of the state, the regional setting, and so on.

As a first approximation, one may distinguish the following socio-economic groups: wage labour in the public sector; wage labour in the private sector; the peasantry; public sector business; and private sector business. Wage labour refers to sheer labour power, divorced from any ownership of the means of production. Two distinct subgroups must be distinguished in view of the different rules of wage determination and unionization: wage labour in government and the public sector; and wage labour in the private sector.

Wage labour in the public sector

Wage labour in the public sector reached 3.7 million in 1984 (CAOA, 1985, p. 7), comprising both employment in general government (including economic authorities) and employment in public sector enterprises. Of this, 2.4 million were employed in the government and about 1.3 million employed in the public-sector enterprises. Government employees are not unionized. Public enterprise sector workers are unionized, but effectively their unions are state-controlled, and strike action is prohibited by law. Labour in both the government and the public enterprise sector accounted for close to 37 per cent of the total labour force around the mid 1980s. According to the 1986 population census, total employment in the economy was 11.77 million, and public-sector employment (government, economic authorities and public enterprise sector) was 3.974 million. This gives a ratio of public-sector employment to total employment of 33.4 per cent in 1986 (Handoussa, 1992, pp. 91–3).

According to the institutional/legal set-up, wages for this group are largely government-controlled (see Appendix 1.1).

Wage labour in the private sector

Wage labour in the private sector is located in agriculture, construction and private manufacturing and service sectors. No direct estimate of the size of this category of labour is available. But we can make a guesstimate on the basis of CAPMAS Labour Force Sample Survey (LFSS). According to the May 1980 round of LFSS, total wage labour in the economy was 5.567

million. If we assume that wage labour in the government and public enterprise sector for 1980 was 3.0 million (which is consistent with the figure of 3.974 million quoted above for 1986), wage labour in the private sector may then be estimated at about 2.6 million in 1980. This represents 26 per cent of the total labour force.

Wages for this category of labour freely adjust to reflect market conditions both in Egypt and in neighbouring countries. There is unionization of labour in certain sectors, but it is not very effective for wage setting.

It is interesting to note that the labour market in Egypt is highly segmented along a public/private axis. Although this segmentation has manifested itself historically in a significant wage differential, there is evidence that the public sector/private sector wage gap has been narrowing during 1973–78 (Handoussa, 1992, p. 104).

The peasantry

Peasants are defined here as owners of less than five feddans of agricultural land.[14] According to the 1980 official data, they number 3.5 million, representing 95 per cent of landowners and owning 53 per cent of total area owned (5.5 million feddans) (CAPMAS, 1983, p. 74). This socio-economic group produced the bulk of the crops marketed by the government (cotton, rice, wheat, sugar cane, broad beans and onions) and *berseem* (Egyptian clover).

Public sector business

This used to be the backbone of the economy outside agriculture. Public sector companies contributed about one-third of GNP on the average during 1975–79. It was particularly significant in industry and mining, energy, construction, transport and communications, supply and commerce and finance. Its share of investment averaged 27 per cent (excluding the government) and it employed 11 per cent of the total labour force in the economy, earning 20–25 per cent of total wages. Capital assets in this sector were estimated at about LE 12 billion in 1979 (see Table 1.14).

Private sector business

For the period under consideration, the private sector was particulary important in certain activities (notably services, construction and small-scale industry). It was also gaining importance in the context of the open-door policy (*infitah*). This group included rather diverse sub-groups: national capitalists in industry and agriculture, *compradors* and even rentiers. For the purpose of discussing the effects of the stabilization measures these sub-groups should be distinguished, as they are bound to be affected differently by various measures.

Table 1.14 Relative magnitude of public sector, 1975–79

	1975	1976	1977	1978	1979
1. Share in gross output (%)	31.2	31.0	31.9	32.1	29.7
2. Share in total investment (%)					
a. including government	85.6	79.4	80.2	83.0	77.5
b. excluding government	15.6	20.0	34.5	33.3	29.5
3. Share in total employment (%)	10.6	11.4	11.6	11.8	11.6
4. Share in total wages (%)	20.5	22.6	23.6	25.3	27.6
5. Value of capital invested (LE million)	4239	5371	6231	9551	12027

Source: Shoura Council, Committee on Financial and Economic Affairs, *Report on Public Sector* (1982, pp. 15–18).

The Approximate Effects on Various Groups

To establish the various effects of the stabilization attempts on the different groups which make up the social matrix, it is necessary to separate these effects from the effects of other shocks to the system. It is also necessary to take into account fully indirect effects on various socio-economic groups. Computable general equilibrium models are frequently used, but they are not without limitations either regarding data requirements or the underlying assumptions (see remarks on the GEM3 model below). On the other hand, econometric models designed for examining the impact of policy are frequently subject to the Lucas critique. For lack of a better alternative, we shall adopt an eclectic approach. The conclusions of this part of the study should be viewed within this context. Some may find them controversial, reflecting both the nature of the problem and the polarization of views between the Fund on the one side and its 'critics' on the other.[15]

It may be useful to think of the stabilization measures as falling under the following main categories:

a. demand-side measures geared to reduce absorption;
b. supply-side measures aimed at restructuring the economy toward producing more tradables; and
c. changes in overall strategy concurrent with the stabilization attempt.

The thrust of the stabilization packages of the 1970s and 1980s belongs mainly to categories (a) and (b), but some of the elements relate to (c). For measures belonging to category (a), we focus only on those measures which strongly impact on the welfare of various socio-economic groups. Uppermost in this regard are: devaluation, raising interest rates, credit restriction and reducing the fiscal deficit through cutting subsidies. Aside from devaluation, which can be viewed partly as a supply-side measure, measures which are supply-side in nature (category (b)) were only vaguely stated; no performance criteria were stipulated for them. It is difficult, therefore, to be specific about their possible effects on various groups, and hence they are ignored here. We end this section by discussing the implication of measures belonging to category (c).

It may be relatively easy to establish the effect of devaluation, raising interest rates, and reducing subsidies on the lot of wage labour in the government and public enterprise sector. It may be observed that all three measures generated cost-push inflation against which this group did not seem able to protect itself. This is due to its weak bargaining position, and other institutional considerations reflected in the fact that government and public-sector employment is basically a fix-price sector (see Appendix 1.1; Hansen and Radwan, 1982, pp. 70–77, 146–7). The share of government wages in GDP dropped to 8.6 per cent in 1979 compared to 9.9 per cent in 1978 (Handoussa, 1992, p. 97).

Over the period 1974–79, annual money salaries in *government administration* grew at about 10 per cent per annum (Hansen and Radwan, 1982, Table 22). Such an increase is less than the official estimate of the annual rate of inflation of 11–13 per cent (measured by the CPI, see Table 1.15). *Public-enterprise sector* workers fared a little better. The average annual wage rate of labour in public-sector manufacturing rose from LE 599 in 1975 to LE 1068 in 1982, at an average growth rate of 11.1 per cent (Hansen and Radwan, 1982, Table 22; and CAPMAS, 1985). Although no data are available for the same period with regard to the average annual wage in other public enterprise sector employment, evidence for 1978 suggests that, overall, the wages of public-sector labour grew faster than wages in manufacturing. However, the weight of evidence suggests that real income of labour in government and white-collar public sector employment has declined (Zaytoun, 1991).

The effect on labour in the private sector is not as clear-cut. Both domestic interest rate increases and subsidy cuts had detrimental effects on this group by engendering cost-push inflation. On the other hand, devaluation may have had a mixed effect on them. While causing cost-push inflation, which hurt this group, the change in the black-market exchange rate consequent on devaluation also accentuated the wage differentials between the domestic and the outside labour markets, contributing to labour migration and hence to a relative shortage of labour. The shortage seems to have contributed to the rapid rise in domestic wage rate in sectors such as construction, agriculture and maintenance-related services. Devaluation *could* have also contributed to

Table 1.15 Inflation trends, 1965/66–1985 (1965/66 = 100)

	CPI				Inflation Rate %	
Year	Rural	Urban	Total	WPI	CPI	WPI
1965/66	100.0	100.0	100.0	100.0		
1966/67	101.8	104.7	103.0	107.8	3.0	7.0
1967/68	103.6	106.8	105.0	110.2	1.9	2.2
1968/69	107.5	111.1	109.0	112.0	3.8	1.6
1969/70	115.5	114.3	115.0	114.6	5.5	2.3
1970/71	120.0	118.9	119.5	119.1	3.9	3.9
1971/72	119.7	121.8	120.6	119.3	0.9	0.2
1973	133.6	128.2	131.3	128.8	8.9	7.9
1974	152.3	142.1	147.9	147.2	12.6	14.3
1975	170.9	155.9	164.5	158.3	11.2	7.5
1976	191.2	171.9	182.9	170.7	11.2	7.8
1977	210.4	193.8	203.3	186.6	11.2	9.3
1978	238.8	215.3	228.7	214.1	12.5	14.3
1979	253.2	236.6	246.1	235.1	7.6	9.8
1980	316.6	285.5	303.2	285.2	23.2	21.3
1980/81	337.8	302.5	322.6	298.5	6.4	4.7
1981	359.8	315.4	339.8	308.9	5.3	3.5
1981/82	383.6	336.7	362.5	320.4	6.7	3.7
1982	410.1	362.2	388.5	337.5	7.2	5.3
1983	520.1	422.1	475.0*	n.a.	22.3	
1984	547.9	505.2	528.2*	n.a.	11.2	
1985	601.8	520.6	564.4*	n.a.	6.9	

Notes:
CPI = Consumer Price Index.
WPI = Wholesale Price Index
* = average weighted by share of population: rural 54 per cent, urban 46 per cent.

Source: 1965/66–1982: CAPMAS, *Measuring Inflation Trends in Egypt*, (January 1993) in Arabic. 1983–1985: CBE, *Annual Report 1984/85*, mid-year figures (1966/67 = 100).

an environment conducive to wage increase had it resulted in a significant enough rise in the production of exportables, which did not happen.

It should be noted, however, that devaluation only encouraged the process of labour migration which was already in full swing anyway. The other demand-side measures, namely reducing the ratio of the public sector deficit to GDP and restricting credit, may have helped this group to the extent that they moderated inflationary pressures. Available evidence suggests that the lot of this group improved during the 1970s. Ministry of Agriculture (unpublished) data show that the daily wage of agricultural labourers more than doubled between 1975 and 1982. But this was mainly due to labour migration, and was not caused by the stabilization measures.[16] As to wage labour in private manufacturing, its annual wage rose by 15.3 per cent between 1970 and 1980, slightly ahead of official inflation figures for the period (CAPMAS, 1985). However, care should be taken not to attribute such developments to the stabilization measures; in fact, had these measures been implemented in full, they would have brought about a deflationary situation detrimental to private-sector labour.

The peasantry, which mainly produced commodities whose prices were fixed by the government under the system of compulsory delivery, did not gain from devaluation, since production-cost increases wiped out the rise in farm-gate prices. It may be argued that the subsidy cut had a detrimental effect on this group, since subsidies account for a significant proportion of total consumption expenditure of the poorest quartile in rural areas. But on the other hand, cutting subsidies would benefit them, given more flexibility in setting farm-gate prices for basic food crops – mainly wheat, rice and broad beans.

Devaluation coupled with import liberalization has dealt a severe blow to the public business sector. As a result of devaluation, the cost of living rose, and at the same time liberalization allowed competitive imports to eat into the home market previously enjoyed by the public sector. The result was rising indebtedness, increased idle capacity, and excessive inventory accumulation. Overall, this sector is a clear loser in the stabilization process.

It is not clear whether the private business sector as such lost or gained on balance. This is a very heterogeneous category. It includes the traditional and the modern sectors; national-capitalists, rentiers and *compradors*, as well as firms established under the foreign investment code (Law 43 for 1974, amended by Law 32 for 1977). However, it is clear that the stabilization measures benefited the *comprador* elements and holders of net foreign currency assets.

Since the above discussion was not based on any explicit model of the economy, attention should be given to its weakest aspect – namely the neglect of system-wide repercussions. However, it is interesting to compare the previous results, thus based, with the results of a simulation exercise based on a computable general-equilibrium model of the Egyptian economy (Hansen and Radwan, 1982, pp. 285–7). The model (named GEM3) is a 12-sector demand-oriented model with perfect factor substitution and price-clearing markets. It leaves out the effect of capital accumulation on capacity, and treats imports as complementary to domestic production. It has neither a money nor a financial sector. In addition, the structure is based on the then outdated 1976 SAM. The model distinguishes three income groups in each of the rural and urban sectors: the bottom 60 per cent, the middle 30 per cent and the top 10 per cent.

With these characteristics, the model may not be strictly suited for analysing the effect of stabilization measures. However, several simulation runs involving stabilization-like measures were conducted for the ILO mission to Egypt in 1980 using it. Of particular relevance to our present discussion is a simulation run involving a 50 per cent cut in consumer subsidies coupled with a 15 per cent increase in government and private wages. The macro effect is slightly contractionary, with real GDP falling by 1.3 per cent. The impact on the import surplus is more pronounced – a 13.5 per cent fall. But there is a 7.4 per cent rise in government deficit. There is also contraction of both sectors' output and factor demand, and an increase in the cost of living. Somewhat unexpectedly, income distribution changes in favour of the urban sector. This is probably because the compensating wage increase is by nature concentrated in the urban sector. The outcome of such stabilization-like policy is clearly both contractionary and inegalitarian.

The last point in the assessment of the effect of the stabilization attempt on the various socio-economic groups relates to changes in overall strategy which amount to deferring to market forces as both the allocative and distributive mechanism. Notwithstanding the merits of the argument in favour of market forces in some important respects, it has its limitations on both theoretical and empirical grounds. On theoretical grounds, the argument is not always in line with the established principles of the theory of second best – that the removal of only some of the constraints while leaving others in place may lead to a less optimal situation. As an example, trade liberalization in the form of outright dismantling of state-trading monopolies by a country which is still in the early stages of industrialization may be harmful to that country. Egypt's experience in the nineteenth century, when she was forced to dismantle the monopolies set up by Mohamed Ali, may provide an interesting example. The ultimate result was the virtual dismantling of Egyptian industry under pressure of competition by the more mature British industry.

On empirical grounds, LDCs suffer the structural rigidities which may limit their production possibilities considerably. In this context, the alternative to the pre-liberalization use of resources may be to become idle, rather than shift to alternative uses. The case for trade liberalization may then rest solely on the benefits accruing from allocation in consumption *à la* Haberler. Linder (1961) has even argued that liberalizing trade is not necessarily better – even from a world welfare point of view. In the absence of well-developed markets, complete submission to market forces may not necessarily produce better results compared to an interventionist stance.[17]

NOTES

1. These are calculated on the basis of CPI development in Egypt and its main trading partners as derived from IMF, *International Financial Statistics (IFS),* and *Direction of Trade Statistics.*
2. Banks were allowed to extend local currency credit to customers using foreign currency-denominated deposits as collateral.
3. McKinnon defines financial growth as the increase in the ratio of time and saving deposits to money supply. Financial growth is measured as $((M_2–M_1)/M_1) \times 100$. For details see McKinnon (1973, ch.7).
4. This overall rate is the average for a higher rate applying to the private sector and a lower rate applying to the public sector. Perhaps the justification for the lower ceiling on credit to the public sector lies in the desire to cut the budget deficit.
5. See, for example, the interesting chapter by Seers in Jansen (ed.) (1983). Seers makes reference to the experience of the USSR and Czechoslovakia in the early years of socialist regimes, and in Chile after Allende.
6. Note that this proportion is derived by applying the unified exchange rate to the 1978 data to ensure comparability with figures for the programme years. But the actual proportion of fiscal deficit to GDP in 1978 was 23 per cent.
7. This definition of public finances was subsequently changed later in the 1980s. According to the new definition, public-sector enterprises were excluded from the government budget.
8. See the classic article by by Francis M. Bator, 'The Anatomy of Market Failure', *QJE* (August, 1958), published in William Breit and Harold M. Hochman (eds), *Readings in Microeconomics* (New York: Holt, Reinhart and Winston, 1968).
9. It should be emphasized that the empirical coverage for this is not exhaustive; it leaves out some agricultural crops such as fruit and vegetables and the cost of agricultural inputs. The latter may be rising as a result liberalization.
10. Available data based on final account rather than budget proposals indicate a much higher ratio of overall budget deficit to GDP for 1985/86 of 27 per cent. In view of the deterioration of the country's foreign exchange earnings and the concomitant fall in government revenue, the ratio of the budget deficit to GDP for 1986/87 was even higher.
11. Before the amendment in May 1987, debtor interest rates were differentially escalating, with a range of 11–13 per cent on loans to agriculture and industry, 13–15 per cent to the household and service sectors, and 16 per cent minimum on loans for trade. According to the new strucure, these old rates continued to apply on loans with maturities less than one year. One percentage point was added for maturity longer than two years.
12. The consumer price index for urban areas rose from 10.1 per cent in 1984/85 to 19.2 per cent in 1985/86. It should be noted that official CPI data considerably underestimate the rate of inflation, because of several factors (the outdated weights used in constructing the index, and the reliance on official prices). Actual inflation should be much higher, possibly in the neighbourhood of 30 per cent, for 1985/86.
13. In recent years there has been striking divergence between budget appropriations and actual figures. According to final government accounts, actual overall budget deficit for the years 1983/84–1985/86 was LE 5.3, 6.9 and 9.8 billion, against planned figures of LE 5.0, 5.4 and 4.9 billion, respectively. Sources of the above data are the published budget documents and the unpublished final government accounts.
14. One feddan equals 1.05 acres.
15. On this see, for example: Carlos Diaz-Alejandro, 'A Note on the Impact of Devaluation and the Redistributive Effect', *JPE*, vol. 71, 1963, pp. 577–80; G.K. Helleiner, 'Stabilization Policies and the Poor', Dept. of Economics, University of Toronto, Working Paper No. B9, April 1985; Omotunde Johnson and Joanne Salop, 'Distributional Aspects of Stabilization Programmes in Developing Countries', *IMF Staff Papers*, vol. 27, no. 1, March 1980; Charles A. Sisson, 'Fund Supported Programs and Income Distribution in LDCs', *Finance and Development*, March 1986; Henry Bienen and Mark Gersovits, 'Economic Stabilization and Political Stability', *International Organization*, vol. 39, no.

4, Autumn 1985, pp. 729–54; G.K. Helleiner, 'Lender of Early Resort: the IMF and the Poorest', *ARE*, vol. 73, no.2, May 1983, pp. 349–553; Lauka T. Katseli, 'Devaluation: A Critical Appraisal of the IMF's Policy Prescriptions', ibid., pp. 359–63.

16. Without belittling the factors on the demand for labour in the labour-receiving countries, labour migration itself may be related to devaluation. Devaluation resulted in increasing wage differentials between the local and foreign labour markets and hence helped to propel labour migration.
17. For a similar conclusion based on the experience of Jamaica, Peru and Portugal, see Girvan (1980), pp. 55–74.

APPENDIX 1.1

Table 1A.1 Price formation during the 1970s and 1980s

	Fixprice	Flexprice	Mark up
I. Commodities			
A. *Agricultural*	Cotton, sugar cane	Maize, sorgum, fruit and vegetables	
	CD: Wheat, broad beans, rice, peanuts, sesame, onions Supply commodities: (flour, oil, sugar, tea, frozen meat)	*FR*: wheat, broad beans, rice, peanuts, sesame, onions	
B. *Industrial*	– energy products – cotton yarn, low quality textiles and fabrics – sugar, edible oil, fat, soap, animal fodder, artificial cleaners, dairy products, sauce, jam, soft drinks, cigarettes – fertilizers, tyres, batteries, leather, matches, pencils, paper – automobiles, buses, trucks, tractors, refrigerators, washing machines, air conditioners, light bulbs. – aluminium, concrete iron – salt – surface glass, cement	Fine textiles and fabrics of cotton and silk, draperies, carpets, perfumes and cosmetics, chocolate, furniture and fixtures, non-essential imports	Imports except: – supply food commodities – fertilizers, pesticides – intermediate goods

II. Factors			
A.	*Labour*	Government public enterprises (until the mid-1970s)	Rural private-sector construction, migrant labour
		Urban private sector (employment adjusts)	Informal self-employment (employment adjusts)
B.	*Capital*	Egyptian-pound assets and liabilities	Foreign currency assets and liabilities
C.	*Foreign Exchange*	Official, parallel	Black market

Notes:
CD = compulsory delivery quota
FR = free retention quota

Sources: Based on information from Shoura Council (1985); Hansen and Radwan (1982).

2. Economic 'reform' in the 1990s

PRELUDE TO ERSAP

As already mentioned in the previous chapter, following a series of protracted negotiations starting in 1989, Egypt concluded agreements with both the IMF (in May 1991) and the World Bank (in November 1991) on a stabilization and adjustment package. These made up the core of the reform programme known as ERSAP.[1] It may be said that such a package represents, in a real sense, a natural extension of the policies that were adopted since the mid 1970s under the open-door policy (*infitah*), and the stabilization and adjustment attempts in the 1970s and 1980s. However, it seems to go much further in reworking the institutional fabric of the Egyptian economy to become a truly private enterprise market-oriented economy. We have argued elsewhere (Abdel-Khalek, 1994), on the basis of Egypt's past experience, that the package failed to take serious account of some important structural features of the Egyptian economy – notably, food deficit, dollarization, and the prevalence of significant idle capacity. It was also maintained that the ERSAP package may have followed the wrong sequencing by stressing trade, interest rate and exchange rate 'reform' long before dealing with the real economy (in other words, *exchange* appears to have taken precedence over *production*). We also argued that the sustainability of the programme could prove problematic in view of the draconian nature of some of the components and the harsh conditionality attached.

In addition to the analysis of Chapter 1, several studies of Egypt's previous stabilization and adjustment attempts are now available (Abdel-Khalek, 1987; Amin, 1987; Handoussa 1991; Korayem, 1986). But there are only a few studies dealing with ERSAP. Furthermore, the impact of ERSAP on industrialization has not been seriously analysed yet. The purpose of this part of the study is to provide a detailed account of the set of measures proposed under ERSAP, to serve as a basis for analysing their impact on industrialization in Egypt in a latter part. Before we do that, it is necessary to set out the circumstances which conditioned the prelude to ERSAP.

By the late 1980s, Egypt faced a crisis situation which prompted the government to engage in negotiations with the Bank and the Fund (see Table 2.1). Real GDP growth fell below population growth, resulting in a deterioration of income per capita. This entailed significant changes in Egypt's

Table 2.1 Selected economic indicators, 1985/86–1991/92

	1985/86	1986/87	1987/88	1988/89	1989/90	1990/91	1991/92
Real GDP growth (%)	2.7	2.5	3.9	3.0	2.5	2.3	0.3
Domestic inflation	16.1	25.2	14.2	20.2	21.2	14.7	21.1
Av. nominal exchange rate (LE/US$)	1.069	1.273	1.761	1.937	2.229	3.009	3.331
Av. nominal deposit rate*	11.0	11.0	11.0	12.0	12.0	16.0	17.1
Av. nominal lending rate*	14.0	15.0	15.0	16.0	17.0	18.0	22.0
M2 growth rate (%)**	16.3	12.4	11.1	12.3	21.4	13.4	34.4
Overall fiscal deficit/GDP (%)	23.1	19.3	24.5	18.1	16.5	20.0	7.2
Current account/GDP (%)	–9.4	–5.2	–4.0	–9.3	–10.5	–7.4	2.8
DOD/GDP (%)	118.0	131.4	155.0	127.9	144.3	119.1	109.5

Notes:
* Rate on deposits and loans with maturity less than one year.
** M2 = Currency + demand deposits + LE time and savings deposits.
Excluding official transfers.

Source: All data are from World Bank (1992), p. 165.

international economic standing. Thus, in 1990 it moved for the first time from the lower stratum of the group of middle-income countries to the group of low-income countries according to the World Bank *World Development Report* classification. Also, it requalified for interest-free resources from IDA, the soft-financing member of the World Bank group. Unemployment appeared on the rise, representing some 10–15 per cent of the labour force.[2] Domestic inflation did not abate. Both the fiscal deficit and the current account deficit showed no sign of improvement. The economy was increasingly overburdened by debt overhang – debt outstanding and disbursed (DOD) hit the US$50 billion mark by the end of June 1990, a staggering 144 per cent of GDP. With only half the annual debt service obligations (of around US$6 billion) actually paid, accumulating debt arrears reached US$11 billion in 1989/90. There is little doubt, therefore, that the country was facing a severe crisis and a drop in its creditworthiness.

All this was against the backdrop of a sharp decline in the terms of trade since 1982. In addition, the country was hit hard by the strongest external shock of its post-Second World War history in the wake of the Gulf crisis of 1990. Estimates of the direct economic cost to the Egyptian economy of the said crisis ranged from $2.5 billion (Abdel-Khalek, 1991) to $3.6 billion (World Bank, 1990b).

In response to these developments, a stand-by arrangement (SBA) with the IMF was concluded in May 1991. It was coupled with a structural adjustment loan (SAL) with the World Bank in November of the same year. This is the first real structural adjustment package (SAP) in the history of Egypt's relation with the Bretton Woods institutions. Together, the SBA and SAL made up the backbone of ERSAP.

ERSAP: THE MAIN ELEMENTS

The ultimate objective of ERSAP was to restore economic growth and to improve living standards in a sustained fashion. It focussed on three policy areas: stabilization, structural adjustment, and social policies.[3] The main components are the following: (a) macroeconomic reforms, (b) public enterprise reform, (c) domestic price liberalization, (d) foreign trade liberalization, (e) private sector reform, and (f) the Social Fund for Development (SFD).

We outline each of these components briefly, and after doing that we turn to offer a number of pertinent critical comments. Our treatment is not exhaustive; we elect to focus on the more important aspects of the programme.

Table 2.2 Fiscal variables under ERSAP (per cent of GDP)

	Fiscal Year						
	89/90	90/91	91/92	92/93	93/94	94/95	95/96
Total Revenue o/w	25.37	29.56	36.89	36.69	38.27	39.29	39.96
CG Tax Rev.	14.91	18.48	23.77	23.12	23.65	23.91	23.95
CG non tax	4.93	7.63	9.59	10.51	11.55	12.32	12.98
Total Expenditure	43.81	51.47	47.12	45.15	44.65	43.45	42.08
Current Expenditure	28.05	32.40	33.80	35.92	35.48	34.75	33.86
o/w Interest	4.60	9.33	11.29	13.20	13.08	12.93	12.54
Capital Expenditure	15.76	19.06	13.32	10.22	9.17	8.70	8.22
Final Deficit o/w	18.44	21.91	10.24	6.58	5.42	3.33	1.52
Bank Finance	9.68	1.81	9.87	0.00	0.00	0.00	0.00

Notes:
Capital Expenditure includes public enterprise investment and structural reform related expenditure. For FY 1991 it includes LE 6.1 billion (= 6 per cent of GDP) as government transfer to the four public sector banks to close their foreign currency exposure. This was mainly financed from Gulf crisis-related extraordinary foreign financing.
o/w = of which.

Source: World Bank (1991).

(a) Macroeconomic Reform

The thrust of macroeconomic reform was to implement a development strategy to achieve sustainable economic growth consistent with the country's ability to service foreign debt. As mentioned, this is the stabilization foundation for ERSAP. It encompasses fiscal policy, interest rates and the exchange rate regime.

The fiscal adjustment lies at the heart of the stabilization package, and involved trimming off the fiscal deficit, both overall and the bank-financed part. As shown in Table 2.2 the target was to bring down the ratio of the overall budget deficit to GDP from an estimated high of 22 per cent for 1990/91,[4] to a mere 1.5 per cent by 1995/96. It stipulated a slight reduction in the ratio of public expenditure to GDP,[5] and a substantial hike in the share of public revenue (from about 25 per cent to about 40 per cent of GDP). But it is interesting to note that, in relative terms, central government non-tax revenue would provide most of the targeted adjustment: namely through price increases, particularly energy prices. The increase in tax revenue was mainly through greater reliance on indirect taxation (a comprehensive sales tax, escalation of stamp tax, and so on).

The large shift envisaged by ERSAP in the structure of total expenditure over the programme period is extremely important on both equity and efficiency grounds. The fiscal component of the programme involved an almost tripling of the ratio of interest payments to current expenditure. In fact, such a ratio actually doubled in just one year (between 1989/90 and 1990/91) corresponding to the liberalization of domestic interest rates and the placement of treasury bills (TBs). According to data of the Central Bank of Egypt, the stock of treasury bills outstanding at the end of June 1992 exceeded LE 17 billion. More than 80 per cent of the outstanding TB stock was held by the banking system, about 6 per cent each by the private business sector and insurance companies and about 4 per cent by the household sector. The tremendous rise in interest payments should have a negative impact on income distribution – because it implies a rise in the share of the rentier or 'clipping class'.

On the expenditure side, measures included cutting food and fertilizer subsidies and reducing public investment outlays. The latter measure is obviously the more significant from a growth point of view. According to the programme, public-sector investment outlays would be reduced by 5 percentage points in real terms between 1989/90 and 1992/93. It was assumed that such a withdrawal of the government will 'crowd in' private investment. The package also stipulated strong wage and salary restraint, actually amounting to a labour squeeze.

With regard to *interest rate and monetary policy* ERSAP encompassed removing all interest-rate ceilings, imposing specific domestic credit ceilings that favour the private sector, eliminating any direct credit line between the Central Bank of Egypt (CBE) and the government, and developing a market for treasury bills. Interest rates were liberalized and the first treasury bills auction was held in January 1991.

In the *exchange rate field*, ERSAP included devaluation, simplifying the exchange rate system and ensuring a competitive exchange rate. Anticipating the formal agreement with the IMF in May 1991, a dual exchange rate system consisting of a primary and a secondary market went into effect on 27 February 1991. This is an interesting example of front-loading of conditionality.[6] The new two-tier system replaced the multiple exchange rate system, involving partial unification and a maxi devaluation of the Egyptian pound of some 20–25 per cent in 1991 (see Table 2.1). The control mechanism for the entire system was the rate in the secondary market, which would be determined freely; the rate in the primary market would be within 5 per cent below the former (CBE, *Report on Monetary and Credit Conditions*, 1990/91).

Unification of the exchange rate was finally effected on 8 October 1991, when the free foreign exchange market was established, involving exchange rate unification and a dirty float. According to the new system, the Egyptian

Table 2.3 Exchange rate for tariff purposes (LE per currency unit)

Year	US$	PSTRLG	DM	FF	100 IL	100 YN
1985	0.71	0.86	0.23	0.08	0.04	0.29
1986	0.78	1.14	0.35	0.11	0.05	0.45
1987	1.50	2.41	0.82	0.25	0.11	0.94
1988	1.89	3.36	1.08	0.32	0.15	1.47
1989	2.24	3.66	1.18	0.35	0.16	1.63
1990	2.68	4.71	1.64	0.48	0.22	1.85
1991	3.18	5.64	1.93	0.57	0.26	2.36
1992	3.34	5.99	2.14	0.63	0.28	2.63
1993	3.36	5.07	2.19	0.61	0.22	2.90

Notes:
PSTRLG = Pound sterling
DM = German mark
FF = French franc
IL = Italian lira
YN = Japanese yen

Source: Ministry of Finance, Customs Department, unpublished data.

pound is pegged to the US dollar. The CBE interferes in the foreign exchange market to stabilize the LE/US$ rate. The exchange rates of the pound *vis-à-vis* other currencies seem to be derived from the exchange rate of the US dollar with these currencies, given the LE/US$ (pegged) rate. Restrictions were relaxed on all payments and transfers for international transactions, both current and capital. Egypt thus moved to full capital mobility for the first time in more than 40 years.

Another important aspect of the exchange rate policy, which is usually overlooked, concerns the exchange rate used for calculating the pound value of imports for tariff assessment purposes. That rate was frozen at the Central Bank rate (of about LE 0.7 per US$) until 1985, and was changed only slightly in 1986. In 1987, there was almost 100 per cent devaluation (from LE 0.78 to almost LE 1.50 per US$), and it gradually moved to parity with the free-market rate in 1991 (see Table 2.3 for details). Although it is an accounting rate, it has clear implications both for resource allocation and government tariff revenue and hence the fiscal balance. Pending the detailed analysis, we only mention here in passing that lowering tariff rates in itself may not necessarily mean reducing effective protection. Devaluation of the pound for tariff assessment purposes raises the pound value of imports, and may even cancel the effect of nominal-tariff reduction.

Table 2.4 Comparison of old and new public enterprise laws

Features	Law 97 (old)	Law 203 (new)
1. Autonomy	Company managers are under the control of their respective public sector organizations (PSOs) and a technical ministry that has supervisory authority.	Company managers are autonomous and free to decide on all business matters; they have no links to technical ministries.
2. Company Objectives	Companies are supposed to help realize the State's economic and social objectives, regardless of the impact upon their own efficiency.	Companies have only one objective: to maximize profits and, as a result, their value.
3. Financial Status	Companies are dependent upon the Government for operational subsidies and the financing of capital expenditure, out of captive sources of funds on subsidized terms.	Companies are financially independent of the Government and parent holding companies; the latter would not be allowed to routinely subsidize their affiliates. Company investments should be financed on commercial terms through capital markets.
4. Corporate Form	Public enterprise established under Law No. 97 of 1983.	Joint-stock company listed on the stock exchange in Egypt.
5. Privatization	Not allowed.	Allowed.
6. Liquidation	Not allowed, except under very special circumstances.	Allowed.
7. Bankruptcy	Not allowed.	Allowed.
8. Employment	Companies are uniformly subject to the provisions of Law 48 on PSE employment.	Law 48 is repealed, and companies are free to set their own terms and conditions of employment.

Source: World Bank (1991, p. 22)

(b) Public Enterprise Reform

Structural adjustment measures related to public enterprise reform addressed the issues of autonomy and restructuring. The autonomy part involved promulgating a new public investment law that gave freedom to public enterprises (PEs) and the establishment of a new regulatory environment common to both the public and the private sector. Thus, the Public Business Sector Law (Law 203 for 1991) replaced the previous one (Law 97 for 1983). Table 2.4 compares, in a summary fashion, the main stipulations of the two laws. According to the new law, PEs were reorganized along a three-tiered structure that includes the apex institution (The Public Sector Office) at the top, holding companies in the middle, and their affiliate companies at the base. The law also allowed for privatization of PEs, including asset sales, divestiture, and management contracts with private management teams. As part of public enterprise reform, PEs would operate under the same rules as the private sector; their managers exercise the freedom to decide on investment, product mix, pricing, staffing and so on. Moreover, it was decided to stop financing PEs' new investment using National Investment Bank (NIB) funds. Instead, they can mobilize their resources from retained earnings, loans from the banking system or placement on the capital market.

(c) Domestic Price Liberalization

Industrial products

Measures in this category included a scheduled full decontrol of ex-factory prices of industrial products produced by the public sector, taking account of the competitiveness of the domestic market and the pace of import liberalization. The target under ERSAP was that, by second tranche release of SAL, only a small number of non-competitive products, basic foodstuffs and/or products benefiting from implicit input subsidies, would remain subject to price controls. Their prices would be subsequently decontrolled more gradually, such that by June 1995 the prices of almost all industrial products would be liberalized except for a limited number of basic foodstuffs, cigarettes, and cotton yarn.

Energy prices

ERSAP stipulated raising domestic petroleum product prices and the price of natural gas gradually to achieve eventual parity with world prices by June 1995 at the prevailing exchange rate. Thus, weighted-average domestic petroleum prices as a percentage of international equivalents were to be increased 11 percentage points by May of each year for the period 1992–95 inclusive. The natural gas price would be increased *pari passu* with that of fuel oil prices. Electricity prices would also be adjusted upwards as a proportion of, and towards eventual equality with, the long-run marginal cost by June 1995. As a proportion of LRMC, these prices as an average would be increased 10 percentage points every year during 1992–95 to reach 100 per cent (from 59 per cent in May 1991).

Agricultural prices

Measures in the agricultural sector included the removal of the delivery quota for rice, raising cotton prices to bring them closer to world prices, and the decontrol of prices and distribution of pesticides, fertilizers, and animal feed.

(d) Foreign Trade Liberalization

The main measures included: (i) reducing the list of commodities protected by import bans from close to 40 per cent to less than 30 per cent of industrial domestic output; (ii) changing the tariff structure so that the maximum tariff rate will initially be 80 per cent and the minimum 10 per cent; (iii) eliminating discretionary allocation of foreign exchange by the banking system; (iv) gradual elimination of non-tariff barriers other than import suspensions and

Table 2.5 Domestic production coverage of NTBs (as per cent of domestic output)

	Public sector		Private sector		Overall	
	(1)	(2)	(1)	(2)	(1)	(2)
Exports						
Export bans	9.5	4.2	1.9	1.1	4.9	2.3
Other NTBs	15.2	4.5	1.5	0.0	7.0	1.9
All export NTBs	24.8	8.8	3.3	1.1	11.9	4.2
Imports						
Import bans	49.2	41.2	29.3	10.3	37.2	22.7
Agriculture	n.a	n.a	n.a	n.a	35.9	9.8
Manuf. and Min.	n.a	n.a	n.a	n.a	37.8	28.5
All import NTBs	76.4	47.5	36.3	10.9	52.5	25.6

Notes:
(1) March 1990
(2) June 1991

Source: World Bank (1991), Tables 4 and 5.

import bans, starting with a 50 per cent reduction in import NTBs before the formal start of ERSAP (see Table 2.5, and Appendix 2.1).

(e) Private Sector

Private enterprise reform encompassed a set of measures designed to eliminate discrimination against the private sector in obtaining licences, purchasing inputs and energy, and in obtaining credits. The ultimate objective is to create a level playing field for all types of business enterprises. Thus, by May 1991, investment licensing requirements for enterprises incorporated under Law 159 (mostly domestically-owned firms) had been effectively dropped – aside from a negative list to be reduced further. Furthermore, all production and product-mix licensing requirements have been replaced by a registration process – with a definite and short time limit. Liberalization of investment, production and pricing was also extended to other private sector enterprises (those subject to Law 45 or Law 230 – mostly joint ventures and foreign-owned). Other measures for private sector reform involved phasing out public trading monopolies – particularly for cement and fertilizers.

(f) The Social Fund for Development

This is the palliative for the bitter medicine of ERSAP. It is a temporary measure to provide a short-term and temporary relief to target groups that will be negatively affected by the above measures and/or the Gulf crisis. Financial resources of $600 million (the equivalent of LE 2 billion) were pledged to the Social Fund for Development (SFD) by the Egyptian government, UNDP, IDA and other bilateral and multilateral donors. SFD was initially conceived as a temporary organ with a life span of four years.

ERSAP: FURTHER REMARKS

The detailed assessment of the impact of ERSAP is undertaken in the next three chapters. In anticipation of such detailed assessment, we make a number of critical comments, both with regard to the *nature* of the package and its *likely effects*. These comments may also help us address the issue of an alternative adjustment strategy.

It should be noted that, perhaps, the most immediate and tangible result of the stand-by arrangement with the IMF (as part of ERSAP) is that it paved the way for debt reduction and rescheduling through the Paris Club. In the Paris Club meeting of 24–25 May 1991, creditor countries agreed to restructure Egypt's official and officially guaranteed medium and long-term debt,

Paris Club

including arrears. Outstanding debt considered for restructuring excluded the remainder of US debt or debt contracted after a cut-off date established at the previous rescheduling in May 1987. The debt stock eligible for restructuring totalled some US$ 20–25 billion, and it was agreed to reduce its present value by 50 per cent in three consecutive phases, commensurate with progress in adjustment: 15 per cent in July 1991, another 15 per cent after 18 months, and the remaining 20 per cent to follow at the beginning of 1994. The phasing of the reduction is designed to guarantee that Egypt will continue the adjustment process to the end. The second reduction (of 15 per cent) came into effect in September 1993, following the signing of a new agreement between the Egyptian government and the IMF. The third and last reduction (of 20 per cent) took place in October 1996. Although this debt relief effort may not in and of itself solve Egypt's external debt problems, there is little doubt that it gave the country a reasonable respite.

As already explained before (Abdel-Khalek, 1994), the stabilization and adjustment package making up ERSAP carries a high probability of overkill. One critical factor is whether the package eventually sacrifices growth for stabilization. This issue is drawing increased attention in the literature – witness the proceedings of the 1990 World Bank development economics conference (particularly contributions by Dornbusch and Corden).

In anticipation of the detailed analysis of the impact of ERSAP on industrialization in a subsequent part of this study, some preliminary remarks are especially relevant at this stage.

i. The package reveals a strong bias against the government and the public sector and in favour of the market and the private sector. A case has been made elsewhere for a *restructuring rather than an across-the-board reduction* of the government role (Abdel-Khalek, 1990). The distinction often made between a soft state and a hard one may be very relevant in this context. A government may be large, indeed too large, and less effective. The right question is therefore 'how to reconstruct a *developmental state* that can consistently implement the right policies', to quote Albert Fishlow (1991, p. 169; emphasis added). From the standpoint of the purpose of our research, that is studying the effect of ERSAP on industrialization, effective measures by the state in the areas of trade, investment and industrial policies are extremely vital.
ii. Deference to the market mechanism, which is the hallmark of the package, abstracts from the structural characteristics of the Egyptian economy. Trade liberalization and a reduced government role are *assumed* to ensure a better allocation of resources based on comparative advantage, and hence foster growth. In the presence of structural rigidities and the absence of competition, this remains only a theoretical proposition – not

to say idle curiosity. As an example of an important rigidity, take the marketing of locally produced wheat. It was widely reported in the local press that farmers who shifted to wheat production in response to higher farm-gate prices encountered difficulties in marketing their grain. The infrastructure for handling grain was geared more to imports than to local production, for which packing material was in short supply, storage facilities inadequate, and finance lacking. Government procurement facilities could only achieve 40 per cent of the 1993 target (see *Al Akabar* daily, June/18/1993).

iii. Further, the package may be based on a misconception about the nature of the relation between the private sector and the public sector – the crowding out thesis. At best, crowding out may be true only partly as far as the competition for resources, particularly credit, is concerned. Recent empirical work on determinants of private investment in Egypt indicates a somewhat mixed effect of government policy on private investment. The government appears to crowd out the private sector with regard to credit; but government investment in infrastructure crowds in private investment (see Shafik, 1992).

iv. Moreover, although the package aims at boosting the private sector, it contains a number of measures that could be disadvantageous to it – especially in commodity-producing activities generally and in manufacturing particularly. Thus raising domestic interest rates, raising energy prices, imposing a general sales tax and trade liberalization, may only lead in one direction: de-industrialization. The only advantage such a package offers to private industry is perhaps cheap labour; but the latter can also mean a thin market, and hence carries the threat of contraction of domestic activity.[7] Such a contraction cannot be overlooked since there is strong evidence of significant idle capacity in manufacturing. According to CAPMAS estimates, idle capacity in the public manufacturing sector averaged 15–19 per cent in the second half of the 1980s. For the private sector it was even higher, averaging 19–26 per cent. The main causes of idle capacity were shortage of material (42 per cent), lack of demand (28 per cent) and aging capital (10 per cent) (Shoura Council, 1992). Idle capacity in public-sector engineering industries during the early 1990s averaged 37 per cent, the main cause being lack of demand.

v. Apparent 'success' of ERSAP has been claimed by the government and the Bretton Woods institutions in stabilizing the value of the pound, improving the current account balance, reducing the budget deficit and curbing inflation (see CBE, n.d.). With some important qualifications to be elaborated in the next chapter, such a claim may be correct. However, there are serious doubts about *the sustainability of the programme.* Indeed, there is a real danger of backsliding. The real economy has been largely neglected, with much emphasis put on monetary and financial aspects. The sequencing of various measures is defective: liberalization of foreign exchange transactions – both current and capital – has proceeded long before the necessary changes in the productive side of the economy. In fact, *trade liberalization under ERSAP may have been pushed too far too fast,* threatening the recovery of economic activity. It is interesting to note that such trade liberalization has proceeded much beyond Egypt's commitments under GATT 1994. Further, it took place against the backdrop of protectionist tendencies in industrial countries. According to World Bank estimates, the trade coverage ratio of industrial countries' NTBs facing developing countries rose; the corresponding ratios rose from 26.5 per cent in 1981 to 28.0 per cent in 1990 for manufactures. For textiles, the ratios were 53.5 per cent and 56.9 per cent, respectively; and for clothing 61.0 per cent and 65.5 per cent, respectively (World Bank, *Global Economic Prospects and the Developing Countries 1992*, p. 20).

vi. With full capital mobility, and adopting a nominal exchange rate anchor since October 1991, the only way to avert capital outflow is by keeping the real interest rate significantly above the interest rate abroad. The scope for monetary policy is thus severely curtailed. This is for two reasons. The first is that monetary authorities lose effective discretionary powers over the interest rate, both because of balance of payments and fiscal considerations. The second is that fully mobile capital flows, unless sterilized, render the money supply largely endogenous. Little, therefore, remains of the instruments of monetary policy. If domestic inflation continues to edge above inflation in Egypt's main trading partners (not a remote possibility indeed), this may cause real appreciation of the pound. One of the consequences may be a sudden wave of hot capital outflow in anticipation of a maxi devaluation. This is the hard lesson of Latin America's Southern Cone (Argentina, Chile and Uruguay) in the late 1970s and of Mexico in the mid 1990s.

NOTES

1. ERSAP stands for Economic Reform and Structural Adjustment Pogramme, in official language. It was launched in March 1990.
2. Unemployment data in Egypt are a bit confusing. Main sources for unemployment data (Population Censuses and Labour Force Sample Surveys) are not comparable. According to the Population Census of 1986 total unemployment amounted to 11.1 per cent of labour force (15 years and over). The figure based on the 1987 Labour Force Sample Survey (LFSS) is 10.5 per cent, as compared to only 8.6 per cent on the basis of the 1990 Employment Sample Survey (ESS). But the latter defines labour force as 6 years and over. The incidence of unemployment is dangerously much higher among the youth, hitting 31 per cent for those

aged 20 and less than 25, according to the 1990 ESS. For more discussion of the size and nature of unemployment in Egypt, see the introduction by Handoussa in Handoussa and Potter (1991). During the early 1990s (early phases of ERSAP) the total unemployment rate was 10.6 per cent in 1993 and 11.3 per cent in 1995, according to the ESS. So far, unemployment does not seem to be abating; in fact the unemployment rate may be on the rise.

3. Information in this section is drawn from various unpublished material of the Bank, the Fund and the Egyptian government. Most important is the letter of intent of April 1991. The Central Bank of Egypt's annual submission of the People's Assembly, *Report on Monetary and Credit Conditions*, was also used, especially that for 1991/92.
4. Data concerning the fiscal deficit leave much to be desired. The figures reported in Tables 2.1 and 2.2 are taken from two documents of the World Bank, and they differ for the two common years, 1988/90 and 1990/91. Figures in Table 2.1 seem consistently about 2 percentage points below those of Table 2.2. We could not satisfactorily account for the discrepancy, or reconcile the figures.
5. Abstracting from the exceptionally high ratio in 1990/91, for the reasons explained in the note to Table 2.2.
6. In fact, the SBA, the foundation of ERSAP, provides an interesting example of conditionality. Cross-conditionality seems to be excessive. The IMF requires approval of the World Bank with regard to measures for privatization and adjustment of energy prices, while the Bank in turn insists on the Fund agreeing to the exchange-rate and interest-rate measures. With regard to the budget, the Bank examines expenditure measures while the Fund monitors revenue measures.
7. A study by a World Bank team, using a multi-sector two-household groups' economy-wide framework (called MISR2), concluded that a predominant result associated with the increase in public-sector prices is similar to increasing taxes (Ahmed *et al.*, 1985).

APPENDIX 2.1

Table 2A.1 Trade Liberalization Measures Under ERSAP, 1991–98

March 1991	Reduction of the production coverage of import bans from 35.6 per cent to 33.3 per cent of tradable goods output.
March 1991	Lift suspension of letters of credit on LE 140 million worth of output.
May 1991	Import duty rates restored to levels in effect in early 1989, prior to their reduction by approximately 30 per cent, and the tariff range reduced from 0.7–120 per cent to 5–100 per cent.
May 1991	Number of products subject to export bans were reduced from 20 to four.
May 1991	Number of products under quantitative annual export quotas was reduced from 17 to four. The remaining four products were raw and waste wool, tanned skin, cotton waste and paper waste (newspaper only).
May 1991	All exports prior to approvals that were imposed on 37 product categories were eliminated except for one (cotton yarn and fabrics) which is pending further study.

May 1991	The suspensions of letters of credit were eliminated.
May 1991	The list of products requiring adherence to certain special conditions for import was shortened from 12 to three.
May 1991	Production coverage of import bans was reduced from 37.2 per cent in March 1990 (of total manufacturing and agricultural production) to 22.7 per cent in June 1991.
May 1991	Twenty-nine of the total 90 BTN lines having tariff preferences were eliminated.
May 30,1991	The advance import deposit rate for imports that are settled with letters of credit was reduced to 10 per cent from 35 per cent in respect of import for own use and to 20 per cent in respect of imports for trade.
July 4, 1992	All export quotas except on treated hides were eliminated.
August 8, 1992	The advance import deposit requirement for opening of letters of credit was abolished.
August 1992	The number of footnotes (preferential tariff rates) was cut from 60 to 30 and duty rates were increased on about 100 items with a revenue impact of LE. 200 million.
August 1992	Further seven items removed from list of items requiring prior government approval for imports (nine products remain).
August 1992	Further four items have been removed from export bans list. Scrap metals and raw hides are the two remaining items.
August 1992	32 preferences have been removed from tariff preference list; 29 items remain.
August 1992	Export restrictions on cotton yarns and fabrics were eliminated.
August 1992	The drawback and temporary admissions system had been further improved and simplified.
1993	Export quota on the only remaining item (treated hides) eliminated.
February 1993	The tariff range was reduced from 5–100 per cent to 5–80 per cent.
December 1995	The tariff range was reduced from 5–80 per cent to 5–70 per cent.
October 1996	The tariff range was reduced from 5–70 per cent to 5–55 per cent.
1997	Only remaining item on export bans is raw hides. Number of items subject to prior government approval is down to one.
1997	Tariff range reduced to 5–50 per cent.
July 1998	Tariff range reduced to 5–40 per cent.

3. The macroeconomic effects of ERSAP: structural reform or Dutch disease?

INTRODUCTION

In this part of the study, we shall examine the most important effects of ERSAP at the macroeconomic level. Some aspects of the economic impact of ERSAP were discussed before, dealing with effects on the balance of payments, the budget deficit, inflation and output and employment (Korayem, 1993). Special emphasis will be placed here on particular elements of the programme which we deem critical for studying the impact of ERSAP on the prospects of industrialization in Egypt. Foremost among these are trade policy reform, foreign exchange reform and financial liberalization. Monetary and fiscal policies under the programme will only be dealt with in the context of examining the other elements just mentioned.

Some guiding principles will be adopted as criteria for judging the effects of ERSAP at the macroeconomic level. These include growth, equity, and employment generation (Abdel-Khalek, 1994). In addition, the main structural features of the Egyptian economy will be highlighted in order to serve as a background for determining the likely effects of ERSAP. Three such features deserve attention, namely: the large food deficit, heavy reliance on imported intermediates and the importance of external shocks.

EXTERNAL SHOCKS – NATURE AND MAGNITUDE

As a background to the analysis of the impact of ERSAP, it is necessary to examine the external shocks which impacted on the Egyptian economy in the second part of the 1980s and the policy responses to these shocks. In this context, it is important to emphasize that the Egyptian economy has become rather exposed to external shocks. Its prospects have grown strongly bound to the ebb and flow of oil and related factors – especially since the mid 1970s. This situation led to the observation that many of the well-known symptoms of Dutch disease have become manifest in the Egyptian case – most notably the rising share of non-tradables' sectors in GDP (Abdel-Khalek, 1982; El-Khawaga, 1996; Hansen, 1991).

The following factors play an increasingly important role in conditioning the equilibrium of the economy: oil revenues, workers' remittances, Suez Canal dues and tourism proceeds. All of them are largely beyond the country's control.

The strongest adverse shock is oil-related. The force of external shocks operating through oil exports may readily be seen from the perusal of Table 3.1. Oil exports exhibited a roller-coaster pattern of behaviour. They plummeted from $1664.3 million in 1985/86 to $634.1 million in 1986/87, a strong 62 per cent drop in a single year. Two years later, oil exports sustained another drop at the rate of 32 per cent in 1988/89, followed by an almost 65 per cent increase in 1989/90 and another 61 per cent increase in 1990/91. Oil exports exceeded their 1985/86 level only in 1990/91. This pattern of volatile movement was largely reflected in the value of total exports, which exhibited a similar pattern. Egypt's barter terms of trade deteriorated by 24 per cent between 1987 and 1990. Within the group of low-income countries according to World Bank classification, Egypt fared only slightly better than Burundi and Ghana. Cumulative terms of trade adjustment (1987=100) reached $4 billion during 1988/89–1990/91, representing about 1 per cent of GDP.

Table 3.2 summarizes the performance of the Egyptian economy over the decade straddling the beginning of ERSAP. Several macroeconomic indicators are used to gauge performance, and distinction is made between the first and second parts of the decade. Although the impact of external shocks on macroeconomic performance is quite clear, some important observations are in order. *First*, real GDP growth fluctuated rather sharply during the period 1985/86–1995/96 reaching a trough of 1 per cent per annum at the beginning of the programme but gradually recovering after that. It is our judgement that the extent of recovery may be a bit less than the figures in Table 3.2 indicate, partly as a result of exaggerated GDP growth at current prices and partly as a result of underestimation of inflation. *Second,* domestic inflation subsided, with the inflation rate falling from a double-digit level to single-digit levels starting 1993/94. *Third*, the overall fiscal deficit was brought down very drastically, reflecting the tough fiscal stance under ERSAP. The figures in the table indicate that the budget deficit was sharply reduced from 20 per cent of GDP to 7 per cent in just a single year (between 1990/91 and 1991/92). It approached 1 per cent of GDP around the mid 1990s.

However, those estimates of the budget deficit should be considered with caution, as they are based on budget *proposals* not *actuals*. The deficit figures based on actuals are severalfold those based on proposals. For example, the 1995/96 actual deficit LE 6 billion, compared to only LE 600 million according to the budget proposal. Nevertheless, the fiscal performance under ERSAP is actually quite remarkable compared with Egypt's past stabilization efforts in the 1970s and 1980s which showed little fiscal discipline. *Fourth,* the

Table 3.1 *Trade balance, 1985/86–1995/96 ($ million)*

		1985/86	1986/87	1987/88	1988/89	1989/90	1990/91	1991/92	1992/93	1993/94	1994/95	1995/96
Export:	value	3575.7	2264.4	3273.9	2545.9	3144.8	3886.8	3636.4	3416.7	3337.3	4947.0	4592.8
	index	100	63.3	91.6	71.2	88.0	108.7	101.6	95.6	93.3	138.6	128.5
Oil:	value	1664.7	634.1	1093.9	756.4	1228.6	1970.7	1615.1	1803.0	1772.0	2175.5	2225.6
	index	100	38.1	65.7	44.8	73.8	118.4	97.0	108.3	106.5	130.7	133.7
Imports:	value	8554.1[a]	7952.2	9841.0	10078.9	11443.1	11424.5	10054.1	10728.2	10647.1	12810.5	13826.4
	index	100	93.0	115.0	117.8	133.7	133.6	117.5	125.4	124.5	149.8	161.6
Trade Balance:		–4978.8	–5687.8	–6567.1	–7533.0	–8296.3	–7537.7	–6417.7	–7311.5	–7309.8	–7853.5	–9233.6
TOT Adjustment		3833	2456	0	–1240	–1599	–1186	724	715	718	312	616

Note: a. Excludes commodity imports as grants in kind.

Source: Central Bank of Egypt, *Economic Review*, and *Annual Report*, various volumes, except for terms-of-trade adjustment which is from The World Bank, *World Development Indicators, 1998 CD-ROM*.

Table 3.2 *Selected economic indicators, 1987/88–1995/96*

	1985/86	1986/87	1987/88	1988/89	1989/90	1990/91	1991/92	1992/93	1993/94	1994/95	1995/96
Real GDP growth (%)	3	3	5	5	6	1	4	3	4	5	5
Domestic inflation	13	31	14	19	19	15	20	10	7	9	9
Av. nominal exchange rate (LE/US$)	1.069	1.273	1.761	1.937	2.229	3.009	3.331	3.33	3.38	3.39	3.39
Av. nominal deposit rate*	11.0	11.0	11.0	12.0	12.0	16.0	17.1	16.3	13.9	11.0	10.4
Av. nominal lending rate*	14.0	15.0	15.0	16.0	17.0	18.0	22.0				
M2 growth rate (%)**	16.3	12.4	11.1	12.3	21.4	13.4	34.4	16.4	12.4	11.1	10.5
Overall fiscal deficit/ GDP(%)	23.1	19.3	24.5	18.1	16.5	20.0	7.2	3.5	2.1	1.3	1.3
Current account/GDP (%)#	–9.4	–5.2	–4.0	–9.3	–10.5	–7.4	2.8	0.6	–1.2	0.8	–2.0
Resource balance/GDP	–10	–10	–18	–14	–13	–8	–3	–3	–5	–5	–5
DOD/GDP (%)	118.0	131.4	155.0	127.9	144.3	119.1	109.5	65.6	58.0	55.7	47.1

Notes:

* Rate on deposits and loans with maturity less than one year, except for 91/92 where 3-month LE deposit rate is used.

** M2 = currency + demand deposits + LE time and savings deposits.

\# Excluding official transfers.

Sources: Real GDP growth, inflation, and resource balance, World Bank, *WDI 1998 CD-ROM*. All other data from IMF (1997).

current account deficit was reduced significantly. Prior to ERSAP, the current account deficit averaged 7–8 per cent of GDP; it improved dramatically after 1990/91, thanks to ERSAP. It is actually significant that the current account deficit of 7.4 per cent of GDP was transformed into a surplus of 2.8 per cent; a remarkable turnaround indeed. But that should not camouflage the widening trade deficit (see Table 3.1). *Finally,* external debt was reduced significantly, partly due to ERSAP, with the DOD/GDP ratio falling from 144 per cent in 1989/90 to 47 per cent in 1995/96.

FOREIGN EXCHANGE REFORM

As Annexes I and II indicate, both the foreign exchange regime and the exchange rate have undergone fundamental changes since 1945, reflecting several attempts to devalue the pound and unify the rates. Even before the official start of ERSAP, measures were taken which involved moving from fixed parity to a flexible peg and from multiple rates to a unified rate. There was a number of maxi devaluations in the process (for more details see Abdel-Khalek, 1987, Annex I; El-Rifaie, 1992).

Exchange Rate: Regime and Changes, 1973–97

As mentioned, attempts to streamline the exchange rate regime predate ERSAP. Although they may be traced back to the measures taken in 1987, it may be useful to refer to 1979. The steps leading to the unification-cum-devaluation of 1979 have been discussed already elsewhere (Abdel-Khalek, 1987). Here we focus on the development thereafter, particularly since the second half of the 1980s. The history of the exchange rate system over this period, and until October 1991, may be characterized as one of repeated failed attempts at establishing a unified exchange rate. But the trend over the period since 1979 has clearly been one of recurring devaluation of the pound.

The year 1985 witnessed a maxi devaluation of about 60 per cent in the authorized banks' exchange rate, which at the time covered about 50 per cent of transactions (El-Rifaie, 1992, p. 187). Another maxi devaluation of more than 60 per cent came about with the establishment of the free banking market for foreign exchange, which started in May 1987 to replace the authorized banks' pool. The devaluation of the exchange rate in the Central Bank pool by 64.6 per cent in August 1989 (from LE 0.70 per dollar to LE 1.15 per dollar) and by another 73.6 per cent in July 1990 is relatively less significant since this rate accounted then for less than 15 per cent of total transactions (El-Rifaie, 1992). More important perhaps is the move to a two-tier exchange rate system (primary/free market) in February 1991, and finally the unification of the exchange rate in October of the same year. This involved a devaluation of about 15 per cent.

Some observations are now in order regarding exchange rate policy in Egypt under ERSAP. The culmination of exchange reform with the establishment of the free market of foreign exchange ushers in a new phase. The Egyptian pound has been pegged to the American dollar since the unification of the exchange rate on October 8, 1991. The Central Bank of Egypt intervened in the foreign exchange market to maintain a stable pound/dollar exchange rate, that is using the nominal pound/dollar exchange rate as an anchor. The bilateral exchange rates of the pound *vis-à-vis* other currencies follow straight from the pegged pound/dollar rate and the corresponding rates of exchange between the dollar and these currencies prevailing on international currency markets. Monetary authorities thus only decide on the pound/dollar rate; the pound rates against other currencies follow. In order to deepen the foreign exchange market, non-bank foreign exchange dealers have been officially allowed, with restrictions on their operations increasingly liberalized. Until very recently, the pound/dollar rate has been fairly stable since the exchange rate unification in 1991. It may be said that Egypt adopts a managed float around a dollar peg, or a *de facto* nominal anchor. Both current and capital transactions have been almost completely liberalized.[1]

Assessment of the impact of the change in the exchange rate (devaluation) and the change in the exchange rate regime (liberalization) calls for examining the behaviour of balance of payments – with emphasis on the trade balance. The impact on the competitiveness of manufacturing and on macroeconomic balance has to be considered as well. In approaching these questions, special emphasis should be placed on the sustainability of reform measures in this field.

Because of the lack of sufficient data, we cannot calculate the average nominal exchange rate over the period of multiple rates through 1991/92; detailed information necessary to estimate relative shares of trade transactions taking place according to the various rates are hard to come by. As a second best alternative in order to trace out the changes in the 'average' nominal exchange rate of the Egyptian pound, the 'implicit' exchange rates for exports and imports were calculated for the period 1978–1991/92. The 'implicit' exchange rate is in effect a weighted-average rate which arises from a system of multiple exchange rates. In such a system, data may not be available regarding the relative weights of transactions subject to the various individual rates. Within this context, a direct calculation of the average exchange rate will be impossible. Alternatively, the implicit exchange rate is thus calculated by dividing the Egyptian-pound FOB value of trade (exports or imports) by the corresponding dollar value. In a sense it is analogous to the implicit GDP deflator.

Table 3.3 Trade balance, implicit exchange rates and export/import ratios, 1978–1991/92

	Exports (X)			Imports (M)					
	LEm (1)	$m (2)	Implicit X rate (LE/$) (3)=(1)/(2)	LEm (4)	$m (5)	Implicit M rate (LE/$) (6)=(4)/(5)	Trade balance $m (7)	(8)=(2)/(5) (%)	(9)=(6)/(3)
1978	776.2	1983.7	0.3914	2 067.1	5 282.7	0.3914	–3299	37	1
1979	1 758.4	2512.1	0.7000	4 672.6	6 675.2	0.7000	–4162	38	1
1980	2 697.1	3853.1	0.7000	5 304.4	7 577.9	0.7000	–3725	51	1
81/82	2 765.1	3846.7	0.7189	6 569.0	8 618.2	0.7622	–4772	45	1.060
82/83	2 682.9	3741.9	0.7170	6 382.5	8 269.3	0.7718	–4527	45	1.076
83/84	2 859.8	3960.4	0.7220	7 384.8	9 519.3	0.7719	–5559	42	1.069
84/85	2 837.8	3927.8	0.7225	7 495.9	9 640.6	0.7775	–5715	41	1.076
85/86	2 885.4	3575.7	0.8071	9 221.4	8 554.1	1.0780	–4979	42	1.336
86/87	2 076.6	2264.4	0.9171	8 296.1	7 952.2	1.1328	–5688	31	1.236
87/88	3 766.0	3274.0	1.1507	17 737.7	9 841.0	1.8024	–6567	33	1.566
88/89	3 383.4	2545.9	1.3298	19 869.8	10 078.9	1.9714	–7533	25	1.482
89/90	5 567.2	3144.8	1.7706	25 516.9	11 443.1	2.2303	–8298	27	1.260
90/91	9 438.9	3886.8	2.4285	31 392.0	11 424.5	2.7478	–7538	34	1.131
91/92	11 554.6	3636.4	3.1775	33 074.1	10 054.1	3.2944	–6418	36	1.037

Source: 1978–1988/89, El-Rifaie (1992), Table 8, p. 156. 1989/90–1991/92, CBE, *Eco. Rev.*, vol. 32/4, Tables 4/1 and 4/2.

The results of these calculations are shown in Table 3.3, and they reveal some interesting features. *First,* the nominal exchange rate of the Egyptian pound has been brought down significantly since the mid 1980s. Aside from the short episode of the unified exchange rate during the late 1970s–early 1980s, a bias against exports clearly manifests itself in the fact that the average exchange rate implicit in the case of exports is less than that in the case of imports. The import exchange rate reached one-and-a-half times the export exchange rate during 1987/88–1988/89. This points to the significant distortion during the 1980s, which was reduced significantly during subsequent years and was completely eliminated by the unification of the exchange rate in October 1991. Although a special exchange rate is still in force for liquidation accounts under terminating bilateral payments agreements, this is a minor deviation.

Effect of Devaluation

Some macroeconomic effects of the devaluation of the Egyptian pound were discussed elsewhere (Korayem, 1993). We focus here on a number of neglected aspects of the Egyptian devaluation, notably its effect on the cost of domestic production and the cost of living. But it should be reiterated that since the 1991 devaluation under ERSAP, the Egyptian pound has been pegged to the US dollar and has significantly appreciated. The extent of appreciation will be determined below. Nominal devaluation of the pound contributed to increasing the cost of production, significantly in some sectors, in view of the high intermediate import content of domestic production. Examining the structure of production in 1989/90 provides supporting empirical evidence to this contention. Analysis based on the input–output matrix for that year reveals a relatively high direct content of domestic production – something in the range of 13–14 per cent. The total requirements (both direct and indirect) are much higher. It is useful to examine the case of some sectors in 1989/90 (see Table 3.4) in order to gauge the order of magnitude of the impact effect of devaluation on the cost of intermediate inputs. Some important sectors stand out. Transport equipment tops the list, with a coefficient of total intermediate inputs of 0.551. This is followed by wood and furniture (0.544), chemicals except oil (0.479), paper, printing and publishing (440), food (0.438), machinery (0.383), leather except shoes (0.292), and other manufacturing (0.276).

Although there are other sectors where the total import requirements per unit of domestic production is much lower, the significance of the sectors singled out above is because they are the most important tradables sectors. This is also supported by field survey results which indicate even a much higher import dependence of manufacturing during the 1990s. A recent

Table 3.4 Direct and total intermediate import requirements, 1989/90

		Direct import coefficient	Total import coefficient
1.	Food plant production	0.023497	0.041320
2.	Non-food plant production	0.019837	0.035784
3.	Animal production	0.082466	0.116512
4.	Crude oil & natural gas	0.303796	0.340406
5.	Other extraction	0.002320	0.024216
6.	Food	0.376107	0.437758
7.	Beverages	0.165368	0.255399
8.	Tobacco	0.109368	0.163163
9.	Ginning	0.000349	0.045810
10.	Spinning & weaving	0.113563	0.167937
11.	Ready-made clothes	0.038620	0.101967
12.	Leather except shoes	0.188587	0.292112
13.	Shoes	0.053730	0.185870
14.	Wood & furniture	0.532004	0.544213
15.	Furniture	0.333315	0.380303
16.	Paper, printing & pub.	0.360132	0.439872
17.	Chem. exc. ref. oil	0.436003	0.479313
18.	Refined oil	0.192441	0.216624
19.	Plastic & rubber	0.078332	0.253572
20.	Porcelain & china	0.054479	0.093487
21.	Glass products	0.111531	0.167947
22.	Mining exc. metal	0.023925	0.063451
23.	Iron & steel & basic metals	0.066679	0.151248
24.	Machinery & equipment	0.323759	0.383060
25.	Transport equipment	0.532561	0.551454
26.	Other manufacturing	0.162650	0.275775
27.	Electricity, gas & water	0.114922	0.193758
28.	Construction & building	0.214284	0.276258
29.	Wholesale & retail	0.019967	0.0389253
30.	Hotels & restaurants	0.025934	0.148681
31.	Trans. & storage	0.116281	0.177261
32.	Communication	0.010021	0.026060
33.	Financial enterprises	0.155944	0.174326
34.	Insurance	0.000682	0.012924
35.	Housing & real estate	0.027169	0.053512
36.	Social services	0.007421	0.010446
37.	Cultural & entertainment	0.066373	0.125614
38.	Personal services	0.135597	0.204621

Source: Calculated on the basis of the 1989/90 input–output table for Egypt.

sample study on industry in one pioneering industrial town revealed that imported intermediates account for 65 per cent of total intermediates as an overall sample average, but reaching 95 per cent in some industries. Import content in machinery and equipment is much higher, averaging 94 per cent for the sample study (Fawzi, 1993, p. 88).

With these structural characteristics, devaluation must have had important cost-push effects – particularly in the short run. Unless supported by other measures to cut costs and/or raise productivity, this would reflect negatively on the competitiveness of domestic production both in foreign markets and also in the local market – given the rate of protection (tariffs, and so on).

In addition to imported intermediates, the shares of *food imports* and *capital goods imports* are also relevant for assessing the cost-push impact of devaluation. According to the Central Bank of Egypt, food imports accounted for 21 per cent, intermediate inputs 46 per cent, and capital goods imports 24 per cent of total imports on the average for the period 1987/88–1991/92. The rest is the share of other imports, notably fuel and consumer goods other than food.

Given these structural characteristics, one would expect imports to be inelastic with respect to exchange rate changes. According to estimates by the Central Bank of Egypt using data for the period 1975–1991/92, the value of this elasticity was about – 0.3.[2] Another study using data for the period 1967–93 concluded that the exchange rate is insignificant in determining total imports (El-Shawarby, 1997, p. 100). On the other hand, the propensity to import is high for Egypt compared to other countries. For Egypt, the share of imports in GDP is around 0.30, whereas for a comparable case like Turkey it was only about 0.20 on the average during 1981–91. All this may provide partial evidence that the Marshall-Lerner condition did not apply in the case of total imports.

With a low exchange rate elasticity and high import propensity, the impact of devaluation on the general price level cannot be ignored. This in itself partly undermines the efficacy of devaluation as an expenditure-switching measure, since it leads to an increase in the cost of domestic production. We conclude therefore that import-substitution industrialization by itself sets rigid limits to the effectiveness of devaluation as a means of dealing with balance of trade disequilibria. With regard to exports, devaluation was actually irrelevant for Egypt's major export item (oil), which accounted for at least 50 per cent of exports during the period of devaluation. The impact of devaluation on exports may be most felt in the case of non-traditional manufacturing items, provided there is a reasonably high supply elasticity. If we examine the evidence in Table 3.1, we observe that the impact of the 1990–91 devaluation lasted through 1993–94. But it seems to have quickly dissipated thereafter.

The foregoing analysis should be qualified in at least two important ways. *First,* in the long run, devaluation may contribute to the streamlining and rationalization of the industrial structure – but only if supported by appropriate monetary, fiscal and trade/industrial policy measures. *Second,* since there is no real wage indexation in Egypt's case, the increase in the cost of living resulting from devaluation coupled with the stickiness of nominal wages may have resulted in a fall in the real wages. *Ceteris paribus,* all this may thus improve the country's competitiveness on this score.

The Real Exchange Rate

Why was the effect of devaluation on the trade balance only temporary, as we concluded above? The answer lies in the fact that nominal devaluation did not translate into lasting real depreciation. We thus have to look closely at the behaviour of the real exchange rate for the Egyptian pound.

At the outset, it is important to note that the real exchange rate calculations are based on a number of assumptions: in particular a small economy, for which world prices of imports and exports are given (the country is a price taker), and whose tariff structure is given. The latter assumption may be relaxed, and changes in the tariff structure may be built into the formula for the RER.

In the literature, reference is often made to the concept of the effective exchange rate and hence to the nominal effective exchange rate (NEER) and the real effective exchange rate (REER). The effective exchange rate takes into account changes in other currencies' exchange rates. Distinguishing the effective exchange rate has become almost common practice after the collapse of the fixed parities system of Bretton Woods and the ensuing wide variations in individual currencies' exchange rates. The rationale for this is that the exchange rate is basically a relative price which is supposed to be an indicator of competitiveness, and thus it is important to take into account the changes in other currencies' nominal exchange rates as well. The concept of the effective exchange rate makes good sense in the context of an adjustable-peg system; but it becomes rather fuzzy under a floating regime.[3]

In the context of this study, the real effective exchange rate (REER) is measured in the usual way by adjusting the nominal effective exchange rate (NEER) by differential inflation rates (that is, the ratio of domestic to foreign price indices). The formula used to calculate the real effective exchange rate (REER) is the following:

$$\text{REER} = \text{NEER} \times P_f / P_d \qquad (3.1)$$

where

REER = real effective exchange rate index
NEER = nominal effective exchange rate (LE/foreign currency) index
P_f = foreign price level index, and
P_d = domestic price level index, measured by CPI.

Equation (3.1) may be interpreted as follows: a rise in NEER (REER) means nominal (real) depreciation, and a fall in NEER (REER) means nominal (real) appreciation. It is a common practice in applied work to use the wholesale price index (WPI) as a measure of the foreign price level. In our application reported in the text, we had to use the CPI for Egypt's major trading partners as a substitute for the WPI, which was not available.[4]

Table 3.5 provides estimates of the REER of the pound for the period 1973–96. The table provides calculations of the real exchange rate of the pound *vis-à-vis* the currencies of Egypt's main trade partners (countries accounting for about 80 per cent of Egypt's trade). Several interesting conclusions may be reached based on such estimates; but we focus here on the episode of ERSAP. The last column of Table 3.5 shows that the devaluation of 1990/91 did not translate into lasting real depreciation. According to our results, it is clear that the real exchange rate of the pound *vis-à-vis* Egypt's main trading partners has declined, signalling real appreciation by about 20 per cent during 1991–96.

We argue here that one aspect of financial liberalization – namely the liberalization of interest rates in conjunction with liberalizing capital transactions in the balance of payments – and the adoption of a nominal exchange rate anchor by the Central Bank of Egypt have contributed to this appreciation of the Egyptian pound. Whether that amounts to an overvaluation of the pound depends on whether the initial rate was an equilibrium one. This issue is open to debate.

With the liberalization of interest rates on pound deposits and loans by the Central Bank of Egypt as part of ERSAP effective from January 3, 1991, banks have become free to set pound deposit interest rates.[5] As a result of the tight monetary policy under ERSAP, interest rates on pound deposits in the domestic banking system rose steeply. For example, the rate on three-month pound deposits jumped from 8.5 per cent on an annual basis at the end of December 1990 to 13.6 per cent at the end of June 1991 – a 60 per cent increase. It peaked at the end of January 1992, reaching 17.2 per cent annually. There was a declining tendency thereafter. When compared to the LIBOR interest rate on US dollar deposits, the interest differential jumped from 0.59 percentage points at the end of December 1990 to 13.02 percentage points at the end of January 1991 (see Table 3.6). The major factor behind the movement in the interest rate on pound deposits is the auction for government treasury bills (TBs), which determines the rate on treasury bills. The latter in

Table 3.5 Real effective exchange rate, 1973–96

Year	Nominal exchange rate (LE/$) (1)	Nominal LE/$ index (2)	Nominal $/FC index (3)	CPI_{LE}/CPI_{FC} (4)	NEER (5)	REER (6)
1973	0.436	14.5	142.1	35.3	20.6	58.4
1974	0.436	14.5	139.4	33.8	20.2	59.8
1975	0.436	14.5	140.9	33.1	20.4	61.7
1976	0.450	14.9	131.0	33.4	19.5	58.4
1977	0.450	14.9	131.1	34.3	19.5	57.0
1978	0.455	15.1	138.8	35.2	21.0	59.5
1979	0.705	23.4	142.3	35.1	33.3	94.9
1980	0.742	24.6	172.7	45.9	42.5	92.6
1981	0.753	25.0	147.9	44.7	37.0	82.7
1982	0.764	25.4	130.3	46.2	33.1	71.6
1983	0.773	25.6	117.2	48.8	30.0	61.5
1984	0.781	25.9	102.7	51.6	26.6	51.5
1985	0.806	26.7	94.0	52.9	25.1	47.4
1986	0.538	31.2	106.7	62.4	33.3	53.4
1987	1.090	36.2	115.0	71.2	41.6	58.5
1988	1.573	52.2	122.8	84.6	64.1	75.8
1989	2.048	68.0	109.8	91.0	74.7	82.4
1990	2.390	79.4	108.6	93.2	74.0	92.5
1991	3.011	100.0	100.0	100.0	100.0	100.0
1992	3.304	109.7	94.1	102.6	103.2	100.6
1993	3.334	110.7	81.9	103.4	90.7	87.7
1994	3.339	110.9	80.0	101.0	88.7	87.8
1995	3.339	110.9	76.4	104.9	84.7	80.8
1996	3.339	110.9	77.6	107.5	86.1	80.1

Notes and sources:
Column (1): Nominal LE/$ exchange rate calculated as a transaction-weighted average of exchange rates derived from Annex II. It is not the official rate only, as is normally done.
Column (2): Nominal exchange rate figures in column (1) normalized for 1990/91 as the base year. This is the year with the largest proportional nominal devaluation.
Column (3): Index of the nominal trade-weighted exchange rate (measured as $ per national currency) of Egypt's main trading partners. Exchange rates from IMF, *IFS 1998 CD-ROM*, and trade weights from IMF, *Direction of Trade Statistics 1998 CD-ROM*.
Column (4): Ratio of Egypt's CPI to major trading partners' weighted average CPI, normalized for 1990/91.
Column (5) = column (2) × column (3).
Column (6) = column (5) ÷ column (4).

Table 3.6 Deposit interest rate on Egyptian pound and libor rate for US$

End of	3-month pound deposits (1)	3-month US$ libor (2)	Interest-differential (3) = (1) – (2)	LE/$ exchange rate (4)
Dec. 90	8.5[a]	7.91	0.59	
June 91	13.6	6.20	7.40	3.3409
Jan. 92	17.2	4.18	13.02	
June 92	16.7	3.99	12.71	3.3211
Dec. 92	15.1	3.63	11.47	
June 93	13.5	3.24[b]	10.26	3.3525

Notes:
a. Adopted since January 1981.
b. March 93

Sources: (1) Central Bank of Egypt, *Annual Report*, various years. (2) IMF, *IFS*, various issues.

turn determines the discount rate (since the Central Bank of Egypt sets the discount rate at 2 percentage points above the rate on three-month TBs), and hence the pound lending interest rate.

Even after the ensuing decline in the interest rate on domestic pound deposits, the differential was still more than 10 percentage points by mid 1993. The interest differential seems to have finally stabilized around 5 percentage points. At the same time, following a nominal exchange-rate anchor effectively eliminates foreign exchange risk. With free capital mobility, this policy resulted in large short-term capital inflow, driven by uncovered interest arbitrage.

Against this backdrop, we observe that monetary policy during the latter phase of ERSAP had three main targets: (i) to control monetary expansion; (ii) to stabilize the pound/dollar (nominal) exchange rate; and (iii) to bring down the pound interest rate in order to encourage investment. The instruments used are credit ceilings and treasury bills issuing (CBE, 1992/93, p. 40). This is a classical example of too few instruments chosen to achieve a given set of targets.[6]

In the Egyptian case, the interest rate differential resulted from the confluence of a jump in interest rates on pound deposits and a drop in interest rates abroad. Such a differential opened the possibility of making profits through interest arbitrage, by moving funds between the domestic and foreign money markets. The general formula for interest arbitrage (in the case of three-month deposits) may be expressed as follows (Salvatore, 1995).[7]

$$m = (r - r_a)/(4 + r_a) - (e_f - e)/(e) \quad (3.2)$$

where

m = arbitrage margin per dollar per year
r = interest on 3-month pound deposits, annualized
r_a = interest on 3-month dollar deposits, annualized
e = spot exchange rate (LE/\$)
e_f = forward exchange rate (LE/\$).

In applying this formula to the Egyptian case, it has to be noted that $e_f = e$, thanks to the nominal exchange-rate anchor. This is the special case of uncovered interest arbitrage, where speculators need not buy foreign exchange forward in order to hedge against exchange risk. Ignoring transactions cost, the 'profit' margin from arbitrage operations in Egypt's case exceeded 3 percentage points (on an annual basis) in the first half of 1992. Although the arbitrage profit margin has declined since January 1993, it is still significant.

Interest arbitrage may thus explain or at least shed interesting light on two important consequences of ERSAP, namely the shift from foreign currency denominated deposits to pound denominated deposits in the domestic banking system (de-dollarization), and massive short-term capital inflows and accumulation of foreign exchange reserves with the Central Bank.

The Egyptian experience under ERSAP may be reminiscent of the Mexican experience of the mid 1990s. We are not necessarily predicting a scenario similar to the debacle leading to the 1994–95 financial crisis in Mexico, nor are we implying that the Egyptian case is a 'clone' of the Mexican one. But one has to underscore the fact that in Egypt now as in Mexico in 1994–95, economic fundamentals do not seem to be properly aligned. The pound is appreciating, domestic public debt is mounting, and there is a widening trade deficit counteracted by short-term capital inflows. In addition, there is a fall in the savings rate, and stagnation in the rate of investment. Such a combination is extremely fragile and eventually unsustainable.

Let us look at this process in action, and consider the orders of magnitude involved. To avert nominal appreciation of the pound, the Central Bank intervened in the foreign exchange market, buying dollars in exchange for pounds. Under the nominal exchange rate anchor, such capital inflows led to the accumulation of foreign currency reserves with the monetary authorities. Thus, the international reserves of the Central Bank of Egypt (excluding gold) rose from the equivalent of only US$ 2.684 billion at the end of 1990 to US$12.904 billion at the end of 1993, equivalent to about 120 per cent of annual imports. Estimates for June 1996 come close to US$19 billion, the equivalent of more than 16 months' worth of imports. This level of foreign international reserves is unprecedented in Egypt's recent economic history – the sterling balances aside.[8]

With both nominal exchange rate anchor and capital mobility, the stage was set for the endogenous determination of foreign exchange reserves (Blejer and Leiderman, 1981). Domestic debt accumulated in parallel, representing the other side of misaligned economic fundamentals: interest rate, inflation rate and nominal exchange rate. To avoid unwarranted monetary expansion, foreign exchange inflows were largely sterilized. The government issued treasury bills well in excess of the needs of financing its fiscal deficit largely to sterilize capital inflows. Domestic debt accumulated, in part representing the other side of accumulated international reserves with the Central Bank. The other part was excess pound liquidity in the domestic banking system (see Table 3.7).

Table 3.7 Treasury bills issues, interest rates and international reserves

	1991/92	1992/93	1993/94
Total TBs issued (LE billion)	13.1	13.4	4.6**
To cover deficit	3.6	2.6	n.a.
To mop up liquidity*	9.5	10.8	n.a.
Interest rate on 3-month TBs %	20.7	18.3	14.8
International reserves ($ billion, end of June)	10.5	15.0	16.8

Notes:
* Mostly government deposits with the Central Bank of Egypt.
** Change in stock of outstanding TB.

Sources: (1) CBE, *Annual Report*, 1991/92 and 1992/93, (2) CBE, *Economic Review* vol, 35, no. 3 (1994/95).

In its effort to stabilize the nominal value of the pound in the face of capital inflows attracted by the interest rate differential (see Table 3.6), the Central Bank of Egypt bought US$4.7 billion during 1991/92, raising its foreign exchange reserves to US$10.5 billion at the end of June 1992. Net purchases during 1992/93 amounted to US$5.2 billion, raising foreign exchange reserves to some US$15 billion at the end of June 1993 (see Table 3.7).

The increased pound liquidity in the banking system was used largely to buy treasury bills, with tax-free income. Of treasury bills issued during 1991/92 amounting to LE 13.1 billion, only LE 3.6 billion of treasury bills' proceeds were used to cover the budget deficit for the same year. As a result, government deposits with the Central Bank increased by LE 7.2 billion in 1991/92, which was more than half the value of treasury bills' issues for the same year.[9] This means that only about 27 per cent of the proceeds of treasury bills issued during 1991/92 were used to cover the fiscal deficit; the rest went to sterilize foreign capital inflows. The figures for 1992/93 show more increase in the proportion of treasury bills' issues motivated by monetary rather than fiscal considerations (that is, mopping up liquidity rather than covering the budget deficit).

Fiscal policy was thus subordinated to monetary policy, and the cost of such a policy mix must be carefully considered in the overall assessment of ERSAP. This may be reminiscent of Mundell's famous model, where capital mobility frustrated either monetary policy (under a fixed exchange rate regime) or fiscal policy (under a flexible exchange rate regime).[10] On the basis of the proceeds of TB issuing to mop up liquidity and the average interest rate on 3-month TBs, one can estimate the fiscal cost of such policy. For example, in 1991/92, LE 9.5 worth of treasury bills was used to sterilize capital inflows (representing 73 per cent of TB issues for the year), and the interest rate on this debt averaged 18.4 per cent. Hence, the interest payments on this addition to the domestic debt for 1991/92 runs in the order of LE 1.75 billion. Against this interest cost, one should consider the interest income that the government received on her deposits with the Central Bank, made possible by issuing TBs in excess of the need to finance the fiscal deficit. The interest rate on such deposits was set at 2 percentage points below the rate on TBs. Government deposits with the Central Bank (LE 7.2 billion during 1991/92) carried a return of 16.4 per cent yielding total interest receipts of LE 1.18 billion. Hence, there was a net direct fiscal cost of LE 0.57 billion for 1991/92 alone.

The World Bank has recently estimated the annual loss (caused by the Central Bank of Egypt holding excess international reserves) to be in the range of 1–2 per cent of GDP (World Bank, 1997, vol. II, p. 22). These represent government resources that could have been devoted to better or more desirable alternative uses. There are also clear distributional aspects involved in such a policy; if these funds have to be raised by collecting taxes, as they should in the final analysis, then Egyptian taxpayers are in effect subsidizing, through this policy, the holders of TBs – the foreign and local rentiers or 'clipping class'.

What has been the impact of exchange rate policy adopted under ERSAP? As mentioned above, since there is capital mobility (thanks to the liberalization of capital transactions in the balance of payments) and a nominal exchange rate anchor, financial liberalization leads to capital inflows. The money supply increases in the process, except for sterilization, thereby increasing inflationary pressures in the economy. If we add to that the impact of price liberalization as part of the structural adjustment component of ERSAP (see Korayem, 1993), we should expect build-up of inflationary pressures which, if not arrested, may result in a steadily rising price level. The inevitable consequence of a nominal exchange rate anchor and high domestic inflation relative to Egypt's major trading partners was the appreciation of the Egyptian pound.

It seems that this appreciation of the pound has become one of the central tendencies under ERSAP (see World Bank, 1995, 1997; IMF, 1997). As a result, devaluation became for some time a contentious issue between the Egyptian government and the IMF: the latter pushing for devaluation and the former strongly resisting it. Concern has been voiced regarding the potential loss of competitiveness as a result of the deterioration of the real exchange rate. This point may be further explained with reference to equation (3.1) above.

Assuming that the world price level expresses the price of tradables, and that the domestic price level is a good proxy for the price of non-tradables or home goods, we may obtain a slightly modified version of (3.1) in the following form:

$$\text{RER} = P_t / P_n \qquad (3.3)$$

where

$P_t = \text{NER} \times P_f =$ price of tradables (in local currency)
$P_n = P_d =$ price of non-tradables.

RER as expressed in (3.3) is the familiar Salter ratio. Using that ratio, we may derive the following conclusion. *On the basis of available empirical evidence, the relative price of tradables vis-à-vis non-tradables in Egypt has gone down by about 20 per cent over the period 1991–96, which is the first phase of ERSAP.* Results of recent studies concur with our conclusion (compare World Bank, 1997, vol. II. pp. 14–15; El-Khawaga, 1996, Ch.3).

Caution should be observed when interpreting these results. The appreciation of the pound may imply that the country is losing competitiveness in international exchange. This, however, should be qualified in an important respect, namely, the behaviour of wages. To demonstrate this point, a slightly modified version of (3.1) may be used. Consider

$$\text{RER} = \text{NER} \times P_f / W \qquad (3.4)$$

where *W* stands for wage index in the home country. The version expressed in (3.4) may be more suitable where wages constitute a major component of production costs; manufacturing may be one such case. With reference to equation (3.4), we observe that nominal wages in Egypt seem to be lagging behind the cost-of-living increases, as expressed for example by the CPI. Official estimates by the Central Agency of Public Mobilization and Statistics (CAPMAS)[11] indicate that, over the quinquennium 1986/87–1991/92, total nominal wages increased at an average annual rate of 15.9 per cent, while the consumer price index recorded an average annual increase at the rate of 18.4 per cent. Real wages have thus been falling steadily at a rate averaging 2.5 per cent per annum. This deterioration in real wages should be expected to continue under ERSAP, since the programme explicitly stipulates that wage increases be kept below the rate of inflation.

Barring a commensurate drop in labour productivity (which we assume away), a fall in real wages means a decrease in the cost of production, *ceteris paribus*. It may be difficult therefore to argue that the loss of competitiveness was actually to the extent indicated by the real appreciation of the Egyptian pound. But there definitely has been some loss of competitiveness, nevertheless.

The conclusion we can safely draw on the basis of available evidence is that the maxi devaluation of 1990–91 did not stick; the period representing the first phase of ERSAP witnessed real appreciation of the Egyptian pound. Such real appreciation entails some loss of competitiveness in international exchange. This may sound as if it contradicts the reservations already expressed on devaluation because of its inflationary effects (see above and also Chapters 1 and 2). But there is really no contradiction; our objection was to the exchange rate regime (nominal anchor) in the context of liberalization in the capital account. From a trade balance point of view, a policy of export subsidization may be superior.

The implication of this for capital flows and currency substitution is interesting. In this aspect, we reiterate that the main factor for the real appreciation of the pound is the financial liberalization of capital transactions in the balance of payments. Real appreciation was taking place against the backdrop of a widening trade deficit. With the pound pegged to the American dollar, foreign exchange risk was virtually eliminated, opening the door for massive capital inflows driven by interest arbitrage.

Interest rate differentials between pound deposits and deposits denominated in foreign currency in the local banking system triggered a shift from the latter to the first. The latter process is a process of de-dollarization encouraged by the perception (expectation) of negligible exchange risk. De-dollarization may be measured by either one of two indicators. The first is the change in the ratio of foreign currency deposits to total deposits in the banking system. The second is the change in the ratio of foreign currency time deposits to total time deposits. According to the first indicator, which emphasizes *foreign currency as a means of payments,* the ratio of foreign currency deposits dropped from a peak of 61 per cent of total deposits in June 1991 to 43 per cent in June 1992 and further to 32 per cent in June 1993. It stabilized at about 30 per cent during 1993/94–1995/96. According to the

Table 3.8 Deposits in the banking system, 1989–93 (LE million)

End of June	1989	%	1990	%	1991	%	1992	%	1993	%
Total pound	22.127	44	26.260	44	30.764	39	63.127	57	88.070	68
Current	4.534		5.177		5.234		8.963		10.605	
Time	17.593		21.083		25.440		54.164*		77.465*	
Total FC**	28.238	56	34.564	56	48.839	61	47.044	43	41.304	32
Current	2.995		3.288		4.725		6.813		7.100	
Time	25.243		31.276		44.114		40.231		34.204*	
Grand total	50.365	100	60.824	100	79.603	100	110.171	100	129.374	100

Notes:
* Includes retained or frozen deposits.
** FC means foreign currency.

Source: CBE, *Annual Report*, 1990/91, tables 5/3–5/4 and 1992/93, p. 59.

second indicator, which stresses the function of *foreign currency as a store of value*, the share of foreign currency time deposits took a real plunge: from 63 per cent in June 1991 to 42.6 per cent in June 1992, and further to 30.6 per cent in June 1993. It seems to have stabilized around 25 per cent during 1994–96 (see Table 3.8 for details).

This clearly demonstrates the remarkable sensitivity of the ratio of foreign currency deposits to pound deposits with respect to the interest rate differential. It should be emphasized that such sensitivity was only made possible by using the nominal exchange rate as an anchor and maintaining capital mobility.

The magnitude of capital inflows induced by interest rate differentials has been steadily rising, posing serious and growing problems of managing such flows. This is perhaps what inspired the World Bank to refer to Egypt's experience with capital inflows as an 'embarrassment of riches' (World Bank, 1997). Private unrequited transfers amounted to US$3.751 billion during 1990/91, US$5.748 billion during 1991/92 and US$7.260 billion in 1992/93, averaging $5.6 billion annually. In relative terms, this amounted to 150 per cent of merchandise exports on the average for the years 1990/91–1992/93 (see Table 3.1). By the standards of the Egyptian economy, these were really quite massive inflows. The rate of capital inflows exhibited some decline during 1993–95, but showed signs of a rebound thereafter. Although it is difficult to ascertain the exact nature of such inflows, partial evidence suggests that some significant proportion was in the form of portfolio investment (IMF, 1997).

The scale and nature of capital inflows into Egypt during the first phase of ERSAP and through the present may provide yet another version of the Dutch disease. Massive capital inflows led to an appreciation of the pound, which we estimated above to be in the order of 20 per cent over the period. Put differently, with reference to equation (3.3) above, the relative price of non-tradables has been rising under ERSAP. As should be theoretically expected, this must initiate a resource pull into sectors producing non-tradables. We may therefore predict an increase in the share of non-tradables sectors in GDP under ERSAP, which makes the task of reducing the trade deficit all the more difficult.

TRADE LIBERALIZATION

Trade liberalization under ERSAP involved a number of measures which essentially reflect the conventional mainstream trade policy stance. According to this view, trade liberalization is defined as a process of replacing a system of quota and other non-tariff restrictions, at possibly a disequilibrium exchange rate, with a system relying only on tariffs at an equilibrum exchange rate (Bhagwati, 1986; Krueger, 1978). Obviously, one problem with this conception is that the equilibrium exchange rate may be clear as a theoretical concept, but is often very difficult to estimate in practice.

Anticipating ERSAP, elimination of non-tariff barriers proceeded in earnest and continued strongly under the programme. Thus, almost all non-tariff barriers were eliminated including: (a) nearly all import bans, all prior approvals, all export bans, and most tariff preferences: (b) institutional checks on imports, and (c) foreign-exchange budgeting and limitations on foreign trading companies.

Under ERSAP phase II, which was covered by the extended arrangement for the period September 1993–September 1996 and a World Bank Structural Adjustment Monitoring Programme (SAMP),[12] the government has embarked on a three-year programme for trade reform. As already mentioned before, the main contours of the programme were announced in July 1993. The general objective of the reform remains the enhancement of efficiency in production and export performance, by increased reliance on tariffs and other price-based instruments, and elimination of quantitative restrictions on foreign trade.

Tariff Reform

Recent tariff reform in Egypt dates back to 1986, when a new tariff schedule was introduced. According to the tariff schedule, imports were classified into 99 divisions lumped into seven commodity groups, in addition to non-classified items as shown in Table 3.9. As part of the programme, the Harmonized System of Commodity Classification was adopted in February 1994, and customs procedures were reviewed and streamlined to facilitate the importation process.

Tariff rates were changed almost annually since 1989 – all of such changes except that of 1989 were part of ERSAP. As a result of these changes, the average tariff rates at the commodity-group level were higher in 1993 compared to 1986, except for commodity group IV (wood, cork, paper, weaving material and products), which was lower in 1993 as compared to 1986. But the overall average nominal tariff rate increased throughout the period 1989–1993, and the dispersion was reduced. Table 3.9 gives the details.

It is rather misleading, however, to take the data in Table 3.9 as evidence of the true extent of trade liberalization. Specifically, such data should not be interpreted as indicating that the trade regime in Egypt has become less liberal under ERSAP. Many reasons may be put forth to support this statement. *First,* the increase in the average nominal tariff in almost all commodity groups does not mean that the trade regime has grown less liberal. This is

Table 3.9 Development of nominal tariff rates mean and dispersion

Commodity Group	Designation	Divisions	Year 1986	1989	1991	1992	1993
I	Live Animals; Animal & Plant Kingdom; Food & Beverages	10–14, 16–24	20.85	21.89	25.08	36.76	38.76
II	Oils; Fats; Oil & Fat Products; Minerals & Fuel	15, 25–27	26.11	22.22	26.67	33.33	31.67
III	Chemicals; Rubber & Skins	28–43	24.90	22.44	23.14	25.54	25.14
IV	Wood, Cork; Paper; Weaving Materials & Products	44–63	50.76	51.52	52.93	50.98	45.87
V	Machinery & Transport Equipt	84–89	38.52	35.29	36.13	25.67	40.99
VI	Metals & Metal Products	73–83	23.28	26.97	27.43	28.16	31.13
VII	Assorted Manufactured Products	90–99	51.11	55.00	55.00	47.78	51.39
Other	Other Manufactured Products	64–72					
Mean			33.65	33.62	35.18	36.89	37.85
Coef. of variation			38.90	42.40	38.30	25.60	24.20

Source: Calculated on the basis of data obtained from the Ministry of Finance.

because most non-tariff barriers were actually converted into their tariff equivalent, and this by itself will result in a higher mean tariff. Thus, simply comparing the average tariff rates over the period does not reflect the true extent of trade liberalization. *Second,* a sales tax was introduced in 1991 (by Law 11/1991) as part of ERSAP fiscal measures, and extended to imported

Table 3.10 Nominal and effective protection, 1986–96

	Nominal protection		Effective protection	
	1986	1996	1986	1996
1. Plant production	27.48	18.74	27.90	18.81
2. Animal production	29.15	23.91	27.85	24.60
3. Food processing	50.34	32.61	69.16	43.72
4. Beverages	110.00	55.00	145.75	69.40
5. Tobacco	195.00	70.60	204.28	73.19
6. Cotton ginning	5.00	5.00	–120.10	–71.42
7. Spinning & weaving	54.46	34.30	76.02	46.74
8. Ready-made clothes	89.09	53.80	100.78	60.30
9. Leather & prods., except shoes	43.44	30.90	55.50	37.90
10. Shoes	66.87	51.00	86.78	67.41
11. Wood & prod., except furniture	37.50	29.15	38.31	29.81
12. Wooden furniture	110.00	48.02	143.87	57.26
13. Paper & printing	35.13	27.53	36.65	28.79
14. Chemical & prods. exc. refining	17.03	15.30	13.17	13.82
15. Rubber, plastic & prods.	30.10	20.10	42.54	24.56
16. China, porcelain & pottery	51.90	32.80	77.07	47.25
17. Glass & prods.	36.43	30.60	40.32	34.06
18. Non-metallic mineral	28.63	22.30	39.15	29.96
19. Iron, steel, non-ferrous metals	28.54	19.70	32.42	21.99
20. Machinery & equipment	24.95	15.74	22.40	13.07
21. Transport equipment	30.82	28.85	31.35	30.88
22. Other manufacturing	54.50	34.97	61.32	38.02
23. Crude oil & natural gas	0.00	0.00	–1.20	–0.96
24. Other mining	5.00	5.00	4.00	3.27
25. Refined oil products	9.55	11.90	11.43	14.73
Import – weighted average	39.18	25.29	46.80	29.40
Standard deviation	42.30	17.00		

Source: Calculated on the basis of the input/output table of 1989/90.

goods at a flat rate of 10 per cent calculated on the basis of the CIF price plus tariffs. *Third,* import bans were reduced considerably over the period, from 210 items to just 26 in 1993. *Moreover,* the exchange rate used for customs' valuation was substantially revalued, from LE 1.853 per US$ at the start of the new tariff schedule (in August 1986) to the monthly average of the unified rate in the free market starting November 1, 1991.

Allowing for this last factor (the revaluation of the customs' exchange rate) effectively means a significant increase in protection, which the standard estimates of the mean tariff rate may not reflect. But the tariff dispersion (measured by the coefficient of variation) has been reduced. Table 3.9 also shows the development of the mean tariff rate and the coefficient of variation between 1986 and 1993, and Table 3.10 measures the change in the level of both nominal and effective protection between 1986 and 1996. The conclusion we may derive is that, under ERSAP, there was an initial slight increase in the tariff height, but a significant reduction in tariff dispersion. But as the programme gained momentum, there has been a significant reduction in both nominal and effective protection.

In addition, tariff dispersion was further reduced quite considerably. The reduction in tariff dispersion was brought about by a number of measures. First, and foremost, was the step-wise reduction of the tariff range (which was 0–160 per cent prior to ERSAP) from 0.7–120 per cent to 5–100 per cent in May 1991, and to 5–80 per cent in February 1993 and further to 5–70 per cent in December 1995, and to 5–55 per cent in October 1996, and then to 50 per cent. In July 1998, the maximum tariff rate was reduced to 40 per cent. Second, out of the 90 BTN (Brussels Tariff Nomenclature) lines with tariff preferences (or *footnotes* in the jargon of Egypt's Customs Department) prior to the implementation of ERSAP, 29 were removed in May 1991 and more lines were removed in August 1992. This brings down the number of BTN lines with tariff preferences from 90 to less than 30. All remaining tariff preferences, except those governed by international treaties and those on health and tourism, were eliminated at the end of June 1993.

Non-Tariff Barriers

As already mentioned, the rise in the mean tariff may be explained by the tariffication of non-tariff barriers as part of import liberalization under ERSAP. The production coverage of import bans was reduced from 37.2 per cent of tradable output (total manufacturing and agricultural production) in March 1990 to 33.3 per cent in March 1991, 22.7 per cent in June 1991, and further to 13 per cent in August 1992. Except for textiles, garments and poultry, all import bans were removed at the end of June 1993, reducing the production coverage of such bans to 4.7 per cent of total agricultural and manufacturing output. Import bans on remaining items were removed, with the exception of cotton yarn. Previously banned import items were assigned equivalent tariff rates within the adopted tariff structure.

At the same time, the list of products requiring compliance with certain special conditions for import was brought down from 12 to 3. In addition suspension of letters of credit was partially lifted in March 1991, and totally eliminated in May 1991. Moreover, the advance import deposit rate for imports which are settled with letters of credit was cut from 35 per cent to 19 per cent in the case of imports for own use and to 29 per cent in the case of imports for trade; it was totally abolished on 8 August 1992.

With regard to exports, liberalization also proceeded in earnest (see Appendix 2.1). The number of products subject to export bans was reduced from 20 to 4 in May 1991, and by August 1992 only 2 export bans remained: those on scrap metals and raw hides. In May 1991, all export prior approvals on 37 product categories were dropped except for raw cotton and fabrics, which were eliminated in August 1992. Finally, the number of products subject to quantitative annual export quotas was reduced from 17 to 4; the remaining products are raw and waste wool, tanned skin, cotton waste and paper (newsprint only) waste.

These are, in some detail, the main components of Egypt's trade liberalization programme under ERSAP. An assessment of the programme is now in order. But as we do that, it is well to put the programme in comparative perspective. It may therefore be illuminating to cast it against recent experience with trade liberalization.[13] In addition to the general considerations set out at the beginning of this chapter, the assessment of the programme involves dealing with issues of design, speed, sequencing and sustainability.

In certain respects the design of the programme follows the usual pattern borne out by other country experiences. Specifically, emphasis was placed at the outset on dismantling quantitative restrictions, notably import bans. This was accompanied by the tariffication of NTBs, involving an initial increase in the mean tariff rate and a decrease in dispersion (Michaely et al., 1991, p. 3). The pattern depicted in Table 3.9 is the same, implying that, initially, liberalization of the trade regime involves changing the *form* rather than necessarily reducing the *level* of protection. In other words, in the initial phase of trade liberalization, emphasis is placed more on shifting protection to the price mechanism than reducing the absolute level of protection. *Ceteris paribus,* this shift to the price mechanism renders the system more transparent and predictable. Whether this encourages more efficient production remains to be proven, but it may eliminate some rent-seeking behaviour and thus has important income redistribution implications.

On the basis of the Egyptian experience, we shall make the important distinction between trade liberalization and import liberalization. We suggest that in the Egyptian context, trade liberalization was in effect import liberalization; *the programme did not include enough measures to promote exports.* One important exception, perhaps, is the correction of exchange rate bias against exports. As shown in Table 3.3, in the late 1980s a dollar dedicated to buy imports was worth 50 per cent more of local currency compared to a dollar earned from exports, reflecting a very strong bias against exports. With the unification of the exchange rate, exports became treated almost on par with imports by 1991/92. This reduces effective protection for import substitutes, and may *in principle* attract resources towards exportables, *ceteris paribus*.

But the reduction of protection of import-substituting activities brought about by ERSAP has in actual fact led to shifting resources more to non-tradables than to exportables – thanks to the misaligned exchange rate. This is a typical Dutch disease symptom. The balance of trade suffered as a result, and was actually aggravated by a fall in the real exchange rate (that is, an appreciation of the pound) as concluded in the previous section. The data in Table 3.1 provide ample evidence to support this contention.

The role of the real exchange rate in the sustainability of trade liberalization is crucial. According to the country experience reported in Michaely et al., where a major nominal devaluation was another element in the reform package alongside trade liberalization, the real exchange rate almost always increased, remaining high during the liberalization episode (Michaely et al., 1991, p. 275). This means a real depreciation of the national currency which helps turn around the trade balance. By contrast, in Egypt's case the real exchange rate did not rise but fell as noted above, implying real appreciation of the Egyptian pound. This was explained by the adoption of a nominal anchor almost concurrently with financial liberalization. Liberalizing capital transactions in the balance of payments was actually rushed in before completing the liberalization of the goods market.

The consensus view now is that the liberalization of the capital market should be introduced *only after* much of the liberalization of the goods market has been completed (Michaely et al., 1991, p. 277; McKinnon, 1991, p. 105). To quote McKinnon: 'free inflows of foreign financial capital should be allowed *only at the end* of an otherwise successful programme of liberalization. *During liberalization, stringent controls on suddenly increased inflows (or outflows) of short-term capital are warranted*' (McKinnon, 1991, p. 117, emphases added).

The justification of this view is that the liberalization of capital transactions in the balance of payments may trigger large-scale inflows of short-term capital, leading to a fall in the real exchange rate (currency appreciation). With trade liberalization still in its beginning, import-competing activities facing reduced protection will suffer, and so also will be exportable. The sustainability of trade liberalization may actually be at stake. It may be for these reasons that only a few of the episodes of trade liberalization analysed in the study of Michaely et al. have been accompanied by liberalization of capital transactions in the balance of payments.

McKinnon observes that a country undertaking a successful stabilization-liberalization programme may be inundated with foreign capital. Referring to the experience of South Korea during 1966–70 and Southern Cone countries (Argentina, Chile, and Uruguay) in the late 1970s and early 1980s, particularly Chile during 1977–81, he characterized an 'over-borrowing syndrome': as the profitability of the economy suddenly rises, foreign lenders attempt to capitalize on this situation by increasing their claim on the newly liberalized economy (McKinnon, 1991, ch. 10).

We have to note, however, that capital inflows in the 1990s are largely in the form of private investment, often portfolio investment. This contrasts with the 1970s and 1980s (before the Mexican debt crisis), when capital inflows were loan finance to a large extent. But because of the exchange regime (adopting a nominal anchor), sterilizing capital inflows resulted in Egypt's case in the accumulation of domestic public debt beyond the requirements of financing the fiscal deficit. In this different sense, Egypt's may be one of the 'over-borrowing' syndrome.

The inflow of capital may be greatly exaggerated when there is a major financial stabilization effort through which either interest rates are moved from low pegs to high pegs, or interest ceilings are removed altogether. An example of the former is the experience of South Korea in the mid-1960s, and the classic example of the latter is Chile in the late 1970s. We may also note that these examples are reminiscent of a much earlier and a highly relevant case for the present study – that of Egypt in the second half of the nineteenth century.[14] In this earlier episode, the dismantling of controls established under Mohammed Ali, including controls on capital transactions in the balance of payments, led to massive capital inflows both in the form of loan finance and foreign direct investment. This episode of Egyptian economic and political history may even be considered a forerunner of the over-borrowing syndrome noted by McKinnon. It eventually culminated in a severe debt crisis, foreign intervention and the re-institution of controls.

Sequencing and Sustainability

Within this perspective, we should look at Egypt's experience of trade liberalization under ERSAP. Unlike the earlier experience of the country in the late nineteenth century when trade liberalization led and financial liberalization followed, in the more recent experience the two types of liberalization were introduced almost concurrently. In fact, after 1991, Egypt was quick to take the easier step of liberalizing capital transactions in the balance of payments. Meanwhile, trade liberalization – though adopted at a relatively fast pace – is not yet complete. Furthermore, the liberalization of interest rate against the backdrop of continued (though falling) inflation and the use of the domestic reserve tax drove a wedge between interest rates on domestic and foreign currency deposits, and between domestic deposit and loan rates. On the other hand, the introduction of treasury bills as a manifestation of a strong fiscal stance further boosted the interest rate on domestic currency deposits. With the pound pegged to the American dollar, exchange rate risk was virtually eliminated. As short-term capital started pouring in, the Central Bank had to intervene to stabilize the exchange rate. In the process, the treasury had to borrow more than warranted by fiscal needs in order to sterilize capital inflows. But in the face of such relatively large inflows, sterilization was only partial, about two-thirds of the inflows, and monetary expansion thus remained well above the programme target under ERSAP (IMF, 1993, p. 7).

It is important to fill the empirical gaps in the analysis given above, especially the scale of short-term capital inflows.

Unfortunately, balance of payments statistics in Egypt are notoriously confused. But as an approximation of the order of magnitude of short-term capital inflows, we may take the accumulated Central Bank gross foreign reserves. These reserves more than doubled during the first phase of ERSAP, and even exceeded US$20 billion later at some point – equivalent to more than one-and-a-half years' worth of imports. Most of this short-term capital inflow was sterilized by accumulating government domestic debt. The level of such debt rose from LE 113.7 billion at the end of June 1993 to LE 170.8 billion at the end of June 1997. As a proportion of GDP, domestic public debt approached 78 per cent in 1997. Under ERSAP, domestic public debt has become of shorter maturity, less securitized and less marketable. Treasury bills in particular have reached an alarming proportion, threatening a Ponzi-type situation. We warn therefore that domestic debt may be approaching dangerous levels (Abdel-Khalek, 1998).

As already mentioned, this may be considered another version of the 'over-borrowing' syndrome described by McKinnon. Although over-borrowing by the government in local currency is largely backed by the foreign reserves of the Central Bank, such a policy raises two important issues: the high fiscal cost and the disincentive to investment. According to IMF estimates, the cost of sterilizing capital inflows may have exceeded 0.3 per cent of GDP per US $1.0 billion (IMF, 1997, p. 27). As to disincentive effects, it has been demonstrated that domestic-debt service clearly crowds out public expenditure on investment and social services (Abdel-Khalek, 1998). Furthermore, the equity implications of this policy are quite interesting: interest payments on domestic public debt almost equalled allocations for wages, or four times total subsidy expenditure, or almost five times non-wage expenditure on health and education in 1997.

Are trade liberalization measures under ERSAP as documented and analysed above sustainable? And what is their likely impact on the industrial structure? Regarding sustainability, it is our contention that the answer to the question is in the negative for a number of reasons. First, Egypt's trade liberalization programme is too rushed, and may perhaps result in an overkill. We have shown that non-tariff barriers, particularly import bans, were substantially reduced within a short span of 2–3 years only.

Based on the stylized facts and the lessons of experience, a period of 6–7 years for shifting from a restrictive trade regime to one approaching free trade would not be unreasonable. While minimizing the transition cost of trade liberalization, especially high unemployment rates and low growth rates, a trade liberalization package put in place over 6–7 years would also avoid long delays in reaping its full benefits (Michaely et al., 1991, pp. 280–81). We argue that, in view of the relatively high transition cost in the case of Egypt, with an unemployment rate of about 15 per cent and too slow a rate of GDP growth, the duration of the trade liberalization component of ERSAP should have been made longer. Perhaps even much longer.

Second, the fall in the real exchange rate (the appreciation of the pound) in the course of trade liberalization has perhaps undermined the potential incentive effects of the programme.[15] With inflation differentials between Egypt and its main trading partners continuing unabated while interest rate differentials continue to narrow, pressure will tend to mount on the pound. Eventually, the pound may have to be devalued, controls may have to be re-instituted, or some combination of both. The end result may be a breakdown of the liberalization effort.

Finally, we consider the second question, that of the impact of the trade liberalization on industrial structure and the prospects for industrialization. The major difficulty with addressing this question satisfactorily is the lack of any real guidance from theory. In almost no other field is the economics profession as divided as in the area of trade policy.

On the one hand, there is the mainstream view, represented by the neoclassicists; strong believers in the Heckscher–Ohlin model (Little et al., 1970; Krueger, 1986; Bhagwati, 1986). They provide the intellectual legitimization of trade liberalization packages usually advocated by the World Bank and the IMF. Their paradigm is marginalist, assuming full employment and competition. As a corollary, arbitrage ensures the operation of the law of one price. In this fictitious world, trade liberalization is conceived as a regime of equal incentives to exports and import substitutes, which derives its rationale from the (static) allocative welfare gains measured by the famous little triangles. The mainstream view claims that economic liberalization enables the economy to achieve higher growth and enhances its ability to adjust to external shocks.

This position has been challenged by a number of authors. Scitovsky (1954), arguing from within the neo-classical tradition, stressed the importance in practice of market failures due to non-trivial factors (such as externalities, economies of scale, and imperfect tradability of most goods). Market prices are thus stripped of their ability to guide the economy to an efficient equilibrium. From another perspective, Pack and Westphal (1986) have argued that mastering technology is non-tradable. Therefore, price-based investment decisions will not be optimal. Getting the prices right, which is the hallmark of economic liberalization in the manner of the Bretton Woods institutions, is left with only shaky theoretical foundations. More recently, this position was further characterized as no panacea (Banuri, 1991). Empirical evidence on the relation between liberalization or economic openness and economic performance (growth) appears inconclusive (Taylor, 1991).

On the other hand, the 'new' trade theorists, following Linder (1961), stressed product differentiation, monopolistic competition, the role of demand and structural rigidity. According to this view, the dynamic transition following trade liberalization may prove rather costly – involving the disappearance of import-competing industries without necessarily shifting resources into new sectors. Moreover, according to the theoretical literature on strategic trade policy, *departing* from neutral-incentive regimes (that is, regimes with low and uniform tariffs) may enhance economic performance in situations where economies of scale, technology-mastering, externalities or monopolistic elements are important (Krugman, 1986). In a small country, protection may actually be beneficial if the resulting rise in profits attracts new entrants. In this context, 'the crucial policy issue is not that of setting the prices right, but that of *charting a developmental role for the state*' (Fishlow, 1991, emhasis added).

At a more practical level, the experience of what the World Bank calls high performing Asian economies (HPAEs)[16] provides partial support to this view. According to a recent World Bank study (World Bank, 1993), HPAEs (except Hong Kong and Singapore) all adopted protectionist trade policies for industrialization. As these countries moved along the path towards industrialization, they experimented with mixed trade regimes, which combined duty-free imports of capital and intermediate goods for exporters with protection of consumer goods.

There were, however, wide variations within this general pattern. For example, in Japan and Korea there is strong evidence summarized in Itoh and Kiyono (1988) for Japan and in Pack and Westphal (1986) for Korea that the government in both cases selectively protected industries that it wanted to promote, using tariff and non-tariff instruments. Moreover, all the HPAEs except Hong Kong followed active industrial policies, as distinct from trade policies, in an attempt to promote productivity-based growth and structural change in the industrial sector (World Bank, 1993, p. 304). Instruments of industrial policy varied from one case to another, but generally they included directed credit, foreign exchange allocations, free advice and information, limitation of entry and relatively high levels of protection.

Against this background, and in the light of empirical analysis of the Egyptian case, we may conclude that ERSAP is more likely to have a negative impact on industrial growth in Egypt. We have shown that the exchange rate policy, financial liberalization and trade policy components of the programme may at least not be conducive to industrial growth. They may eventually prove obstructive. Two more considerations may be added here to complete the argument regarding the likely impact of ERSAP on industrial growth and structure. First, trade liberalization has been pushed too fast, long before the necessary reforms in the real sector of the economy. For example, pushing trade liberalization before the restructuring of public sector enterprises is completed simply forces these enterprises to compete from a position of disadvantage. This carries a real danger of collapse of such enterprises. Also, when non-tariff barriers (such as import bans) are lifted before putting in place the necessary safeguards: system, anti-dumping and countervailing duty mechanisms, as legitimate defences against unfair trade practices, the position of domestic enterprises may be weakened considerably.

Second, ERSAP does not include an industrial policy component in any real sense of the word, for example as in the case of HPAEs. Instead, one is struck by a hands-off stance for the government. This is ill-suited to the conditions of Egypt which is a low-income country trying to develop. If development is defined broadly to encompass growth with structural change and equity, then a neutral-incentive regime, the essence of trade liberalization under ERSAP, may eventually amount to the de-industrialization of Egypt.

CONCLUDING REMARKS

The experience of the Southern Cone countries (Argentina, Chile and Uruguay) in the late 1970s–early 1980s and the Mexican experience of the mid 1990s clearly demonstrate that bad management of capital inflows and large domestic debt may lead to instability detrimental to development. In the present context of increasing globalization of financial markets, interest-rate differentials trigger short-term capital movements. The absence of exchange risk, such as under a nominal exchange rate anchor encourages uncovered interest arbitrage. In such an environment, short-term capital becomes highly elastic.

It is one of the hard lessons of the 1994–95 Mexican crisis that there is a real danger in continuing to use a nominal anchor even after domestic inflation has subsided (Cardoso, 1996). If a restrictive monetary stance is adopted to reduce aggregate demand and maintain external balance, real domestic interest rates will rise. The persistence of high real interest rates produces a number of negative effects. First, high real interest rates can only make fiscal adjustment more difficult. Second, a rise in real interest rates results in a deterioration of bank portfolios, and hence necessitates subsidized recapitalization of banks, Third, high real interest rates induce short-term capital inflows, which are usually sterilized, leading to domestic debt accumulation parallel to the piling up of foreign reserves.

On the other hand, real appreciation propagates numerous problems throughout the economy. First, it may reduce the savings rate, as consumers substitute present for future consumption (in anticipation of devaluation), and engage in speculative activities (in real estate and the stock exchange). The force of real (exchange rate) appreciation in encouraging consumption may be gauged by referring to available evidence. Banking credit denominated in Egyptian pounds to the household sector rose by 47.4 per cent in 1994/95 (from LE 8.4 billion to LE 12.3 billion). A significant proportion of these credit facilities was used to finance the purchase of consumer durables and real estate (CBE, *Annual Report 1994/95*, pp. 44–5). The World Bank (1995) reports a fall in national savings (including official transfers) by 7 percentage points over the period 1990/91–1994/95. The implication of this for sustainable growth is rather disquieting.

NOTES

1. Only three restrictions remain: (a) the bilateral payments agreement with the Sudan; (b) the special liquidation accounts from expired bilateral payments agreements; and (c) outstanding arrears with non-Paris Club members and non-conclusion of a bilateral agreement with one Paris Club member.
2. This estimate is derived on the basis of a double logarithmic aggregate import function relating the dollar value of total imports to both GDP in 1981/82 Egyptian pounds and the nominal exchange rate LE/$. The estimate of the elasticity of imports with respect to the exchange rate quoted in the text is a point estimate (at the average), based on data for the period 1975–1991/92 (Central Bank of Egypt Review, 32(4), 1991/92).
3. The RER may be expressed in several formulae, depending on how the exchange rate is viewed. For example, if the exchange rate is viewed as the price of the foreign currency (measured in units of local currency), then RER may be viewed as the price of a real dollar in terms of real domestic currency units. According to this perspective, RER is simply the relative price variable in the standard supply-demand analysis applied to foreign exchange.
4. We experimented with the producer price index in one case where it was available (that of the United States), since it is supposed to be a better proxy for the WPI. Although it made some difference in the numerical results, we believe that it did not really alter the main conclusion of the analysis.

5. Initially, this was subject to a minimum of 12 per cent annually for three-month deposits. This minimum level was dropped in 1992/93. See CBE, *Annual Report 1992/93*, p. 41.
6. Furthermore, there may be a built-in conflict among these targets under conditions of free capital mobility. With an initial high interest rate, a nominal exchange rate anchor may lead to monetary expansion. Interest rate differentials attract short-term capital inflows (hot money) which tend to push up the value of the pound.
7. But the formula developed by Salvatore suffers from a mathematical error, as he failed to make the transformation from 3-month investment to one-year investment properly. Thus, instead of multiplying all elements of the formula through by 4, he just knocked 4 off the denominator of some elements only (see Salvatore, 1995, p. 441). Using the same notation as in the text, his formula would read:

$$m = (1 - r_a)/(1 + r_a) - [(e_f - e)/e].$$

8. The sterling balances piled up during the Second World War. They represented the sterling equivalent of Egyptian-pound expenditure by the British and allied forces in Egypt during the war, and amounted to LE 430 million in 1946. M.Z. Shafei, *An Introduction to Money and Banking*, Cairo: Dar Al-Nahda Al-Arabia, 1986, p. 205 (Arabic).
9. This is the difference between the stock at the end of June 1992 and 1991, LE 17.1 billion and LE 4 billion, respectively. The source of figures in this paragraph is the Central Bank of Egypt, *Annual Report 1991/92*, especially pp. 40, 79, 87 and 225.
10. But there are some differences between the Egyptian case and the theoretical model: in the Mundell scheme, capital mobility meant the same interest rate at home and abroad – that is, there is only one type of assets. In the Egyptian case, on the other hand, the problem is complicated by the coexistence of two competing assets (dollar and pound positions). See Robert A. Mundell, 'Capital Mobility and Stabilization Policy under Fixed and Flexible Exchange Rates', *Canadian Journal of Economics and Political Sciences*, vol. XXIX, no. 4 (Nov. 1963).
11. See CAPMAS, *Statistical Yearbook, Arab Republic of Egypt, 1952–1992*, Cairo: CAPMAS, June 1993; and *Study Measuring Inflation Trends in the Arab Republic of Egypt, 65/66–91/92*, Cairo: CAPMAS, January, 1993.
12. The main areas of reform to be covered by SAMP include public enterprise reform and privatization, trade liberalization and tariff reduction, and financial market liberalization.
13. The most extensive study is that of Michaely et al., 1991. The study deals with 19 countries covering Asia and the Pacific (seven countries), Latin America (six countries), and the Mediterranean (six countries). It is published in seven volumes, the first six devoted to country experiences, and volume 7 is a synthesis volume subtitled *Lessons of Experience in the Developing World*. Reference in the text is to the last volume.
14. The case of Egypt has been widely studied and documented. See, for example, A.-M. Hamza, *The Public Debt of Egypt 1854–1876*, Cairo, 1944; E.R.J. Owen, *Cotton and the Egyptian Economy 1820–1914*, London; Oxford University Press, 1969.
15. This contrasts, for example, with the trade liberalization experience of Mexico in the mid 1980s. There, the peso depreciated significantly – thanks to controls on the capital account of the balance of payments (Ten Kate, 1992).
16. HPAEs include Japan, Hong Kong, the Republic of Korea, Singapore, Taiwan, Indonesia, Malaysia and Thailand. The last three became part of the group only during the 1980s and 1990s.

4. The main features of the manufacturing sector

INTRODUCTION

As early as 1983, a World Bank study on Egypt underscored the need for a concentrated effort over the following two decades to achieve an investment rate of 30–35 per cent (World Bank, 1983, p. 45). The study also pointed out that, according to the most desirable scenario based on an optimal growth path of the Egyptian economy, Egypt would have to raise the share of merchandise exports in domestic production of tradables from 13 per cent to 35 per cent over the planning horizon to 2012 (World Bank, 1983, p. 23).

In addition to the World Bank study mentioned above, several other studies were undertaken to deal with various aspects of the manufacturing sector in Egypt. The most important are CAPMAS (1985); World Bank (1983, 1984, 1987); USAID (1979); Papanek (1981); Jones (1981); and Ministry of Industry (1986 and 1998). The essence of all these studies is that there are a number of problems besetting the manufacturing activity and inhibiting its dynamic growth.

In 1991/92 industrial output actually amounted to LE 21 409 million and industrial exports LE 5762 million, or about 27 per cent of industrial output. The five-year plan 1992/93–1996/97 rekindled the old hopes by targeting industrial exports to reach 40 per cent of industrial output by 1996/97, implying a growth rate of industrial exports averaging 16 per cent per annum in real terms during the plan period (see Appendix, Table 4A.1). The plan document, however, did not spell out the policy instruments which make this ambitious export target realistically achievable. It may have been initially assumed that ERSAP will furnish the policy environment necessary to achieve such ambitious targets. But that remains to be seen.

In view of the relatively large public ownership in the manufacturing sector, the issues of public sector reform and industrial, investment and trade policy reform are strongly intertwined. As already mentioned, ERSAP was intended to address these issues. But in addition, it included other elements which have strong potential implications for manufacturing. Among the most important are fiscal and monetary policy, exchange rate policy and trade liberalization. The manner in which these policy changes impact on the manufacturing activity (both public and private) and on the prospects of industrialization, is the focus of our research.

The purpose of this part of the study is to highlight the basic contours of manufacturing on the basis of data for the past 10–15 years. This will serve as background for the analysis which will follow.

THE BASIC CONTOURS OF EGYPT'S MANUFACTURING

This section is divided into two parts: the first deals with the macro indicators related to manufacturing in Egypt, and the second analyses the salient features of the structure of the sector.

Macro Indicators

These indicators are the manufacturing sector growth rate and its shares in value added, investment, employment and exports. With regard to value added, we put the contribution of manufacturing alongside those of the other sectors of the Egyptian economy over the period 1981/82–1995/96 (Table 4.1). This period covers the decade which preceded ERSAP and resumption of planning with the implementation of the country's so-called first five-year plan (1982/83–1986/87).[1] It also covers the first and second phases of ERSAP. Some remarks on the data are essential before we discuss the various indicators.

The data source (MOP, 1992b) gives the figures for 1981/82–1986/87 in 1981/82 prices, and figures for 1986/87–1991/92 in 1986/87 prices. Estimates of GDP for 1991/92–1995/96 in 1991/92 prices were also obtained from the Ministry of Planning. Using the chaining method, the data sets for 1986/87–1991/92 and 1991/92–1995/96 were converted to the 1981/82 basis. Although this was the only option given the data available, there are some problems with this treatment. It involves serious distortions in the GDP data for the oil sector. MOP constant-price data for GDP in the oil and oil products sector show a significant real increase (at a rate of 42 per cent) between 1981/82 and 1986/87. But current price output and GDP figures for the same period show considerable decline – by 15.5 per cent and 31 per cent, respectively. During 1981/82–1986/87, the combined effect of the depreciation of the dollar and the slight decline in output of the sector (because of the oil glut) implies that constant-price GDP should have declined – contrary to MOP estimates. During 1986/87–1991/92, the increase in the LE value of oil GDP conceals the significant devaluation of the Central Bank exchange rate from LE 0.70 per US$ in March 1988 to LE 1.10 per US$ in August 1989 and to LE 2.0 per US$ in August 1990. On 8 October 1991 the Central Bank rate became identical with the Free Market

Table 4.1 *GDP growth and structure, 1981/82–1995/96 in constant 1981/82 prices (LE million)*

	1981/82		1986/87		1991/92		1995/96	
	Value	%	Value	%	Value	%	Value	%
Agriculture	4053	19.6	4695	16.9	5397	16.1	6087	15.4
Industry & mining	2736	13.3	4250	15.3	5393	16.1	6737	17.1
Petrol. & products	2713	13.2	3863	13.9	3935	11.7	4340	11.0
Electricity	178	0.6	253	0.9	338	1.0	405	1.0
Construction	1170	5.7	1445	4.1	1848	5.5	2170	5.5
Total	10800	52.7	14506	52.1	16911	50.4	19739	50.0
Trans. & comm.	1525	7.4	2250	8.1	2709	8.1	3259	8.3
Suez Canal	642	3.1	668	2.4	786	2.3	722	1.8
Commerce	2653	12.9	3701	13.3	4364	13.0	5208	13.2
Finance & insu.	873	4.7	1093	3.9	1296	3.9	1684	4.3
Hotels & rest.	226	1.1	299	1.1	663	2.0	715	1.8
Total	5919	28.7	7991	28.8	9818	29.3	11588	29.4
Real estate	372	1.8	580	2.1	967	2.9	1160	2.9
Public utilities	50	0.2	83	0.3	121	0.4	161	0.4
Social services	2360	11.4	3195	11.5	4071	12.1	4848	12.3
Personal services	1127	5.5	1473	5.3	1648	4.9	1972	5.0
Total	3909	18.9	5331	19.1	6804	20.3	8141	20.6
Grand total	20628	100	27828	100	33533	100	39468	100
Population (million)	44.4		50.6		57.6		61.5	
Per capita GDP(LE)	464.6		550.0		582.2		642.0	

Notes and Sources:
For 1981/82–1991/92, MOP, 1992b, Tables 5 and 6, pp. 68–69. Table 6 gives 1991/92 GDP figures in 1986/87 prices. These were transformed into 1981/82 prices using the chaining method. For 1995/96, MOP estimates in 1991/92 prices. They were transformed into 1981/82 prices using the chaining method.
Population figures are the average for mid-year population that is, the population for 1981/82 is the average of the mid 1981 and mid 1982 population figures, and so on. Source of population data is CAPMAS, *Statistical Yearbook 1952–1992* (June, 1993), Table 18, p. 28. 1995/96 figure was estimated by incrementing the 1991/92 figure by the growth rate implied by the 1996 population census.

rate averaging LE 3.32 per US$ (see CBE, *Economic Review*, vol. 32, no. 2, 1991/92, p. 248).

With the important caveat in the preceding paragraph, we proceed to discuss the macro indicators of manufacturing over the decade preceding ERSAP. According to the data of Table 4.1, the Egyptian economy grew at a compound average annual rate of 5 per cent over the decade 1981/82–1991/

92. Overall, per capita GDP grew at a rate of 2.3 per cent per annum. It is difficult to accept that the growth and structural change recorded in Table 4.1 was actually *planned*; the impact of a number of external shocks was perhaps more significant than the plan. Let us consider in some detail the pattern of growth and structural change over this period.

i. GDP growth has decelerated in the second half of the period, which raises many questions. Was the slowdown deliberate, via the contractionary policies which the government adopted starting in the second half of the 1980s? Was it the impact of the external shock? Was it the result of import strangulation or, was it simply the case of an economy going through another phase of a longer cycle? For lack of a better alternative, it is probably reasonable to postulate that the slowing down of growth in the latter part of the period is the outcome of these forces taken together.
ii. The commodity producing sectors (both primary and secondary) lagged behind the rest of the economy, growing at an average rate of 4.6 per cent per annum during the whole period. As a result, their relative share in GDP fell steadily from 52.4 per cent in 1981/82 to 50.4 per cent in 1991/92. The other side of this coin is the rising share of the service sectors, which grew at average annual rates of 0.5–1.0 percentage points above that of commodity producing sectors. This reflects what may be called *a process of tertiarization of the economy*, a process which actually predates the period. There is strong evidence that it has been underway for a much longer period (Abdel-Khalek, 1982). It may be considered a special version of Dutch disease.
iii. During the sub-period of fast growth (1981/82–1986/87), the three groups of sectors were growing at a very close pace. By contrast, during the sub-period of slow growth (1986/87–1991/92), the differential in growth rates of the three groups of sectors was much larger. The standard deviation of the sectoral growth rates jumped from 0.153 for the fast-growth period to 0.954 for the low-growth period. In order to explain this pattern, we may hypothesize that the tertiary sectors play the role of buffer or stabilizers which help dampen cyclical changes in economic activity. Whatever the explanation, it is evident that the repeated attempts to improve the structure of production by increasing the share of the commodity sectors were not successful. Consecutive five-year plans failed to achieve the persistent target of raising the GDP share of commodity producing sectors.
iv. Industry, including mining, grew at an average rate of 7 per cent per annum over the entire period, but its growth was much slower during the second half compared to the first (4.8 per cent *vs* 9.2 per cent per

annum).[2] Tourism was the fastest growing sector by far, followed by electricity and public utilities and real estate. With the exception of tourism, these sectors are largely non-tradables. It is therefore interesting to approach the question of sectoral growth from a Dutch disease perspective. Hansen visited the problem using data for the period 1975–1983/84 (Hansen, 1991, pp. 526–8). Basing his analysis on such indicators as tradables/nontradables price relatives, agricultural wages (as indicators of non-tradables prices) and tradables/non-tradables share of gross investment, he concludes that both data on tradables/non-tradables price relatives and gross investment shares support the Dutch disease hypothesis.[3] Methodologically, it is risky to give a Dutch disease explanation to a falling share of investment in tradables activities, especially during 1980/81–1983/84, because the five-year plan which started 1982/83 *deliberately* focused on rebuilding the infrastructure. Moreover, trade restrictions have been reduced during the period examined in the course of the open-door policy (*infitah*). This particular change in trade policy in itself, *ceteris paribus*, should be expected to result in a reduction in the relative price of tradables. The latter is a necessary, but not sufficient condition for Dutch disease. According to the Dutch disease literature, the essence of the malaise is an appreciation of the real exchange rate due to the expenditure effect of the foreign exchange boom (Corden, 1984; Gelb and Associates, 1988). According to a more recent study, the price index for tradables rose to 237.2 while that for non-tradables reached 272. 3 in 1993 (1987/88 = 100). The relative price of tradables thus fell to 87 in 1993 (El-Khawaga, 1996, p. 90).

The contribution of the manufacturing sector to the growth of GDP and its share therein, though important, is not enough to gauge the extent of the industrialization of the economy. To do that, one has to examine the relative share of manufacturing in employment generation, capital formation and export earnings, in addition to value added. Table 4.2 provides the relevant data for the period 1960/61–1995/96. The main conclusion which can be drawn from examining the data is that the evidence is mixed. On the basis of income generation and capital formation, the Egyptian economy was perhaps less 'industrialized' during the 1980s compared to the 1960s and early 1970s. On the other hand, based on employment generation and export earnings, one may conclude the reverse. This conclusion may have to be qualified in respect of the margin of error involved in the data.

The share of manufacturing in total value added in the economy has shown a trend decline during 1960/61–1981/82. Although it has tended to increase since the early 1980s, it never regained its 1960/61 share. In 1991/92 the contribution of manufacturing to value added was still much less than in

Table 4.2 Contribution of manufacturing to the economy, 1960/61–1995/96

	Value added % of GDP	Employment % of total	Investment % of GFI [c]	Exports % of merchandise
1960/61	20.1	10.0	26.7	20.0
1973	18.7	12.6	28.1	31.6
1981/82	13.3	12.1	27.0	9.9
1986/87	15.3	12.7[a]	23.7	30.4
1991/92	16.1	13.7[b]	22.4	34.5
1995/96	17.1	13.7	19.7	39.9

Notes:
a. 1986 CAPMAS, *Population Census 1986, Final Results*, vol. 2, ref. # 863/90/AMT, Table 7 (Employment = 6 years and more).
b. 1990 CAPMAS, *Quarterly Bulletin of Employment Sample Survey*, ref. # 68–12525/90, Table 16 (Employment = 12–64 years).
c. Figures are averages for, respectively, the periods: 1960/61–64/65, 1970/71–1976, 1977–81/82, 1982/83–86/87 and 1987/88–91/92.

Source: MOP (1992c), except for employment share as noted in a and b above.

1960/61. Data on the share of manufacturing in investment is even more disturbing – exhibiting a steady decline since the early 1970s and through the early 1990s. It is only on the score of employment that the share of manufacturing appears to have shown a steady trend increase over the period.

With regard to the share of manufacturing in export earnings, the 1981/82 and 1986/87 figures give conflicting and misleading signals; the share suddenly rising from 9.9 per cent in 1981/82 to 30.4 per cent in 1986/87. The former year witnessed the peak of the oil boom of 1979–81, and the latter coincided with the trough of the oil slump which started in 1985.[4] These oil-related external shocks impacted on the entire economy, and they manifest themselves directly in a sudden change in the share of the non-oil sectors in value added and exports. The rise in the share of manufacturing exports is, at least in part, more apparent than real – simply a reflection of the arithmetic of fluctuating shares.

If allowance is made for this fact, for example by adjusting the data to exclude oil value-added and oil exports, the trend is clear: the Egyptian economy may have become less industrialized in the 1980s. This calls for an explanation. Perhaps part of the explanation lies in the reduced attention given to manufacturing, and the institutional changes bearing on the sector in the wake of the open-door policy (*infitah).* In 1975, public enterprises lost a great deal of their autonomy – thanks to the abolition of public sector organizations (El-Issawy, 1988, p. 100). As a result, public-sector firms grew increasingly subject to bureaucratic controls regarding output and pricing. For example, in the early 1980s, public-sector firms faced three different price regimes for their products: centrally controlled prices, applying to 19 important products representing some 30 per cent of the total output of companies affiliated with the Ministry of Industry; mark-up prices, applying to some 900 products with 5–10 per cent margins; and negotiated prices for most other products (Handoussa, 1991, pp. 144–55). Such a system was gradually modified beginning in 1984/85.

The rising share of the value of manufactured exports in the second half of the 1980s is the result of both the real increase in manufactured exports and the nominal increase in the pound price of merchandise exports due to the devaluation of the Egyptian pound. Separating the two is not really easy, especially given that devaluation (depending on the elasticities) may have a quantity-enhancing effect. *Devaluation of the Egyptian pound* over the period did not take the form of an across-the-board proportional change, but was more complex. This has been discussed at length already in Chapter 3. As to the point at hand, we suspect that the devaluation of the pound has had a more differential effect on manufacturing exports; that is, raising the pound value of manufacturing exports more proportionally compared to other merchandise exports whose value was calculated largely on the basis of the Central Bank exchange rate. This should help manufactured exports.

Structure of the Manufacturing Sector

Identification of the main features regarding the structure of manufacturing requires analysis of such aspects as overall output growth and growth of particular individual manufacturing activities, ownership (public *vs.* private activity), factor use and productivity. The basic source of information used in the analysis in this part is the Census of Annual Industrial Production (CAIP), produced by CAPMAS. A note on this source is necessary before we start. The Census of Annual Industrial Production (CAIP) does not represent full coverage of the whole of manufacturing activity in Egypt. Data reported in CAIP cover only part of the formal manufacturing sector, that is, all public sector enterprises and only private sector enterprises employing 10 persons or more. Enterprises covered by CAIP account only for some 55–60 per cent of employment in manufacturing. According to the 1986/87 CAIP, total employment in the sector was 929 169 compared to 1 511 239 in the 1986 population census (age 10 years or more). This should be kept in mind when dealing with the structural characteristics of manufacturing.

Pattern of ownership

According to the Census of Annual Industrial Production (CAIP) data (see Table 4.3), industrial production grew at an average annual rate of about 21.5 per cent, value added increased at a slightly higher rate of 23.2 per cent and wages rose at the slightly lower rate of 20.2 per cent. Labour absorption in the sector increased at the disappointingly low rate of 2.7 per cent, not significantly higher than the average population growth rate for the period. Data for production, value added and wages are in current prices. If allowance is made for inflation during the period, the real increases in those variables will be at much lower rates. *Real wages may have either fallen or stagnated at best.*

The fact that gross value added appears to have risen slightly faster than wages may mean an *improving wage competitiveness of the manufacturing sector as a whole*. But this average behaviour for the period conceals significant variations between 1976–1981/82 and 1981/82–1988/89.

Since the mid 1970s, private sector manufacturing has outpaced public sector manufacturing. If we look in more detail, we observe that the share of the private sector has been increasing over the period: in production from one-eighth to one-third; in value added from one-tenth to more than one-quarter; in employment from one-seventh to one-quarter; and in wages from one-eighth to one-fifth. A caveat is important in this context, since the private sector was largely free of the restrictions which constrained the behaviour of the public sector – particularly regarding pricing. Although it still has a long way to go, the Egyptian economy is increasingly becoming more mixed.

It is interesting to note that the growth in these indicators was not uniform throughout the period. If we distinguish sub-periods 1975–1981/82 and 1981/82–1988/89, we observe a manifest pattern that calls for explanation. Value-added growth lagged behind wage increase during 1975–1981/82 but was ahead of it during 1981/82–1988/89 (17.7 per cent annual increase in gross value added against 25.1 per cent annual growth in wages during the first sub-period, and 28 per cent against 16.1 per cent, respectively, during the second sub-period). How do we interpret this pattern?

It probably suggests that the Egyptian economy has experienced a tight labour market prior to 1981/82, thanks to massive labour migration and fast economic growth. Together with import liberalization under *infitah,* this pushed down the relative price of capital. In response to the changing relative factor prices, this period witnessed significant capital deepening (CAPMAS, 1985, pp. 54–8). Capital was substituted for labour in the private sector through the expansion of 'foreign' investment under Law 43 for 1974, and in the public sector through the rehabilitation of public-sector enterprises. Competitiveness in Egyptian manufacturing deteriorated during this sub-period, but recovered during the second sub-period. As a rough indicator of changes in

Table 4.3 *Pattern of ownership in the manufacturing sector, 1975–1995/96*

		1975	1981/82	Growth 1975–81/82	1986/87	1988/89	Growth 1981/82–1988/89	Growth 1975–88/89	1995/96
Output[a]	Pub.	87.1	81.0	19.7	74.7	67.7	18.7	19.1	49.8
	Priv.	12.9	19.0	29.8	25.3	32.3	31.4	30.4	50.2
	Tot.	100.0	100.0	21.1	100.0	100.0	21.8	21.5	100.0
Value added[a]	Pub.	90.2	80.3	15.4	81.3	73.5	26.4	21.2	49.7
	Priv.	9.8	19.7	32.1	18.7	26.5	33.4	32.9	50.3
	Tot.	100.0	100.0	17.7	100.0	100.0	28.0	23.2	100.0
Labour	Pub.	83.8	81.4	2.5	78.7	74.4	1.0	1.7	60.0
	Priv.	16.2	18.6	5.5	21.3	25.6	7.1	6.3	40.0
	Tot.	100.0	100.0	3.0	100.0	100.0	2.3	2.7	100.0
Wages[b]	Pub.	87.6	86.0	24.7	82.0	78.5	14.6	19.1	66.9
	Priv.	12.4	14.0	27.7	18.0	21.5	23.5	25.4	33.1
	Tot.	100.0	100.0	25.1	100.0	100.0	16.1	20.2	100.0
Labour productivity		100	222		525	1066			n.a.
Wage rate		100	319		606	774			n.a.
Competitiveness		100	0.66		0.87	1.38			n.a.

Notes:
a. Output and gross value added are at factor cost in current prices.
b. Wages include payments in kind and fringe benefits.

Source: CAPMAS, *Census of Annual Industrial Production*, various years.

competitiveness, the index of unit labour cost (i.e. the average ratio of labour productivity to the wage rate) is used. It fell from 1 in 1975 to 0.66 in 1981/82. Although it improved to 0.87 in 1986/87, it reflected a worsening of competitiveness compared to 1975. Drastic improvement apparently was achieved in 1988/89, with the index rising to 1.38. But this was really hard to explain exclusively in terms of wage-productivity differentials. It may well be the result of some problems with the data – at least partially.

One final remark relates to labour absorption in the manufacturing sector. For the period as a whole, the rate of labour absorption is modest. But the rate of increase in labour absorption fell in the second sub-period compared to the first; curiously the result of a fall in the rate of growth of employment in the public sector and a rise in the private sector. The public sector/private sector distinction is highly relevant here; while public sector employment rose by a negligible 25 per cent during the entire period, private sector employment more than doubled. In the public manufacturing sector, the growth of employment dropped from an average annual rate of 2.5 per cent during 1975–1981/82 to a modest 1.0 per cent during 1981/82–1988/89. This sharp drop in the growth of employment in the public sector may be explained by a number of factors (CAPMAS, 1985; Handoussa, 1991).

First, it may have also been in response to fast-rising wages in the first sub-period, probably under the pressure of competition for labour from *infitah* projects and regional demand through labour migration – both factors being strong manifestations of labour mobility.

Second, throughout the first sub-period, public sector enterprises were forced to follow the government's employment policy of job guarantees for high school and university graduates. That policy was abandoned in the early 1980s with respect to public sector enterprises, and only a few years later with regard to government departments. As a carry-over from the era of guaranteed full employment, many public sector enterprises were actually over staffed. Hence, many enterprises in the public sector gradually re-adjusted labour closer to the desired level by putting the lid on new recruitment. In fact, the textile industry (ISIC 32), the largest manufacturing sub-sector in Egypt in terms of employment,[5] reduced its employment level in absolute terms after 1984/85. By 1988/89, employment in this industry was only 80 per cent of its peak level in 1981/82. Employment in the metals and metal products (ISIC 37+381) and in printing and publishing (ISIC 34) almost stagnated since 1980/81.

Third, many public sector enterprises have undergone rehabilitation in the late 1970s – early 1980s, going mostly for modern capital-intensive technology. This obviously reduces the need for labour, given capacity output. In fact, there is evidence that capital intensification in Egyptian industry during this period exceeded the optimal rate; it has actually proceeded so fast that it resulted in a fall in total factor productivity (CAPMAS, 1985, pp. 57–58).

We conclude this section on the pattern of ownership by making an important *caveat*. One has to be extremely cautious in making any inferences based on public/private distinction in the Egyptian setting. On the one hand, enterprises established under the foreign investment code (Law 43 and its sequels) are by definition private firms even if the public equity share exceeds 50 per cent. Also, after 1991, privatization measures under ERSAP imply expansion of the private sector *at the expense of* public ownership.

Types of industry

How did the structure of manufacturing industry change over the period? We begin by considering the public sector, then the private sector. The analysis of the data in Table 4.4 reveals some interesting trends.

a. The textile industry has consistently, and in fact rapidly, lost its leading position as a producer of value added. Its share in value added plummeted from 34 per cent in 1975 to only 5 per cent in 1995/96. This indeed is a significant development, and calls for further investigation as to the causes behind this trend and its likely consequences. For the time being, it is well to lament that the fate of the textile industry in Egypt seems to be running parallel to the fortunes of Egyptian cotton.[6]
b. Non-metallic and mineral products, metals and metal products and equipment have all gained importance over the period, both in terms of value added and employment. Their combined share of public sector value added rose from 22 per cent in 1975 to 33 per cent in 1995/96, and their share in employment increased from 25 per cent to 34 per cent over the same period. This may be construed as implying a growing degree of sophistication in Egypt's industrial structure. In view of the stronger backward- and forward-linkage effects of these industries compared to food and textiles, one may hypothesize that the structure of industrial production in Egypt has become more interdependent.
c. It is hard to explain the sudden jump in the share of value added in chemicals. With respect to the private sector, the values fluctuate over a wide range, making it extremely difficult to identify general trends with any degree of confidence. Given that, what can we learn from the data regarding the development of value added and employment in the broad (ISIC 2–digit level) manufacturing activities in the private sector?
d. Some industries have definitely gained in importance through the 1980s. Food, beverages and tobacco (ISIC 31) is the most notable example: its share of value added rising from about one fourth to one third of total value added in private sector manufacturing by 1988/89. But its leading

Table 4.4 Relative importance of various manufacturing activities 1975–1995/96

ISIC			1975		1981/82		1986/87		1988/89		1995/96	
Division			Pub.	Priv.	Pub.	Priv.	Pub.	Priv.	Pub.	Priv.	Pub.	Priv.
(31)	Food	VA	25.0	23.0	19.9	28.6	24.5	25.1	27.7	32.6	15.3	18.4
		LAB	16.7	29.0	16.8	29.0	18.1	29.9	18.7	27.6	16.6	22.0
(32)	Textiles	VA	34.0	19.7	25.7	14.0	21.1	10.0	17.1	13.2	4.9	17.1
		LAB	43.3	27.9	39.3	24.2	33.8	23.9	29.3	27.8	30.6	28.6
(33)	Wood	VA	0.7	3.4	0.8	2.2	0.9	2.2	0.7	5.7	0.2	1.0
		LAB	0.8	3.5	0.9	2.7	1.0	2.7	1.0	3.4	0.6	3.0
(34)	Paper	VA	3.4	16.7	1.7	21.9	2.3	11.9	1.6	5.4	1.7	8.2
		LAB	2.1	11.9	2.0	11.9	1.9	10.3	1.8	8.7	2.0	4.7
(35)	Chemicals	VA	14.5	13.6	13.6	5.1	19.3	17.1	13.9	15.4	44.6	14.3
		LAB	12.1	4.6	14.7	7.1	14.7	9.4	14.2	9.5	16.5	9.5
(36)	Non-metal	VA	5.2	11.8	8.7	15.0	7.2	13.4	8.4	7.8	10.8	8.5
	Minerals	LAB	4.2	10.9	4.5	13.3	4.9	12.7	5.5	8.4	6.5	10.1
(37)	Metal	VA	5.6	6.6	11.8	7.2	14.1	6.3	16.7	16.0	11.0	4.2
		LAB	11.1	8.5	11.7	7.8	13.8	6.9	11.4	8.2	9.1	3.2
(38,39)	Met-prod.	VA	11.3	5.3	17.7	6.0	10.7	13.9	13.9	4.0	11.6	28.3
	& equipt	LAB	9.7	3.8	9.9	4.1	11.8	5.3	18.0	6.2	18.3	18.9

Notes:
VA = Value added
LAB = Labour

Source: Calculated from data of CAPMAS, *Census of Annual Industrial Production*, various years.

position seems to have eroded during the 1990s. Its share in employment remained stable around 28–29 per cent of total employment in private sector manufacturing through 1988/89. Basic metals (ISIC 37) is another industry which expanded over the period through the 1980s in terms of value added, but took a real plunge during the 1990s.

e. Two private-manufacturing activities exhibited trends that run counter to what is widely believed, or even casually observed: textile and non-metallic minerals. The private sector appears to have made significant progress over the past ten years in ready-made clothes and garments, and in ceramic tiles and related products. For example, from a modest starting level of LE 15 million in the mid 1980s, exports of ready-made clothes reached LE 322.4 million in 1990/91 (see MOP, 1992b, p. 40). But surprisingly, the data of Table 4.4 do not provide supporting evidence of such developments.

The developments in the manufacturing sector, both private and public, which we have discussed above may be used to shed some light on the crowding out thesis. If the public sector really crowds out the private sector, we may expect their respective shares to be negatively correlated – other things being equal. Results of empirical analysis of aggregate private investment in Egypt for the period 1960–86 provide mixed evidence of crowding out. With financial repression, which involved fixed interest rates and credit rationing, the government did not crowd out well-established firms in the private sector, while it may have crowded out newer ones. Through infrastructure investment the results seem to suggest some crowding in. But this may just be the result of government investment simply coinciding with private investment during the boom (Shafik, 1992, p. 49).

Examination of the data in Table 4.4 does not seem to support the crowding out hypothesis, since booming industries and lagging ones are almost the same for both the public and the private sectors. What is more plausible perhaps is that the public sector is crowding in the private sector in specific manufacturing activities. This is particularly true in the case of metals and metal products. The public sector is largely dominant in basic metal production (the share of the public sector in value added in 1987/88 was about 88 per cent), while the private sector uses such material for further processing in various product lines. Furthermore, the fact that the share of food processing in value added has been steadily rising and that of textiles falling for most of the period in both private and public sector manufacturing in parallel does not support the crowding out hypothesis. This conclusion may also be relevant for the current debate on privatization in Egypt.

Table 4.4 reveals yet another interesting feature of the manufacturing sector in Egypt over the period since 1975. Public sector manufacturing was more concentrated than private sector in 1975. Over time, public sector manufacturing activity became significantly more diversified while private sector activity became slightly more concentrated. The combined share in value added of the two top-ranking industries in the public sector fell from 59 per cent in 1975 to about 45 per cent in 1988/89, while the combined share of the two top-ranking industries in the private sector rose from about 43 per cent to around 49 per cent. The two industries in 1975 were the same for the public and the private sector: food and textiles. Both industries also maintained their lead in public-sector manufacturing in 1988/89. For private sector manufacturing in the latter year, metals replaced textiles as the second top-ranking industry. This pattern appears to have changed in the 1990s.

Factor proportions

An important aspect of the structure of manufacturing is factor proportions. Previous studies have established the trend rise in the capital–labour ratio over the period 1973–1986/87 (see Table 4.5). We examine here the latest detailed data available – that for 1987/88 and 1995/96. Before we embark on this task, it should be noted that the factor proportions (capital–labour ratios) which are derived here do not reflect exclusively technological characteristics. These are data for a single year and do not necessarily represent equilibrium conditions. Moreover, data on capital stock are based on book values, which distorts the measure of capital and makes inter-industry comparisons rather risky. This is particularly more so the wider is the discrepancy of the age of the capital stock in various industries. Also, the value of the imported components of the capital stock (basically machinery and equipment) may exhibit a different behaviour over time from that of local components (basically land and buildings). Furthermore, the value of fixed assets at the end of the census year equals net capital formation during the year plus fixed assets at the end of the previous year. Net capital formation includes net inventory change, which may be abnormally high, resulting in overestimation of the capital stock.[7] In short, capital stock data are subject to various elements of 'noise'. For simplicity, we assume here that such 'noise' affects all industries equally. Only if this assumption is accepted as a good approximation can we compare values of the capital stock across various branches of manufacturing.

According to the data sets for 1988/89 and 1995/96 (Table 4.6), the total capital stock (fixed assets) in all branches of manufacturing more than doubled between the two dates. It is significant to note that the capital stock is highly concentrated; the bulk of it is in industries 31, 32, 35 and 36 according to the two-digit ISIC classification.

In 1987/88, the non-metallic minerals industry accounted for one quarter of the capital stock in manufacturing. This, in relation to the industry's level

Table 4.5 *Annual compound growth rates of the capital–labour ratio, total factor productivity and average labour productivity, 1970–1986/87*

	Capital–labour ratio		Total factor productivity		Average labour productivity	
	Pub.	Priv.	Pub.	Priv.	Pub.	Priv.
(1) 1970–80						
311/312	n.a.	n.a.	n.a.	n.a.	n.a.	n.a.
321	3.734	17.174	1.70	0.49	4.828	7.607
322	3.979	13.920	0.28	0.58	0.901	11.149
324	6.401	27.692	6.19	2.12	3.868	10.111
332	10.080	18.019	–4.57	–1.48	6.797	6.500
342	4.168	2.660	–0.15	–0.38	7.091	2.055
352	5.380	4.339	0.62	1.20	7.656	11.261
362	3.332	16.063	0.04	0.44	0.168	2.109
369	12.193	10.929	–0.57	–0.69	3.685	5.551
381	4.908	6.716	–1.48	1.57	3.118	9.986
382	3.285	11.470	1.64	0.17	7.246	9.872
383	5.100	10.925	3.11	0.62	6.965	3.879
(2) 1979–86/87 (in 1982/83 prices)						
	5.640	22.309	0.50	–4.40	4.903	9.444

Sources: (1) CAPMAS (1985), Tables 1–6; (2) Abdela'tty (1990), Tables 4.4b and 4.5.

of employment, puts the capital–labour ratio at LE 71 000 per worker, making such industry by far the most capital-intensive among Egyptian manufacturing industries (see Table 4.6). The dominant place which the textile industry occupies in Egypt's manufacturing is illustrated well by the fact that it is the largest in terms of employment and the fourth largest in terms of the capital stock. If we assign equal weight to the various industries' share in capital and labour and combine them in one scale indicator for each industry, scale ranking in 1987/88 was as follows (see column (4) of Table 4.6): textiles; food; chemicals; non-metallic minerals: metal products: metals; paper, printing and publishing; and finally wood and furniture. The scale ranking in 1995/96 was not fundamentally different.

Column (3) gives the capital–labour ratios in the various manufacturing industries – an indicator of the relative factor intensity. Non-metallic mineral products was by far the most capital-intensive industry;[8] its capital–labour

Table 4.6 Capital intensity in manufacturing, 1987/88–1995/96

Industry (ISIC 2-Digit)			Capital LE million (1)	Capital %	Labour Number (2)	Labour %	Capital–labour ratio (LE 000) (3)=(1)÷(2)	Ranking Scale (4)	Ranking Int. (5)
(31)	Food	a	3 482.2	19.8	215 730	21.6	16.14	2	4
		b	6 224.6	16.3	217 786	18.7	28.58	3	5
(32)	Textiles	a	2 997.3	17.0	301 375	30.2	0.95	1	8
		b	5 247.5	13.7	346 846	29.8	15.13	1	8
(33)	Wood	a	84.9	0.5	18 390	1.8	4.62	8	7
		b	276.6	0.7	18 010	1.5	15.36	8	7
(34)	Paper	a	450.6	2.6	35 261	3.5	12.78	7	5
		b	1 198.6	6.6	35 483	3.0	33.78	7	4
(35)	Chemicals	a	3 354.9	19.0	132 891	13.3	25.25	3	2
		b	10 697.7	28.0	159 576	13.7	67.04	2	2
(36)	Non-met.	a	4 303.6	24.4	60 627	6.1	71.00	4	1
		b	6 475.4	16.9	91 990	7.9	70.39	5	1
(37)	Metal	a	1 554.4	8.8	71 611	7.2	21.71	6	3
		b	3 247.2	8.4	78 655	6.8	40.90	6	3
(38, 39)	Metal prod.	a	1 390.4	7.9	161 327	16.2	8.62	5	6
	& equipt.	b	3 554.1	9.3	215 125	18.5	16.52	4	6
Total		a	17 618.3	100.0	997 212	100.0	20.00		
		b	38 223.9	100.0	1 163 473	100.0	36.00		

Notes:
a. Figures refer to 1987/88.
b. Figures refer to 1995/96.

Source: CAPMAS, *Census of Annual Industrial Production, 1987/88* (May 1990) and 1995/96, 2 vols, (May and Sept. 1998).

ratio stood at more than four times the mean capital–labour ratio for the whole of manufacturing. At the other end of the spectrum, wood products and furniture was the least capital-intensive. It is interesting to observe that the inter-industry spread in terms of the capital–labour ratio is so large that the value of the standard error is almost equal to the arithmetic mean (21.22 compared to 21.26, for 1987/88).

Some insights may be gained regarding the structure of the manufacturing industry in Egypt by comparing the last two columns of Table 4.6. Column (4) shows the scale ranking of the eight major divisions of manufacturing (at the ISIC 2-digit level). The ranking for any one industry is based on a scale indicator, calculated as the simple average of that industry's shares in total capital stock and labour in manufacturing. According to this criterion, the top-ranking industry is textiles – the largest on average, in terms of capital stock and labour. Column (5) gives the intensity ranking of the same set of industries, based on the value of the capital–labour ratio. According to this criterion, textiles ranked eighth. Visual inspection gives the impression that correlation between the scale ranking and the intensity ranking is not very strong. The value of the Spearman correlation coefficient is 0.7; not significant at the 99 per cent confidence level but significant at the 87.5 per cent level.

Table 4.6 may be used to throw some light on the allocative efficiency in Egypt's manufacturing. As is well known in standard neoclassical micro theory, an activity may be viewed as efficient if, *ceteris paribus*, it uses relatively more of the more abundant (and hence cheaper) factor of production. For manufacturing activity, the two relevant factors are obviously labour and capital. It is almost common knowledge that Egypt is a labour-abundant, capital-scarce country. Static allocative efficiency in manufacturing activity would thus mean focusing on labour-intensive activities. According to the data in Table 4.6, the most labour-intensive activities were: wood and furniture followed by metal products; textiles; paper, printing, and publishing; and food processing. In all these activities, the value of the capital–labour ratio is below the mean value for total manufaturing. It is obvious that, at least in the case of wood and furniture and paper, printing and publishing, potential comparative advantage is still largely unexploited. The data in Table 4.4 indicate clearly that those two industries have been lagging behind the whole of the manufacturing sector, either in terms of income generation or in terms of labour absorption.[9]

In a development strategy with clear emphasis on employment and income generation, these industries should receive more attention. What was mentioned regarding wood and furniture and paper, printing and publishing, applies even more strongly to textiles. We noted earlier that this industry has been losing labour and gaining capital, that is, undergoing capital deepening over the past 20 years. In the process, it has become more capital-intensive. We also noted the conclusion of a CAPMAS study (CAPMAS, 1985) that faster mechanization, even automation of certain production processes, may have resulted in lower total factor productivity. This raises the issue of the right pace of technological change.

By contrast, the other labour-intensive industries (the food-processing industry and the metal products industry) have been attracting more resources and generating more income. This trend is in conformity with the requirements of allocative efficiency. This, of course, says nothing about technical efficiency, or more broadly, X-efficiency. The latter depends on factors of organizational/institutional nature, and calls for micro-analysis at the firm level (Leibenstein, 1978).

The metal industry, on the other hand, is obviously among the most capital-intensive industries in Egypt. Studies and reports by some outside agencies, particularly the World Bank and the USAID have invariably maintained that production of basic metals is inefficient and hence investment in these activities is wasteful. In its most extensive and detailed study on the issue, the World Bank (1983) divided manufacturing activity into three main categories. Category I included activities which already appear competitive at international prices. Category II included activities which may become competitive and offer potential for exports. Category III consisted of activities with high domestic resource cost which were unlikely to allow efficient exports. Basic iron and steel and aluminium belong to the third category. Their economic rates of return were much less than the financial rates of return; according to the World Bank, the former was even negative for aluminium (see Annex 4A.2).

The USAID has taken more or less the same policy stance based on comparing the economic and financial rates of return for the Kima fertilizer plant in Aswan and the aluminium smelter at Nag'a Hamadi in Upper Egypt (USAID, 1979). This issue will be examined in more detail in Chapters 5 and 6 when we deal with the case studies of the aluminium and iron and steel companies. At this stage, we offer the following observations with reference to Table 4.6. First, the expansion of the more labour-intensive metal products industry (ISIC 38 and 39) should perhaps be related to the expansion of the more capital-intensive metal industry (ISIC 37), thanks to the strong forward-linkage effects of the latter. It would be incorrect to pass a judgement on the merits of any specific industry treated in isolation from the rest. A more comprehensive approach should be used in order to reach policy-relevant conclusions. Second, the main difference between the financial rates of return and the economic rates of return is that the latter were based on world prices of tradable inputs – in particular world prices for energy. But using world prices of petroleum as a norm for judging efficiency lacks a convincing theoretical justification – aside from the argument that petroleum is a tradable good. As shown by the model and data in Annex III, petroleum is far more scarce in Egypt than it is for the world at large. Third, petroleum may actually be a bad example for invoking the concept of world prices as a norm for efficiency. The so-called world price of oil is not a competitive price but rather an administrative or 'political' price – determined by the various parties on both sides of the market in an oligopolistic setting. The world oil market is far from being competitive.

NOTES

1. 'First' and 'second' should be taken to refer to the resumption of national planning under the then new Mubarak administration. It should be noted, however, that Egypt's very first five-year plan covers the period 1960/61–1964/65.
2. An interesting question to be pursued is the contribution of manufacturing to total GDP growth and the sources of industrial growth – that is, import substitution, export expansion, domestic demand and technical change.
3. Hansen has also attempted to throw additional light on the issue using accounting ratios, ARs (AR = ratio of shadow prices to market prices). His conclusion is that the evidence is mixed: evidence based on unweighted means supporting Dutch disease, while evidence based on medians against it (Hansen, 1991, p. 176).
4. The value of oil exports soared to LE 2402 million in 1981/82 and plummeted to LE 634.1 million in 1986/87. See CBE, *Annual Report 1986/87*, Table 31, p. 85, and Table 35, p. 92. Table 31 gives a higher value for oil exports in 1986/87 (LE 1032 million); such value was disregarded as probably incorrect since the text of the Report explicitly mentions the drop in the value of exports of crude oil and oil products to LE 634.1 million in 1986/87 caused by a combination of a 40.7 per cent fall in quantity and a 44.4 per cent drop in export price (p. 84).
5. In 1981/82 this industry, which includes spinning and weaving, clothing, leather and leather products, accounted for 40 per cent of employment in the public manufacturing sector. But in terms of value added, it was second to food, beverages and tobacco (ISIC 31).
6. Annual cotton production has been falling almost steadily since the early 1980s: coming down from 9.2 million *quantars* in 1982/83 to 5.9 million *quantars* in 1990/91 (one *quantar* of lint = 50 kilograms); see NBE, *Economic Bulletin*, vol. 44, no. 1 and 2 (1991), Table 2/5(B).
7. For example, in 1987/88 inventory change amounted to LE 1.6 billion, or 42 per cent of capital formation in both public and private manufacturing. It is not certain whether making allowance for this factor will not change the basic trend.
8. In fact, the value of the capital–labour ratio in this industry is surprisingly too high. The CAIP gives the following details of the capital stock for 1987/88 (LE.000): ceramics, china and pottery 79 675; glass and glass products 272 945; non-metallic mineral products 3 950 983 (CAPMAS, 1990, pp. 480–88).
9. One needs to clarify this conclusion in the light of what was mentioned above, particularly the fact that CAIP covers only establishments employing 10 workers or more. In the case of wood and furniture, a large proportion of enterprises may employ less than 10 workers (see Davies et al., 1992), and hence do not show up in the CAIP results. It is not certain that allowing for this factor will not change the conclusion.

APPENDIX 4.1

Table 4A.1 Development of manufacturing exports, 1981/82–1991/92 and targets for 1992/93–1996/97 at current prices (LE million)

	1981/82		1991/92		1996/97*	
	Value	%	Value	%	Value	%
1. Spinning & weaving	195.2	49.3	1 910.0	33.1	3 475.0	28.7
2. Engineering	0.3	0.1	299.0	5.2	780.0	6.4
3. Food	51.3	13.0	314.0	5.4	710.0	5.9
4. Chemicals	40.4	10.2	973.0	11.7	1 630.0	13.4
5. Metals	76.8	19.4	742.0	12.9	1 955.0	13.6
6. Others**	31.6	8.0	1 824.0	31.7	3 875.0	32.0
Total manufacturing	395.0	100.0	5 762.0	100.0	12 125.0	100.0
Tot. commodity exports	3987.2	9.9	16 705.0	34.5	23 392.0	51.8

Notes:
* 1996/97 are targets of the 1992/93–1996/97 five-year plan.
** Other exports include minerals.

Source: MOP (1992a), Tables 14 and 17.

Table 4A.2 The divergence between economic and financial profitability: single year estimates, FY 1980/81

	Economic rate of return	Financial rate of return
Cotton textiles	13.6	5.9
Wool textiles	14.1	15.5
Jute products	5.1	17.5
Carpets	4.2	18.3
Oil, soaps & detergents	14.4	–6.6
Sugar	34.2	7.1
Processed vegetables	12.3	2.2
Oils & essences	78.1	17.6
Starch & yeast	45.0	6.2
Artificial fibres	–9.5	1.9
Non-edible oils	–11.1	3.8
Coke	–17.4	–20.7
Leather & tanning	8.3	4.1
Iron & steel	2.7	10.9
Aluminium	–21.0	12.5
Non-ferrous metals	–3.1	15.5
Steel pipes	–2.0	18.9
Formed & shaped steel	6.4	11.7
Ferrous castings	–46.2	–6.7
Road motor vehicles	–32.7	–13.4
Railway carriage	17.3	12.1
Bicycles & motorcycles	–3.2	1.5
Industrial electrical products	52.6	24.4
Electric consumer durables	20.0	15.8
Consumer electronics	–3.6	20.5
Ceramics	–12.8	2.4
China & glass	–16.4	20.6

Source: World Bank (1983, p. XVIII).

5. The microeconomic effects of ERSAP: 1. The aluminium industry

INTRODUCTION

The aluminium industry is by far the most energy-intensive industry in Egypt. Energy, in the form of electricity, represents about more than 25 per cent of unit cost. By comparison, the main raw material (alumina) accounts for about 30 per cent of unit cost. The Aluminium Company of Egypt (EGYPTALUM) is the largest single consumer of electricity. According to the Egypt Electricity Authority (EEA), sale of electricity to EGYPTALUM, the sole producer of aluminium in the country, amounted to kW/h 3312 million in 1997/98. Total electricity sales by EEA for that same year reached kW/h 57 106 million. The share of the aluminium smelting in total electricity consumption thus amounts to 6–7 per cent.

The issue of rationalizing energy use assumes paramount micro and macro significance in this context. Its micro significance has to do with the fact that energy cost per unit output of aluminium is the single largest cost item. Barring efforts to raise energy efficiency at EGYPTALUM, any increase in electricity prices, as part of the package of structural adjustment measures under ERSAP (see Annex IV), will result in a corresponding increase in the unit production cost. Such an increase in cost, if not absorbed somehow, may actually jeopardize the competitiveness of the aluminium industry in the country. At the macro level, any substantial reduction in electricity use in the aluminium industry will factor eminently in the overall energy equation of Egypt. In addition, it will help reduce air pollution and hence improve the environment.

But the incidence of adjusting electricity prices is not the only effect of ERSAP on the aluminium industry. As already mentioned in Chapters 2 and 3, ERSAP additionally includes privatization, liberalizing output and input prices, liberalizing interest rates, devaluation of the Egyptian pound, and trade liberalization. Naturally, these measures push in various directions, and their effects in the short run may be different from their effects in the long run. In the present chapter, we focus our analysis exclusively on the *impact effects* of the various relevant ERSAP measures; these are the immediate or short-run effects. The long-run effects depend partly on the overall design of the programme, and partly on the response of the industry to the policy change envisaged thereby. Before proceeding to analyse these impact effects, a brief account of the development and performance of the aluminium industry in Egypt is in order. It is meant to set the stage for the analysis of the effect of various ERSAP measures on this industry in the remaining parts of the chapter.

THE ALUMINIUM INDUSTRY IN EGYPT: ORIGIN AND DEVELOPMENT

The aluminium industry in Egypt is fairly recent; it was established only in the mid 1970s. Production actually started in October 1975. The project was originally conceived during the 1960s to take advantage of cheap hydroelectricity generated by the Aswan High Dam. It was initiated towards the end of the five-year plan 1960/61–1964/65, when a contract was signed with a Polish corporation on December 15, 1964 to set up an aluminium smelter in Suez with an annual capacity of 40 thousand tonnes. The 1967 war delayed the project until it was reconsidered in the late 1960s (Osman, 1990).

The driving force behind setting up the industry was the availability of hydroelectric power from the Aswan High Dam. Various sites to locate the project were originally considered including Suez, Aswan and Alexandria. But the present location in Nag'a Hamady in Upper Egypt was preferred for the following reasons:

a. proximity to Nag'a Hamady transforming station, a factor that reduces the cost of obtaining electricity;
b. proximity to the port of Safaga on the Red Sea, to be used in handling imports of the main raw material – alumina;
c. development of a desert region, and hence making a contribution to regional development in general;
d. location in a safe area outside earthquake and flash flood activity;
e. availability of land, water and rail transport; and
f. availability of underground water for industrial processes.

Perhaps the most important single factor favouring the establishment of the aluminium industry was the availability of cheap electricity from the High Dam hydroelectric power plant. The construction of the Dam's power station with installed capacity of 2100 megawatts was completed in 1967, almost two years before final completion of the Dam project. For technical reasons, transmission of electric power from Aswan in the south to Cairo and other industrial centres in the north was impossible; such power could only either be used in the south (Upper Egypt) or wasted. Electricity generated by the High Dam thus had almost zero opportunity cost during the late 1960s–early 1970s. As already mentioned, the aluminium smelter was seriously considered during the first five-year plan (1960/61–1964/65). But the eruption of the 1967 war and its aftermath delayed the project and forced a change in its location from Suez to Nag'a Hamady. This background is important for the discussion of the issue of energy use in this industry. We shall do that in a latter part of this chapter.

Aluminium is produced in Nag'a Hamady using imported alumina as the main input. EGYPTALUM's main production facilities consist of five potlines. Each potline has two cell lines containing 46 electric cells each. This brings the total to 460 cells using electrolysis to transform alumina into aluminium. Cells at the smelter at Nag'a Hamady works were originally designed according to the Soderberg technology using 155 k ampere electric current.

The design capacity of the EGYPTALUM smelter was gradually expanded from 33 thousand tonnes/year in October 1975 to 166 thousand tonnes/year in July 1983. The original project had a design capacity of 100 thousand tonnes/year, which was fully reached in April 1977, and further expanded to 166 thousand tonnes/year (see Appendix 5.1). But it was possible to push actual production capacity to 180 thousand tonnes/year, thanks to a number of factors:

i. automatization of cell control;
ii. continuous training of production workers;
iii. reducing time needed for cell rehabilitation significantly, from 22 day/cell to 7.6 day/cell; and
iv. prolonging the operating life of cells from the design rate of 42 month/cell to 60.1 month/cell.

An expansion project is currently being implemented, which will increase the productive capacity of EGYPTALUM to 240 thousand tonnes/year.

In addition to the five potlines, the production facilities at Nag'a Hamady include two electric foundries. The first foundry was established at the start of production in 1975. It had a Russian design that was later modified. This foundry produces ingots, slabs and T-bars. The second foundry came on line in 1982. It is based on Western technology, and produces slabs, billets, wires (9–25 mm) and ingots.

The product mix has changed substantially since 1976, when fabricated aluminium accounted for just 12 per cent of total output. It amounted to 84 per cent in 1993/94. One may distinguish three distinct sub-periods. During 1976–1980/81, the increase in the ratio of fabricated aluminium was modest. The dramatic change in the product mix took place during 1981/82–1986/87.

The rise in the ratio accelerated during that period, but naturally decelerated after 1986/87.

An interesting question is: why the acceleration of the ratio during the second sub-period? In order to answer this question, it should be observed that the pricing formulae for primary and fabricated aluminium are different. The price of primary aluminium is given by quotations on the London Metal Exchange. Fabricated aluminium, on the other hand, sells at a premium above the price of primary aluminium – the premium differing by type of fabricated product. The acceleration in the ratio of fabricated to primary aluminium during 1981/82–1986/87 appears to have been the result of bringing Foundry No. 2 on line during 1982, and the attainment of maximum design capacity of 166 thousand tonnes following the completion of the fifth phase in July 1983.

IMPACT OF ERSAP

The various ERSAP measures were outlined before in this study (see Chapter 2). To recapitulate, the measures which are expected to have an impact on the aluminium industry are: raising energy prices; devaluation of the Egyptian pound; liberalizing output prices; liberalizing interest rates; trade liberalization; abolition of credit ceilings and liberalization of input prices. These measures will affect the aluminium industry in different directions. The nature of the likely effects are indicated in summary form in Table 5.1. We focus here on the first five measures as the most relevant for this industry.

Table 5.1 Likely effects of ERSAP on EGYPYTALUM

Type of measure	Nature of impact effect
(a) Raising energy prices	–
(b) Liberalizing output prices	+
(c) Liberalizing input prices	–
(d) Liberalizing interest rate	?
(e) Devaluation	+
(f) Trade liberalization	?
(g) Abolition of credit ceiling	+
Overall outcome	?

Impact of Raising Energy Prices

It was already mentioned in Chapter 2 of this study that ERSAP has a structural adjustment component relating to price reform. Central to the price reform component in Egypt is the issue of adjusting energy prices. ERSAP adopts two norms for price adjustment in the energy field: world prices for tradables and cost for non-tradables. Specifically, the norm is world prices in the case of petroleum products and natural gas, and long-run marginal cost (LRMC) in the case of electricity.

The economics of using electric energy for aluminium smelting was strongly debated at the start of this industry in the country during the 1970s. We have already made reference to the report prepared by USAID which maintained that if the proper calculations were made, aluminium smelting using electricity would involve a real economic loss (USAID, 1979). We also referred to the World Bank study published in the early 1980s which also suggested (on the basis of comparing estimates of the economic and financial rates of return) that the aluminium industry is not one of the industries in which Egypt has a comparative advantage (World Bank, 1983).

Sales of electricity to the aluminium works at Nag'a Hamady are rather significant, amounting to 6–7 per cent of total electricity sold in the country or the equivalent of 35–40 per cent of electricity generated by the High Dam power plant (see Table 5.2). Electricity is currently supplied (since July 1992) to the EGYTALUM complex in Nag'a Hamady at a flat tariff rate of LE 0.068 per kW/h (ultra-high voltage). This compares with LE 0.047 per kW/h to the Kima Fertilizer plant at Aswan, and LE 0.086 per kW/h of ultra-high voltage electricity supplied to industry in general.

According to ERSAP, the price of electricity is deemed highly distorted – meaning that actual prices are significantly below LRMC. As indicated in Annex IV, ERSAP entailed bringing actual electricity prices up to parity with LRMC by June 1995. But actual implementation deviated somewhat from the original commitments under the programme. To appreciate the extent of the energy price hike required by ERSAP, it may be useful to examine the behaviour of electricity prices charged to EGYPTALUM in recent years (see Table 5.3). Between July 1985 and July 1992, this price has increased almost ninefold (from LE 0.0077 to LE 0.0680 per kW/h). Apparently, EGYPTALUM was able, however, to absorb these increases in electricity prices. A number of factors have contributed to this adjustment to higher electricity prices in an industry that is characteristically the most energy-intensive of all. Such factors are: reducing energy consumption per kilogramme of molten (liquid) aluminium; raising cathode current efficiency (from 84 per cent to 87 per cent); and introducing an automated system to control electrolytic cells every minute. However, more important perhaps

Table 5.2 Electric energy sold by EEA, 1992/1993–1997/98

		1992/93		1997/98	
		kW/h million	%	kW/h million	%
I.	Ultra-high voltage	*6 848.97*	*16.3*	*8 159.63*	*14.3*
	1. EGYPTALUM	3 058.94	7.3	3 312.16	5.8
	2. Kima	1 652.50	3.9	1 619.01	2.8
	3. Dekheila Iron & Steel	1 043.64	2.5	1 478.23	2.6
	4. Other	1 093.89	2.6	1 750.23	3.1
II.	High Voltage	*2 475.20*	*5.89*	*4 268.20*	*7.5*
	Total industry high voltage	1 633.48	3.89	3 274.84	5.7
	5. Hadisolb	n.a.	n.a.	(845.68)	(1.5)
	6. Talkha Fertilizers	(323.57)	(0.75)	(298.74)	(0.5)
	7. Amereya Cement	(301.30)	(0.72)	(320.49)	(0.6)
	Total agri. high voltage	746.62	1.78	(766.65)	1.3
	Total gov't high voltage	95.10	0.23	72.72	0.1
III.	Medium voltage	*212.60*	*0.51*	*240.36*	*0.4*
IV.	Distribution companies	*32 451.72*	*77.29*	*44 438.03*	*77.8*
	Cairo	13 806.96	(32.88)	17 552.50	30.7
Grand total		41 988.49	100.00	57 106.22	100.0

Source: Egypt Electricity Authority, *Annual Report of Electricity Statistics for 1992/93*, and 1997/98.

Total electricity generated	47 096.3	62 362.1
Hydro	10 485.8	12 221.6
(of which High Dam)	(7 640.5)	(8 949.0)
Thermal	36 610.5	50 114.7
Sales	*41 988.5*	*57 106.2*
Total sales/total generated	89.15%	91.16%

was the fact that EGYPTALUM was helped significantly by the decision of the Ministry of Industry to price locally sold aluminium at international prices starting in 1993.[1]

For the future, however, the aluminium industry in Egypt will have to devise new ways and means to absorb the hike in the price of electricity stipulated under ERSAP in order to remain economically viable. The essence of adjustment would have to be to achieve a significant reduction in the

Table 5.3 Development of sale price of electricity supplied to EGYPTALUM (ultra-high voltage), 1976–98

Date	Average price mm per kW/h	Percentage increase	Remarks
1976	2.586	–	mm 3.5 for January, mm 2.5 for other months
August 80	2.932	13	4th potline mm 5 for Jan., mm 4 for other months
December 82	4.435	51	mm 4.435 for all 4 potlines
August 83	4.940	12	mm 7 for 5th potline
March 84	5.906	14	mm 5.261 for old 4 potlines and mm 7 for 5th potline
July 85	7.700	37	uniform rate for all potlines
May 87	10.800	40	uniform rate for all potlines
March 89	18.000	67	uniform rate for all potlines
May 90	28.900	61	uniform rate for all potlines
May 91	46.000	59	uniform rate for all potlines
July 92–June 98	68.000	48	uniform rate for all potlines

Note: mm = millieme = LE 0.001.

Source: Egypt Electricity Authority, *Annual Statistical Report for 1993/94* and memo items:
1976–84 annual average compound rate of increase = 11%
1984–87 annual average compound rate of increase = 20%
1987–98 annual average compound rate of increase = 43%.

specific energy consumption. This may be analysed by referring to the following theoretical relations:

$$E = (2.980)(V/x)\text{kW/h/kgAl} \tag{5.1}$$

where
E = specific energy consumption,
V = cell voltage,
x = current efficiency ratio.

This theoretical relation indicates that specific energy consumption may be reduced by lowering the cell voltage (V), or by increasing the current efficiency (x), or both.

i. *Cell voltage* Cell voltage, *V*, has been theoretically demonstrated to be the primary cause of low electrical energy efficiency and hence high specific energy consumption. Thus the primary cause for low electrical energy efficiency is the very high cell voltage. Excess voltage is due to electrode polarization (that is, polarization at the electrode interfaces). This is essentially a function of operating conditions.

   Heat losses are also among the factors affecting specific energy consumption. Generally speaking, relative heat losses are lower the larger the cell size. In aluminium cells, the main zone of heat loss is the top, followed by the sides. In a 108 kA cell with pre-baked anodes, the top and sides account for 53.9 per cent and 31.8 per cent, respectively, of total heat loss. In a 108 kA cell with Soderberg anodes, the corresponding percentages are 58.1 and 28.1, the balance is the proportion of heat loss occurring at the bottom. Cell operation is the major factor contributing to heat losses at the top and along the sides, since it influences the thickness of the aluminium oxide at the top of the bath and of the ledge of solidified electrolyte covering the inside surface of the side walls of the cell. Skilled and better-trained operators can make a significant contribution to reducing the specific energy consumption in aluminium smelting.

ii. *Current efficiency* The other variable determining specific energy consumption in aluminium smelting is the current efficiency ratio (CER), *x*. Current efficiency ratio is a function of a number of factors, but the most important factor influencing CER is cell temperature. Reported values indicate that, on the average, for every 10°C that the temperature is lowered (within the appropriate range of course) about a 3 per cent improvement in current efficiency can be achieved (Grjotheim and Welch, 1980, p. 88). Careful monitoring of cell temperature can therefore economize on energy consumption.

The comparative data in Table 5.4 indicate that according to established standards of aluminium smelting, there is reasonable room for improving cell performance at EGYPTALUM smelters, and hence for absorbing the increase in energy prices proposed under ERSAP. But this entails substantial investment in physical and human capital. EGYPTALUM is planning to replace Soderberg with pre-baked cells in an effort to cut down on energy requirements of liquid aluminium. This is the potline rehabilitation project, which was to start in January 1996 and to be fully implemented over a three-year period. The estimated total investment cost is LE 456 million. It is also planned to increase annual design capacity by 33 per cent (from 180 to 240 thousand tonnes) by constructing a new potline comprising two cell rooms, each having 36 pre-baked side-by-side cells. The new side-by-side arrangement is

Table 5.4 Standard and EGYPTALUM performance data

		Standard	EGYPTALUM 1993/94
1.	Production per day (kg Al)	1000	1098
2.	Specific energy cons. (kW/h/kg Al)	13–15	16.8
3.	Cathode current efficiency (range)	88–92%	87.8%
4.	Alumina consumption (kg/kg Al)	1.9	1.95
5.	Anode carbon consumption (kg/kg Al)	0.450	0.508
6.	Fluorides consumption (kg/100kg Al)	3	4.5
7.	Purity of aluminium	99.85%	99.8*
8.	Cell life (days)	1000–2000	1800
9.	Current	150 kA	155 kA
10.	Type/technology	pre-baked anode	Soderberg

Notes:
kg Al = kilogramme aluminium
kA = kilo amperes
* Interview of EGYPTALUM officers.

Source: Grjotheim and Welch (1980), p. 6; EGYPTALUM, *Annual Report 1993/94*, p. 22; cell life from Aggag (1991), pp. 27–8.

more energy efficient, compared to the old end-to-end arrangement.[2] In addition, scrap aluminium collected from the local market may also bring about some energy savings.[3]

Furthermore, recent developments in the aluminium industry indicate some of the measures that could be helpful in reducing energy consumption in EGYPTALUM's smelters. These include: substitution of silicon rectifiers for mercury arc rectifiers; installation of heat recuperators; installation of high-pressure sodium lamps; improvement of bath chemistry in primary-reduction cells; improved control of the reduction process; and expanding aluminium scrap recycling.[4]

To conclude this part on the impact of raising energy prices on the aluminium industry in Egypt, we underscore the following in the light of the foregoing analysis:

a. The aluminium industry is an extremely energy-intensive industry; for example, its per unit energy requirements are 3–5 times those of steel and 3–4 times those of plastics.
b. The aluminium industry in Egypt was initially conceived as a means of taking advantage of abundant hydroelectricity from the High Dam which came on stream in 1967, *with virtually zero opportunity cost at that time.* Now, the situation has changed dramatically – electricity currently pro-

duced in Egypt is almost 80 per cent thermal, generated by power plants which burn natural gas and/or fuel oil basically. This primary energy is depletable and hence has a shadow price different from the world price (see Annex III).

c. It is often argued that producing aluminium involves burning natural gas and/or fuel oil. At the world price of primary energy, aluminium smelting has a negative economic rate of return. Hence, so the argument goes, the Egyptian economy would be better off exporting oil rather than burning it to keep the aluminium smelter at Nag'a Hamady in operation (USAID, 1979; World Bank, 1983). This argument warrants careful assessment.

The cost structure of hot aluminium production is shown in Table 5.5. Columns (1) and (2) present data which depict the development in the cost structure typical for the industry worldwide in 1977 and 1970. The data reveal a significant decline in the share of electricity and an increase in the share of anode carbons. The former is the result of a number of factors – most notably, a trend decline in energy requirements in aluminium smelting,[5] and an increase in current efficiency. The latter reflects technological change in the aluminium industry from Soderberg to pre-baked anode. For EGYPTALUM, the cost-coefficient vector (column (3)) indicates that the share of electricity in total cost is 26 per cent at present, which is much higher than the average for the entire aluminium-smelting industry worldwide.

It should be noted, however, that the cost share of electricity reported in Table 5.5 represents only the direct electricity intake to effect the reaction. To

Table 5.5 Cost vector for hot aluminium (per cent)

	World aluminium industry		EGYPTALUM
	1977	1970	1993/94
Cost item	(1)	(2)	(3)
Alumina	39.0	40.5	29.0
Anode carbon	20.4	14.4	20.4
Electricity	18.4	27.5	26.1
Wages	8.3	7.1	10.0
Maintenance	7.5	5.6	14.5 (Maintenance and Miscellaneous materials combined)
Miscellaneous materials	6.4	4.9	
Total	100.0	100.0	100.0

Source: Grjothein and Welch, op.cit., p. 81, and EGYPTALUM, unpublished data.

this, one should add also the energy required to prepare alumina from natural ores and, more importantly, energy used up in the production of anode carbon. Total energy requirements are at least the sum of these two.

Let us first calculate the *direct energy requirements* per tonne of hot aluminium (in units of tonne of fuel oil equivalent). From Table 5.4 above, specific energy consumption at Nag'a Hamady amounted to 16 800 kW/h/tonne in 1994. From the EEA data, fuel consumption per kW/h averaged 0.255 kg foe (fuel oil equivalent) during 1989/90–1992/93. *Direct energy requirements* per tonne of hot aluminium thus are 16.800 × 0.255 = 4.284 tonne foe.

Next, we estimate the *indirect energy requirements* per tonne of hot aluminium (in units of foe). According to the present technology used in aluminium smelting (the Hall–Heroulet technology, which is the one used at Nag'a Hamady), electrolysis uses carbon-anode blocks in the cells. At present, the requirements of carbon anode at Nag'a Hamady is estimated to be 0.660 tonne of pre-baked anode per tonne of hot aluminium, which requires burning 0.180 tonne of fuel oil (Hassan, 1992).

Total energy requirements = direct requirements + indirect requirements
= 4.284 + 0.180 = 4.464 tonne foe

The total energy cost in 1992 domestic prices = 4.464 × LE 130 = LE 580.32 per tonne. The total energy cost in 1992 world prices = 4.464 × LE 260 =

Table 5.6 Electricity consumption per tonne of aluminium

Year	Output (000 tonne)	Electricity consumption (000 kW/h)	Electricity cons. kW/h per tonne
88/89	180.9	3 061 080	16 921
89/90	197.2	3 062 240	17 088
90/91	177.7	3 069 730	17 275
91/92	177.8	3 099 709	17 434
92/93	178.5	3 086 924	17 244
93/94	180.2	3 112 280	17 271
94/95	181.1	3 114 654	17 199
95/96	179.8	3 109 578	16 794
96/97	178.5	3 133 624	17 555
97/98	181.2	3 314 324	18 291

Source: EGYPTALUM, *Annual Statistical Report 1997/98*.

LE 1160.64 per tonne. This implies an estimate of the total cost per tonne of hot aluminium of about LE 4300 in 1994,[6] which is slightly less than the average export price of LE 4385.

It is interesting to note that EGYPTALUM would achieve a significant reduction in energy consumption if it successfully managed to bring specific energy consumption down to the world average (that is, from 16.8 kWh/kg Al to 14 kWh/kg Al – see Table 5.4). But the hike in energy prices under ERSAP did not seem to exert the pressure EGYPTALUM needs to rationalize energy use. As Table 5.6 shows, there is no clear trend decline in electricity consumption per tonne of aluminium. We conclude that the price leverage did not achieve the desirable objective of making the aluminium industry more efficient.

Impact of Devaluation

The aluminium industry in Egypt produces both for exports and for the domestic market. As already indicated, an increasing proportion of its annual output is directed to the domestic market to satisfy the fast rising demand. Devaluation and unification of the exchange rate as elements of ERSAP has affected the aluminium industry in a number of ways. On the one hand, devaluation raised the pound cost of imported inputs – mainly alumina.[7] In addition, devaluation *per se* contributed to raising the domestic price of energy, according to the World Bank formulae for adjusting domestic prices of energy towards parity with international equivalents (see Annex IV). On the other hand, devaluation raised the value of the proceeds of aluminium exports in Egyptian pound. As to the sale price in the local market, we have already noted that as part of the price reform under ERSAP, the multiple-price system applying to the domestic market was replaced effective from July 1993 by single-price regime for aluminium. Moreover, instead of fixing that price administratively, it became linked to the London Metal Exchange base price. July 1993 therefore marks a fundamental change in the pricing regime, from a multiple-price system where various domestic prices were administratively set, to a situation where only one price (based on the world price) prevailed on the domestic market. We ignore the effect of devaluation on the asset/net worth position of EGYPTALUM (to the extent that the company maintains any foreign-currency positions – such as owning deposits or incurring debt).

Impact of devaluation on production cost

We shall ignore the impact of devaluation on the cost of imported equipment and machinery the company may decide to procure for investment purposes, and confine ourselves to study the effect of devaluation on the cost of production. As Table 5.5 indicates, alumina is the main imported input. Since

EGYPTALUM is a price taker on the market for alumina, the Egyptian pound cost of imported alumina increased in proportion to devaluation. It is useful to consider the order of magnitude of the cost increase in this case. The current output of aluminium at Nag'a Hamady is about 180 000 tonnes annually. Given the technical aspects of aluminium smelting by electrolysis, the technical coefficient of production is two tonnes of alumina per tonne of aluminium. Thus annual alumina intake in the Nag'a Hamady smelter is about 360 thousand tonnes of alumina. The Egyptian pound value of alumina intake rose in proportion to devaluation according to ERSAP for two reasons. First, because Egypt is a price taker on the world market for alumina, changes in the exchange rate translate *pro rata* into the domestic currency price of alumina. Second, the technology of aluminium smelting necessitates using a fixed coefficient of two (two tonnes of alumina to produce one tonne of aluminium).

The impact of devaluation on the domestic currency cost of other imported intermediates, notably coke/carbon anode, cryolite and fluorides is less significant, and therefore shall be ignored here. More important is the effect of devaluation on raising the energy cost. As we indicate in Annex IV, the commitment to adjust energy prices was made by the Egyptian government in the 1991 structural adjustment loan agreement known as SAL I. According to this, there is an obligation to change the weighted-average domestic prices of petroleum products and natural gas to reflect their internationally traded equivalents, and to adjust electricity prices to eventually cover LRMC. The difference between domestic petroleum product prices and internationally traded equivalents depends on two factors: the price differential and the exchange rate. Devaluation would in itself require raising domestic energy prices in order to maintain the real price of energy (in terms of internationally traded equivalents).

As shown in Annex IV, between May 1991 and December 1992, the weighted average domestic petroleum product prices and natural gas prices were raised to 83 per cent of world prices. This, at least partly, was a badly needed, even belated, correction of a protracted cost/prices distortion.[8] Average electricity prices more than doubled over an even shorter period. It is important to note, however, that under the World Bank formula for adjusting energy prices, devaluation would become an automatic driver for raising energy prices. In the case of energy-intensive industries, particularly aluminium, devaluation would play a double role as a cost-push mechanism: to raise the pound cost of imported inputs, and to trigger increases in energy prices automatically towards parity with world prices.

Perusal of the data in Table 5.3 reveals an interesting pattern of behaviour of nominal prices of electric energy supplied to the aluminium smelter at Nag'a Hamady. Such prices were almost frozen until 1980. Then there was a moderate annual increase averaging 19 per cent during 1980–84, which was hardly enough to compensate for inflation during that period. One may conclude therefore that the real price of electricity supplied to EGYPTALUM continued to decline through the mid-1980s. It was around the mid-1980s, particularly since May 1987, that the real price of electricity provided to the aluminium smelter started to rise. This corresponds to the period when Egypt attempted to take serious reform measures and when devaluation of the pound featured more significantly.

The impact of devaluation on revenue

Because production of the Nag'a Hamady smelter is mostly for exports (62.25 per cent over the period 1976–1993/94), devaluation has been beneficial to the company in the sense that – given the world price of aluminium – the pound value of its total revenue increased with devaluation. Consider Table 5.7, which provides data on the volume and value of exports over the period 1984/85–1997/98. Aside from the last two years, export volume over the period has fluctuated around 100 thousand tonnes. Export value (FOB) in dollars has declined since 1988/89, because of a decline in world aluminium prices as quoted on the London Metal Exchange. However, export proceeds in Egyptian pound experienced much less of a decline, thanks to the devaluation of the pound from LE 2.604/US$ in 1989/90 to LE 3.359/US$ in 1993/94. The devaluation helped provide a comfortable cushion against the sharp drop in the world price of aluminium after 1988/89 (see Table 5.7).

It would be misleading, however, to imply that devaluation has totally been a panacea for EGYPTALUM. On the one hand, nominal depreciation of the pound as part of ERSAP has helped the company. As already shown, it has actually compensated for the decline in the world price of aluminium – at least partially. It may also explain the rise in export volume during 1988/89–1992/93. But on the other hand, real appreciation of the pound soon started to bite. EGYPTALUM found it necessarily more attractive to sell domestically – especially after domestic price liberalization in 1993. The volume of domestic sales has actually been rising, and correspondingly the volume of export sales falling, since 1993/94. In fact, 1997/98 was a watershed – the volume of domestic sales surpassed exports for the first time ever in the history of EGYPTALUM.

Impact of Liberalizing Output Prices

As already mentioned, EGYPTALUM was until 1992/93 selling its output in two largely segregated markets: the domestic and the world market. In the domestic market a regime of administered, centrally controlled prices prevailed. It was a two-tier system[9] with one price for sales to public and

Table 5.7 Export revenue of EGYPTALUM 1984/85–1997/98

Year	Export 000 tonne	Export value, FOB LE m	Export value, FOB US$ m	Export price, FOB LE	Export price, FOB US$	Implicit exchange rate (LE/$)	Export value index LE	Export value index US$
84/85	115.2	136.4	139.9	1184	2214	0.975		
85/86	116.9	208.6	156.2	2039	1336	1.526		
86/87	102.3	208.6	136.6	2039	1335	1.527		
87/88	96.0	445.4	199.9	4640	2082	2.230		
88/89	108.5	652.8	275.9	6017	2543	2.366	100.0	100.0
89/90	104.6	492.1	189.0	4705	1807	2.604	75.4	68.5
90/91	95.7	496.2	171.4	5185	1791	2.895	76.0	62.1
91/92	123.3	553.8	166.8	4491	1353	3.319	84.8	60.5
92/93	106.6*	474.9	142.6	4455	1338	3.330	72.7	51.7
93/94	89.9*	433.9	129.2	4387	1306	3.359	66.5	46.8
94/95	97.8	620.2	183.0	6344	1871	3.290	95.0	66.3
95/96	99.4	627.5	185.1	6311	1862	3.390	96.1	67.1
96/97	87.2	489.4	144.3	5611	1655	3.390	75.0	52.3
97/98	84.3	499.5	147.4	5928	1749	3.390	76.5	53.4

Note: * Includes quantities exported for Deutsche Mark (DM), whose DM value was recorded separately in the source. To present a full picture, their dollar equivalents were calculated using the exchange rates of DM 1.602/US$1.0 for 1992/93 and DM 1.635/US$1.0 for 1993/94.

Source: EGYPTALUM, *Annual Statistical Report*, various years.

private sector firms, and another for sales to firms established under the foreign investment code. There were also originally two prices for exports: one for cash sales and the other for barter exchange with alumina. Table 5.8 presents the development of these various prices over the period 1986/87–1997/98.

On the basis of the examination of the evidence, we hypothesize that the price of aluminium sold on the domestic market to firms established under the foreign investment code was highly correlated with the cash export price. The price of aluminium sold to firms in the public and private sectors, on the other hand, appears to have been only loosely connected to the cash export price. This is corroborated by comparing the values of the correlation coefficients in the two sectors. The value of the correlation coefficient between cash export price and sale price to public and private business was 66 per cent. This compares unfavourably with a value of the correlation coefficient between cash export price and sale price to firms established under the foreign investment code close to 96 per cent.

Table 5.8 Sale prices of aluminium, 1986/87–1997/98 (LE/tonne)

Year	Domestic sales			Export sales		
	Public and private	Investment companies	Average	Cash	Barter	Average
1986/87	1266.6	1757.4	1373.6	2102.6	1850.5	2039.2
1987/88	1511.6	3507.6	1875.5	4725.3	4303.5	4641.2
1988/89	1714.7	4223.7	2232.9	6102.4	5817.8	6017.7
1989/90	2106.7	4374.4	2424.3	4823.7	4315.6	4704.6
1990/91	2755.7	3426.4	3004.4	5234.9	4894.5	5183.0
1991/92	3334.4	4411.3	3375.4	4490.4	–	4490.4
1992/93	4314.9	4649.0	4374.9	4454.4	–	4454.5
1993/94	4501.0	4465.6	4485.9	4385.4	–	4385.4
1994/95	6185.0	6292.0	6213.0	6344.0	–	6344.0
1995/96	6702.0	6787.0	6722.0	6311.0	–	6311.0
1996/97	6017.0	3056.0	6027.0	5614.0	–	5614.0
1997/98	6353.0	6439.0	6148.0	5928.0	–	5928.0

Source: EGYPTALUM, *Annual Statistical Report*, various years.

The liberalization of aluminium output prices as part of the structural adjustment component of ERSAP started in the early 1990s. Barter exchange of aluminium in exchange for alumina was discontinued starting in 1991/92. Furthermore, in 1992/93 the system of administered prices applying to domestic sales was dismantled. An important distortion in the form of market segmentation was thus removed, thereby creating the potential for more efficient allocation of resources.[10]

Until 1992/93, when the regime of administered domestic prices of aluminium prevailed, domestic prices were significantly below export prices; the law of one price did not apply. The situation changed dramatically when the regime of administered domestic prices was abandoned in favour of a world price base effective July 1993, as already mentioned before. In fact, the average domestic price of aluminium has exceeded the export price since 1993/94.

There is a real danger that EGYPTALUM might be tempted under the new pricing regime to sell on the domestic market, thus avoiding tough competition on the world market. But it may be argued that such a possibility is remote, however, for two reasons. First, the size of the domestic market sets an upper limit to what can be marketed there. Second, trade liberalization both as part of the ERSAP package and according to Egypt's commitments under GATT ensures that the domestic market cannot be a captive market. However, our analysis shows that the danger is more real than apparent in view of the real appreciation of the Egyptian pound.

Impact of Liberalization of Interest Rate

The Aluminium Company of Egypt enjoys an almost unique position compared to most industrial public-sector companies with respect to its capitalization. EGYPTALUM does not seem to have a debt-overhang problem such as in the case of a large number of public companies in the industrial sector. On the other hand, the company has large deposits in the banking system, and hence has benefited from the initial rise in the interest rate which followed liberalization in this area. One may conclude that, in net terms, ERSAP was beneficial to EGYPTALUM on this score.

Impact of Trade Liberalization

As indicated in Chapter 2 of this study, trade liberalization involved two elements: first, elimination of direct trade controls or non-tariff barriers (NTBs) such as permits, quotas, and so on; and second, reduction of the mean tariff rate and tariff dispersion (that is, reducing the difference between maximum and minimum tariff rates). In effect, trade liberalization under ERSAP would mean opening up the domestic market, and hence exposing local producers to strong competition from imports. We have already noted that the aluminium industry in Egypt is basically an export industry. Trade liberalization by itself did not impact directly on the industry.

CONCLUDING REMARKS

The tale of the aluminium industry under economic reform according to ERSAP offers an interesting policy lesson: for an export-oriented firm domestic price liberalization should be supported by the right exchange rate policy. As we have seen in Chapter 3, adopting a nominal anchor and pegging to the dollar resulted in significant real appreciation of the pound, thereby sending the wrong signal to producers of tradables. It becomes more lucrative to sell on the domestic market. We have seen a clear shift in that direction for EGYPTALUM. Improving the performance at the micro level calls for reforms at the macro level.

To conclude our discussion of the effect of ERSAP on the aluminium industry, we note that the most significant effect is to signal that the era of cheap electricity is over. As already mentioned, EGYPTALUM uses up slightly more than 3300 million kW/h; each percentage point increase in the price of electricity supplied to the company (currently LE 0.068) would result in an LE 2 million increase in cost.

Against this background, and in the light of the preceding analysis, we address the crucial question: Should the aluminium industry be *shut down*?

This is a very complicated question to answer; there are many factors involved, economic and non-economic, and some are extremely difficult to assess. We shall focus here first on the economic considerations. According to our calculations, the total primary energy requirements per 1 tonne of Al is about 4.248 tonne of foe. At the world price of $82/tonne (or LE 275/tonne) for fuel oil,[11] the total energy cost of 1 tonne of Al is LE 1178. In the absence of detailed information on other cost items such as alumina, fluorides and anode carbon, we use a simplifying assumption based on the aggregate cost breakdown in Table 5.5. Assuming therefore that electricity accounts for 26 per cent of total production cost, we obtain a cost of about LE 4530 per tonne of Al. This is much lower than export prices recorded during 1995–98, as shown in Table 5.7. But of course the total cost will remain highly sensitive to changes in the world price of energy.

The conclusion therefore is that the aluminium industry has to adjust, particularly to a world of scarce energy resources. Such an adjustment may be achieved through a two-pronged strategy: on the one hand, it would involve cuts in cost, particularly energy costs, and on the other hand it would involve increasing value added (by deepening industrialization *via* product diversification).

Measures to Cut Costs

Perusal of performance data in Table 5.4 clearly indicate that there is significant room for improvement. Foremost is the area of the specific energy consumption, where the rate at EGYPTALUM's works at Nag'a Hamady approaches 16.8 kW/h/kg Al. This is even higher than the upper limit of the standard range of 13–15 kW/h/kg Al. Because of the fact that social benefit (to the economy at large) resulting from reducing specific energy consumption exceeds private benefit (to EGYPTALUM), there are good economic grounds for EEA to provide some incentive to EGYPTALUM on account of energy savings. EGYPTALUM may be granted a discount proportional to the reduction of specific electricity consumption beyond a certain limit. This is not the place to work out the details; it is enough to indicate the merits of such a policy.

Cathode current efficiency and fluorides' consumption are additional areas where some significant savings could be achieved.

Finally, labour training is a basic element in cutting the cost in the areas indicated above and others; it is a critical factor in enhancing X-efficiency.

EGYPTALUM already has an active and promising labour training programme; but it may actually be beneficial to develop it further.

Increasing Value Added

Value added may be increased basically through increasing the proportion of fabricated/semis to total production, and moving further downstream. This is because primary aluminium fetches the basic price determined on the London Metal Exchange, while fabricated products sell at a premium above the basic price. In fact, EGYPTALUM has almost reached the limit of increasing the proportion of fabricated/semis. The ratio of fabricated semis is currently 84 per cent of actual production (see Table 5.9). Further along the road to deepen industrialization, a project for producing aluminium rolls has just been completed, with a design annual capacity of 60 thousand tonnes.

Table 5.9 Development of product mix, 1983/84–1997/98 (%)

Bars (Primary)	1983/84	1997/98
Bars	39	16
T. bars	24	11
Ingots	11	5
Wire	7	18
Drums	16	26
Rolls	–	15
Alloy bars	3	8
Slabs	–	1
Total	100	100

Source: EGYPTALUM, *Annual Statisical Report 1997/98.*

NOTES

1. Ministerial Decree No. 61 for 1993 by the Minister of Industry dated 15 July, 1993, abolished administered domestic aluminium prices. A 3-month average of the basic price of the London Metal exchange (LME) is calculated, to which is added premia, packing and baling, shipping and transport cost, to derive the selling price of aluminium on the domestic market.
2. For more details, see EGYPTALUM, 'Study of the Economics of the Aluminium Company of Egypt in the Context of Implementing the Basic Project from 1993/94 until 2012/2013', mimeo., in Arabic, no date.
3. For interesting details in this respect, see Mahmoud M. Farag, 'Energy Conservation in the Aluminium Industry', in Farag, Mahmoud M. ed. (1980), *Aluminium Industry in*

Egypt: Proceedings of the symposium held at the American University in Cairo 18–19 February 1980, Cairo: AUC Press.

4. After almost twenty years of aluminium production and consumption, a feasibility study of the recycling of aluminium scrap is highly relevant.
5. Electricity requirements per unit output has dropped by almost 50 per cent since the turn of the century: from 28 kW/h/kg Al in 1900 to 13.5 kW/h/kg Al in 1979 (Grjotheim and Welch, 1980).
6. Since direct electricity input accounts for 26 per cent of total cost, total electricity input should account for 27 per cent (=(4.464/4.284) x 0.26). Dividing total energy cost by 0.27 gives the estimate of total cost per tonne reported in the text.
7. The aluminium industry uses other inputs such as coke, cryolite, aluminium fluoride and calcium fluoride. But alumina is by far the most important input; the others will be ignored in our analysis.
8. It was shown that because of the regime of administered prices which used to prevail in Egypt, the relative price of petroleum products declined such that by 1981 the real average energy price was only 76 per cent of its 1960 value. The deterioration in the real price of energy occurred basically after 1974 (Abdel-Khalek, 1988).
9. Actually there was a third price for own use at EGYPTALUM, but it will be ignored here because it is not very significant.
10. See results of the Survey of Industrial Pricing Practices sponsored by the Ministry of Economy and Foreign Trade, October 1994, mimeo.
11. This is the average of world price per tonne of low grade fuel oil (3.5 per cent sulphur) over the period 1995–98.

APPENDIX 5.1

Table 5A.1 Various phases of EGYPTALUM design capacity expansion

Date	Phases	Capacity 000 tonne
October 1975	I	33
May 1976	II	66
April 1977	III	100
July 1980	IV	133
July 1983	V	166

Source: EGYPTALUM, *Annual Statisical Report 1997/98.*

6. The microeconomic effects of ERSAP: 2. The iron and steel industry

INTRODUCTION

The iron and steel industry is an important element in the economic structure of nations – being an industry with strong forward linkage effects. In Egypt, the most important company in the iron and steel industry is the Egyptian Iron and Steel Company (known as HADISOLB). The company is an integrated enterprise: mining pig iron in the Bahariya oases, transporting the ore and producing steel. It is one of the largest companies in the industrial sector of the country, with close to 23 000 workers strong.

HADISOLB is essentially an import-substituting enterprise with a current design capcity to produce 1.2 million tonnes of steel annually. It was established in 1954 in the context of Egypt's drive to modernize and diversify its industrial structure. The industry is both capital-intensive and energy-intensive, catering basically for the domestic market. The financial position of HADISOLB is precarious; its paid-up capital less than doubled since 1982, while its long-term debt both in local and foreign currency has increased twelve-fold. Paid-up capital increased from LE 338 million in 1981/82 to LE 631 million in 1993/94. During the same period, long-term debt (both in local and foreign currencies) skyrocketed from the equivalent of LE 58.4 million to the equivalent of LE 696.4 million.

ERSAP seems to have impacted more strongly on the iron and steel industry than on the aluminium industry. Parallel to the case of the aluminium industry, raising energy prices and liberalizing input prices affected the performance of HADISOLB negatively. But unlike the case of the aluminium industry, both interest-rate liberalization and trade liberalization have impacted negatively on the iron and steel industry. In addition, ERSAP has a deflationary component, which will definitely tend to reduce demand for steel on the domestic market. This is particularly so because of the cut-down in the rate of public investment under ERSAP. On the other hand, liberalizing output prices and devaluation are more likely to benefit HADISOLB.

It may be useful, before examining the impact of ERSAP on HADISOLB, to give an account of the main techno-economic and financial aspects of the company.

THE IRON AND STEEL COMPANY OF EGYPT: MAIN INDICATORS

HADISOLB started production in 1958. It is a vertically-integrated public sector enterprise involved in mining and transporting the ores, and producing pig iron and steel. Production, which is significantly below capacity, is mainly for the domestic market (as an import substitute) where 85 per cent of output is sold.

The original design capacity of the mills was 0.3 million tonnes at the start of production in 1958.[1] Design production capacity was later increased to 0.6 million tonnes in 1973, which was then doubled in 1979. There are various stages of production:

- Mining of iron ore from Guidida mines in the Bahariya oases, Guiza; limestone from Beni Khaled quarries in Minya; and dolomite from Adabiya quarries in Suez.
- Sintering.
- Production of pig iron in blast furnances.
- Steel production.
- Rolling of steel.

Annual production capacity is 2.6 million tonnes of ore, 2 million tonnes of sinter, 1.5 million tonnes of pig iron and 1.27 million tonnes of steel.[2] The Helwan iron and steel works use Russian technology involving the following technical coefficients:

1.5 tonnes of sinter	1.0 tonnes of pig iron
+ 0.6 tonnes of coke	+ 0.4 tonnes of silt
= 1.0 tonnes of pig iron;	= 0.92 tonnes of steel

The iron and steel industry is an energy-intensive activity; it uses coke, natural gas and electricity. Electricity is not essentially used as energy, but as motive power to run motors operating various production facilities. The Helwan iron and steel works are supplied with medium-voltage electric power (6.3 kV) by the Cairo Electricity Distribution Company through four power transformers using high voltage (66 kV) from the national electricity grid (Assaf, 1993).

Coke is fed into blast furnaces along with sinter. It performs the dual function of fuel to provide heat energy and of chemical element needed for the process of reduction to produce pig iron. Natural gas is used (since 1973) as an overall energy input, and is also fed into blast furnaces. Direct requirements of *energy inputs per tonne of steel* are as follows (Abou Zeid, 1990, pp. 26–7):

Coke	0.54 tonne
Natural gas	465 m^3
Electricity	880 kW/h.

Iron ore is now produced by HADISOLB from its own mines in the Bahariya oases in the Western desert since 1973. Previously, ore was obtained from the company's Aswan mines, which are now closed. The Aswan ore had high silica content with metal concentration as low as 40 per cent.

In addition to ore and energy, the industry relies on the following inputs: ferro-manganese, graphite rods, limestone and dolomite. Limestone is locally procured from HADISOLB's own quarries in Beni Khaled (Minya governorate), and dolomite is mined in Adabiya (Suez governorate). Ferro-manganese and graphite rods used to be imported, but are now supplied by local producers in Egypt.

HADISOLB produces mainly for the local market. During 1988/89–1993/94, average annual total sales were 0.897 million tonnes of final products. Exports accounted only for 10–15 per cent of sales and the rest was channelled to the local market (Abou Zeid, 1990, pp. 26–7). HADISOLB is actually a prototype of an import-substituting enterprise operating, until very recently, in a non-competitive environment. Exports only started as late as 1979, and are not really seriously targeted, let alone planned. An interesting and revealing supporting evidence of this statement is the deviation between export targets and actual exports for 1992/93. According to the company's balance sheets and financial statement for that year, the sales targets were 0.722 million tonnes in the domestic market and 0.06 million tonnes for export. As it turned out, however, exports shot up to 0.178 million tonnes, almost triple the planned target. It is also interesting to note that the planned export figure seemed out of line with most recent developments, which showed an average annual rate of growth of almost 24 per cent during 1988/89–1991/92 (calculated from Table 6.1).

Financially, HADISOLB is struggling to turn losses which it has been incurring in recent years into profits. Its bank overdraft has increased according to a geometric series – almost doubling every year. Between 1988/89 and 1991/92, the index of bank overdraft recorded 100, 214, 390 and 726 respectively. In 1993/94 bank overdraft amounted to LE 1036.8 million, nearly double paid-up capital which was only LE 632 million. That this is a phenomenal increase may be ascertained by observing that the level of overdraft was fairly stable at some LE 15–20 million during 1975–1979/80, more than doubling to LE 51 million average annual for the first half of the 1980s, then more than quadrupling to LE 239 million during 1986/87–1991/92. We should remember that the last year of the latter sub-period coincides with ERSAP measures.

Table 6.1 Output, domestic sales and exports (Q = 1000 tonnes, V = LE million), 1984/85–1997/98

		Sales					
	Output of finished	Domestic		Exports		Total*	
Year	products	Q	V	Q	V	Q	V
1984/85	n.a.	620.4	206.1	47.7	7.9	668.1	214.0
1985/86	730.6	675.8	249.0	17.0	6.4	692.8	255.4
1986/87	688.4	613.7	232.0	37.4	15.9	651.1	247.9
1987/88	875.0	788.3	346.0	59.6	39.7	847.9	385.7
1988/89	879.5	828.6	498.1	38.7	34.5	867.3	532.6
1989/90	858.2	800.5	553.9	51.5	47.2	852.1	601.1
1990/91	976.8	835.0	644.0	65.8	65.5	900.7	709.5
1991/92	894.2	724.1	669.0	72.2	70.8	796.3	739.8
1992/93	924.3	800.8	710.7	177.7	155.7	978.5	866.4
1993/94	1067.4	868.9	835.9	120.2	107.6	989.1	943.5
1994/95	1004.9	861.3	943.9	162.9	157.9	1024.2	1101.9
1995/96	893.0	789.7	981.3	65.6	73.0	855.3	1054.3
1996/97	1059.5	808.8	954.6	134.0	123.7	942.8	1078.3
1997/98	1114.9	932.7	1076.9	136.8	128.3	1069.5	1205.3

Note: * Total sales value of finished output, including discounts which could not be allocated to domestic sales and exports.

Source: For 1985/86–1987/88, Abou Zeid, (1990). For 1988/89–1997/98, HADISOLB, *Annual Report*, various years.

HADISOLB has always been operating below its design capacity. Over the period 1988/89–1993/94, output of steel averaged 933.4 thousand tonnes, making up 77.8 per cent of design capacity. Idle capacity thus averaged about 22 per cent during the late 1980s–early 1990s. Table 6.1 shows that there has been a trend increase in the rate of capacity utilization over the period 1985/86–1993/94; the ratio of actual output to capacity output rose from a 67 per cent average for the pre-ERSAP period 1985/86–1989/90 to 80 per cent average for the post-ERSAP period 1990/91–1997/98. At the same time there has been a fall in the ratio of total sales to output, from about 97 per cent average during 1985/86–1989/90 to about 91 per cent during 1990/91–1997/98.[3] Thus, although HADISOLB managed to raise the rate of capacity utilization significantly over the period, it was not successful in raising, or even maintaining, the ratio of total sales to output. As a result, stock of finished products accumulated, rising in value terms from LE 44.4 million in 1989/90 to EL 175.9 million in 1993/94. The volume (quantity) of unsold finished products rose from 37.5 thousand tonnes in 1987/88 to 165 thousand tonnes in 1991/92 and further to 207 thousand tonnes in 1997/98.

According to HADISOLB management, various reasons were given for this undesired stock accumulation, namely: increased cost of production mainly because of the increased energy cost, and mounting competition of foreign steel in the domestic market due to the world economic recession. To these factors one may add the increase in capacity utilization noted above. These factors will be taken up in more detail when considering the impact of ERSAP on HADISOLB.

One of the significant features of HADISOLB is factor intensity, since the iron and steel industry is known to be both capital- and energy-intensive. HADISOLB employs some 23 000 workers in various stages of production. Table 6.2 traces the development of factor use, focusing on labour, capital and factor intensity (measured by the capital/labour ratio). Employment in

Table 6.2 Labour, capital and factor intensity in HADISOLB

Year	Fixed assets* LE million	Employment**			Capital labour ratio (LE 1000)
		Production	Other	Total	
1984/85	376.3	6 927	16 454	23 381	16.1
1985/86	392.7	6 788	16 563	23 351	16.8
1986/87	436.8	6 676	17 382	24 058	18.2
1987/88	647.3	7 076	17 276	24 352	26.6
1988/89	703.7	7 164	17 116	24 280	29.0
1989/90	993.6	7 866	17 193	25 059	39.7
1990/91	1 074.2	7 674	16 647	24 321**	44.2
1991/92	1 323.9	7 464	16 436	23 900**	55.4
1992/93	1 440.2	7 249	16 160	23 409**	61.5
1993/94	1 555.4	7 059	15 723	22 782**	64.5
1994/95	1 649.5	6 859	15 512	22 371	73.7
1995/96	1 713.2	6 613	15 251	21 864	78.4
1996/97	2 123.3	6 502	14 807	21 309	101.4
1997/98	3 472.9	6 529	14 407	20 936	165.9

Notes:
* Include value of fixed assets excluding accounts receivable.
** Employment in current production only (excluding employment in projects).

Source: HADISOLB, *Annual Report*, various years.

HADISOLB peaked in the early 1980s, exceeding the 25 thousand mark in 1979/80. But there has been almost steady decline since 1981/82. The company's employment data distinguish at least four categories of workers:[4] workers in production, workers in so-called productive services, sales workers and workers in administrative and financial services. We shall call the first category production employment and all the rest service employment, for short. The distinction between these two main categories of workers is significant, and it is curious to note the imbalance between production and service workers; the latter represent more than two-thirds of total employment. The total number of workers peaked in 1989/90, then steadily declined throughout the 1990s. The data in Table 6.2 may characterize a situation of underemployment or disguised unemployment, a legacy of the company's employment policy during the 1960s and 1970s.

On the other hand, capital (fixed assets) rose from about LE 376 million in 1984/85 to almost LE 3473 million in 1997/98. Such a large increase in fixed assets took place against the backdrop of stagnant productive capacity during this period. One reason for this development is that HADISOLB has undergone capital deepening through a rehabilitation project implemented with financing from the World Bank, the Soviet Union/Russia and Germany (Abdel-Rahman, 1992). As a result, capital intensity rose tenfold over the period: from about LE 16 thousand in 1984/85 to almost LE 166 thousand in 1997/98. This definitely represents significant capital deepening over the period. If fixed assets were related to production employment only, the capital/labour ratio rises even more dramatically. It should be expected to result in faster labour productivity growth in the industry.

The prospects of HADISOLB suffer from some basic factors. First, and foremost among them, is the company's capitalization. For the period 1984/85–1992/93, its paid-up capital was almost frozen at about LE 540 million. Subsequent increases were too modest compared to borrowed funds. The leverage ratio (the ratio of long-term loans to equity) exceeded unity in 1989/90 (Table 6.3). At the same time, the overdraft increased five times during the 1990s. In fact it exceeded paid-up capital in 1991/92. This rendered the capital structure of the company extremely weak. Table 6.3 has more details. Under such circumstances, the company has become more exposed to the heavy burden of higher interest rates following interest rate liberalization (as part of ERSAP measures) as will be detailed below. Second, according to the company management, part of the design capacity of HADISOLB of 1.2 million tonnes is technically unattainable. Actual annual production of finished products averaged 0.933 million tonnes during 1988/89–1993/94 and 1.028 million tonnes during 1993/94–1997/98. Unused capacity thus averaged about 20 per cent of design capacity over the past decade. In an industry where fixed costs are extremely significant, the existence of technically unat-

Table 6.3 Equity, debt and leverage, 1984/85–1997/98 (LE million)

Year	Equity (1)	Long-term domestic loans (2)	Long-term foreign loans (3)	Total long-term loans (4)	Overdraft (5)	Fixed assets* (6)
1984/85	500	36.5	19.0	55.5	79.5	376.3
1985/86	537	41.6	77.6	119.2	67.3	392.7
1986/87	540	49.9	135.8	185.7	119.8	436.8
1987/88	540	68.1	226.9	295.0	129.1	647.3
1988/89	540	175.4	277.6	453.0	82.7	703.7
1989/90	540	192.3	356.4	548.7	177.2	991.6
1990/91	540	290.1	398.7	688.8	322.1	1074.2
1991/92	540	320.7	409.3	730.0	600.6	1323.9
1992/93	540	335.7	315.9	651.6	712.4	1440.2
1993/94	632	399.6	296.8	696.4	949.7	1555.4
1994/95	632	410.4	360.7	771.1	1094.7	1649.5
1995/96	665	414.8	333.4	738.2	1292.0	1713.2
1996/97	665	428.3	274.5	732.8	1404.6	2123.3
1997/98	665	508.3	334.2	842.5	1588.3	3472.9

Note: * Consists of the sum of total fixed assets in the company's balance sheets, excluding accounts receivable, since these have no techno-economic relation to production.

Source: HADISOLB, *Annual Report*, various years.

tainable capacity puts the company at a competitive disadvantage from the outset.

ENERGY USE IN THE STEEL INDUSTRY

The steel industry is one of the most energy-intensive industries in the economy. It uses natural gas, electricity and coke. We shall focus on electricity and related issues, since pricing and other terms of supply of electricity have always been a matter of contention between HADISOLB and Egypt Electricity Authority (EEA). As already mentioned, HADISOLB is supplied with electricity from the national grid by the Cairo Electricity Distribution Company (CEDC). The HADISOLB works in Helwan are supplied with medium voltage electric power (6.3 kV) *via* four main transformer stations owned by EEA and operated by CEDC. Those transformers receive electricity from the national grid – high voltage (66 kV). There is no contractual relation between CEDC and HADISOLB; changes in electricity rates are decided by the Ministry of Electricity and Energy subject to the approval of the Cabinet.

Table 6.4 indicates the development of total electricity consumption by HADISOLB since 1987/88. Electricity consumption by the steel works in Helwan currently stands close to 25 per cent of the total industrial consumption of high voltage electricity.[5]

Table 6.4 Ouput, electricity consumption and cost, 1987/88–1997/98

	Output (10^3 tonne)	Electricity consumption: Total (10^6 kW/h)	Electricity consumption: kW/h/tonne	Electricity price LE/kW/h	Electricity cost LE/tonne
1987/88	875.0	716.6	819	0.0302	24.7
1988/89	879.5	710.9	808	0.0302	24.4
1989/90	858.2	705.5	822	0.0518	42.6
1990/91	976.8	778.2	797	0.0518	41.3
1991/92	894.2	779.9	872	0.1100	95.9
1992/93	924.3	760.4	823	0.1535	126.3
1993/94	1067.4	613.9	575	0.1535	88.3
1994/95	1004.9	586.8	583	0.1535	88.9
1995/96	893.0	548.1	613	0.1535	94.1
1996/97	1059.5	816.9	771	0.1134	87.4
1997/98	1114.9	850.1	762	0.1134	86.4

Source: HADISOLB, *Annual Report,* various years; and HADISOLB, unpublished data.

IMPACT OF ERSAP

We shall study the effect of ERSAP on HADISOLB by looking into a number of factors, namely:

1. raising energy prices
2. liberalizing input prices
3. liberalizing interest rates
4. trade liberalization
5. deflation of demand
6. liberalizing output prices, and
7. devaluation.

HADISOLB officials were interviewed (using a questionnaire) regarding the effect of ERSAP on their enterprise. They expressed particular concern about the negative effects of trade liberalization, raising energy prices, interest-rate and price liberalization, and devaluation. They also strongly voiced their concern about the effect of the sales tax and the macro elements of ERSAP – notably demand deflation measures. Before undertaking in-depth analysis of the effects of ERSAP on HADISOLB, it is pertinent to summarize the results of the questionnaire representing the views of the company's management (without necessarily endorsing them either in full or in part).

a. HADISOLB officials gave a number of reasons to account for the underutilization of capacity. Aside from the technical reasons referred to previously, they cited mounting stocks of unsold finished products. Since HADISOLB adjusts production to sales, it could not expand output in the face of accumulating stocks of finished products. Various reasons were given for the accumulation of stocks; most notably *import liberalization and economic slowdown*. They maintain that steel originating in Russia and other CIS countries and entering *via* Libya was dumped on the Egyptian market,[6] thanks to import liberalization. Actually, this is a case of trade deflection. In addition, the demand-management component of ERSAP resulted in a slowdown of economic activity associated with a lower rate of expenditure, particularly investment expenditure; hence lower demand for steel products.

   Blame should not be placed *fully* on ERSAP for the accumulation of stocks of finished products and hence the prevalence of significant idle capacity at HADISOLB works. Mention must be made of low X-efficiency due to outdated equipment used in smelting, casting and rolling (Abdel-Rahman, 1992, p. 17). Also, the fact that part of the design capacity of 1.2 million tonnes annually is technically unattainable puts the company at a cost disadvantage. But HADISOLB officials continue to underscore the need for protection against unfair foreign competition.
b. HADISOLB has been adjusting to a situation of *rising energy costs*. Several steps were taken – namely using gas emitted from high blast furnaces to heat air blown into the blast furnaces and to generate steam to drive blowing turbines instead of electricity, and using gases emitted by oxygen converters to generate steam for industrial uses. Despite all this, in the view of HADISOLB officials, the company was troubled by the erratic increases in energy prices at the onset of ERSAP (Table 6.4). They estimate that at the design capacity output (of 1.2 million tonnes), every 0.9 per cent increase in electricity prices (that is by LE 0.001 above the current price of LE 0.1134) will result in an LE 1 million increase in cost, equivalent to 0.07 per cent. Similarly, a 0.2 per cent increase in the price of coke (equivalent to LE 1 above the current price

of LE 450 per tonne) will also increase total cost by about LE 1 million at capacity output. This implicitly assumes zero response to rising input prices, which may not be realistic in a competitive business environment. In addition, these estimates ignore the fact that the price of electricity supplied to HADISOLB was rolled back to about its level in 1991/92. Output prices, on the other hand, cannot be adjusted upward because of world recession and the domestic deflationary policy adopted under ERSAP.

c. The *devaluation of the Egyptian pound* as part of the ERSAP package has resulted in an increase in the pound equivalent of loans committed in foreign currency (foreign loans for short). This applies in particular to the 1980 World Bank loan for the rehabilitation of the company. But this is only a partial assessment; it ignores the effect of the devaluation on the operating surplus of HADISOLB. Devaluation should on the other hand lead to higher pound prices for competing imported finished products, and thus boost the company's competitive position.
d. *Sales tax imposed on inputs* has led to increasing the cost of production. At the same time, sales tax on finished products resulted in higher prices facing buyers of steel. This is the familiar 'excise tax' effect which, *ceteris paribus*, may result in lower sales as may be inferred from the standard S-D model. HADISOLB officials argue that the sales tax should be removed in order to encourage greater utilization of capacity.

With this brief exposition of the views of HADISOLB's management regarding the various ERSAP measures, we proceed to a more detailed and balanced analysis of the impact of the programme on the company.

Energy Pricing Under ERSAP

The concern with energy aspects of the steel industry actually transcends ERSAP. Issues of energy efficiency in this industry are relevant, not only for the micro level (performance of the industry), but also for the macro performance (overall energy utilization for the national economy). At the micro level, any saving in electric energy per unit output will improve the performance of HADISOLB, considering the fact that this is an energy-intensive activity. At the macro level, Egypt is facing a strict energy-supply constraint, with stagnant oil reserves and somewhat uncertain reserves of natural gas. Some oil experts anticipate that Egypt would exhaust its national share of oil and natural gas reserves by the year 2006, if the present policies in the field of energy continued (Abdalla, 1995).

Table 6.5 gives comparative data on electricity requirements per tonne of steel in Egypt and a number of other countries. It shows clearly that electric-

Table 6.5 Electricity requirement per tonne of finished steel products

Country	Electricity requirements kWh/tonnes	Country	Electricity requirements kWh/tonnes
Brazil	563.6	Portugal	492.6
Canada	561.2	South Africa	783.3
Finland	544.3	Spain	641.5
France	537.7	Sweden	902.7
Germany	447.0	United Kingdom	446.7
Italy	745.0	United States	479.2
Japan	545.0	Egypt*	812.5

Note: * Figure includes preparation of ores. Without ore preparation, requirements become 659.1 kWh/tonne.

Source: Assaf (1993, p. 52).

ity requirements per tonne of finished steel products in Egypt is one of the highest in the world. According to the data of Table 6.5, such requirements are 44 per cent higher than that for Brazil, 65 per cent higher than that of Portugal and 27 per cent higher than that of Spain, to take the countries which are not well established in this industry and which may be more meaningfully compared with Egypt.

Based on the above information, it is clear that the integrated steel industry in Egypt, as represented by HADISOLB, should have reasonably good prospects for improving energy efficiency; the real question is how. Obviously, the price leverage is important, but it is not enough by itself. In fact, applying the price leverage only (meaning charging more for energy) may do more harm than good. Surprisingly, the price leverage has been relaxed in recent years – witness the reduction by 26 per cent in the price of electricity sold to HADISOLB effective 1996/97 (Table 6.4). Supplementary measures to increase X-efficiency are vital.

Some measures to increase X-efficiency

This section lists certain measures to reduce energy requirements per unit output. Of course, it goes without saying that raising output to the technically attainable capacity level by itself reduces average total cost. But aside from this, a number of measures are needed in order to reduce average energy input at HADISOLB:

i. HADISOLB may seriously entertain discontinuing the production of electric steel as it requires 2–3 times as much electricity per tonne as oxygen steel. The fact that electric steel output represents less than 10 per cent of total output of steel from the Helwan works makes this measure easier; the gain in electricity savings may outweigh the loss of steel output. If the company is looking for ways to adjust to a slack in demand because of ERSAP, this would be a reasonable measure to take.

ii. Raising the X-efficiency of oxygen converters. It is estimated that the efficiency of materials' use is about 80 per cent (Abou Zeid, 1990, p. 30). Since oxygen converters contribute most (that is, more than 90 per cent) of molten steel produced at the Helwan works, raising the efficiency of the use of materials in this stage should produce significant results.

iii. Improving the efficiency of the rolling mills, where efficiency of materials' use is some 5–10 per cent lower than in foreign steel works.

iv. Cutting down the time loss due to breakdowns, accidents, power failures, and so on. The proportion of lost time ranges between 20 per cent and 40 per cent for various units of HADISOLB (Abou Zeid, 1990). Indeed, this is a fairly high incidence of wasted working time by any standard. Even cutting it by 50 per cent would still leave a significant proportion of time lost, but it would definitely help increase X-efficiency considerably.

v. Raising the ratio of finished products to the output of molten steel. For example, in 1988/89 output of molten steel from oxygen converters was 844 396 tonnes and the quantity of finished products was 766 669 tonnes, representing less than 90 per cent. A 5 per cent increase in the quantity of finished products out of a given quantity of molten steel output would help reduce average cost.

Applying the energy price leverage

As already mentioned, three energy products are particularly critical for the operation of the steel industry, namely coke, electricity and natural gas.

Coke Coke is used in blast furnaces both as energy and as a chemical element to help in the reaction necessary for producing pig iron. HADISOLB obtains its coke requirements *via* a conveyer belt from another public-sector company next door. According to the technical parameters at HADISOLB mentioned above, coke requirements are 0.6 tonne per tonne of pig iron or 0.652 tonne per tonne of steel. According to the average annual production of steel during the five-year period 1989/90–1993/94 of 0.944 million tonnes, average annual consumption of coke is about 0.616 million tonnes. The price

Table 6.6 Energy input prices, 1973–97

	Coke price		Natural gas price	
Date	(LE/tonne)	Index	(PT/m^3)	Index
1966–73	16.00	100	n.a.	n.a.
10/2/74			0.671	100
1976	49.76	311		
1/1/80	50.26	314		
1/7/84	65.00	406		
1/1/85	130.00	813		
26/4/87			2.643	394
1/5/87	155.00	969		
5/9/88	235.00	1469		
24/3/89			3.304	429
22/10/89	290.00	1813		
6/5/90			4.670	696
3/5/91			7.500	1118
1/7/91	380.00	2375		
28/6/92			9.400	1401
18/12/92			12.250	1826
1/7/95	450.00	2813		
1/8/97			14.100	2086

Source: Coke price HADISOLB unpublished data. Natural gas price, Egyptian General Petroleum Corporation (EGPC), unpublished data.

of coke supplied to HADISOLB was fairly stable at some LE 15.0 per tonne for the decade of the mid 1960s to the mid 1970s, then trippled to some LE 50–60 per tonne through the mid 1980s. Since 1984 the price of coke has been adjusted upward almost every year until 1991, when it reached LE 380 per tonne (see Table 6.6). It remained at this level until July 1995, when it was increased to the current level of LE 450 per tonne. It is curious that the price of coke has risen much faster and more frequently before ERSAP compared to the period under the programme, and even more curious that the price rose by only 30 per cent at the beginning of ERSAP.

What has been the response of HADISOLB to the big hikes in the price of its main input, coke? Since coke accounts for 57 per cent of the cost of inputs for the production of pig iron (Abou Zeid, 1990), effective adjustment to the increased cost of coke should prove highly rewarding. Such an adjustment may take the form of either passing the increase through to the final users of steel, or increasing the efficiency of using coke (and hence reducing the coke requirements per unit), or a combination of both.

The evidence suggests that the response of HADISOLB was a mix of both; there was some effort to reduce coke requirements per tonne of steel, as well as raising the price of steel on the domestic market. As the price of coke rose by 132.1 per cent, input of coke per tonne of steel went down by 32.7 per cent over the period 1985/86–1988/89 (Abou Zeid, 1990). The domestic price of steel was raised by 60 per cent over the same period.

If we assume that the reduction of coke input per tonne was exclusively in response to the increase in the coke price, we may estimate that the arc elasticity of 'demand' for coke by HADISOLB was approximately –0.25. Given the coke input requirement per tonne of steel, the increase in coke price by 132 per cent noted above implies an increase in total production cost of steel by about 33 per cent.[7] Against this, we should consider the decrease in cost due to reducing coke input of tonne of steel by 18.6 per cent (= 0.327 × 0.57). We may thus conclude that about half the cost effect of the increase in coke price was neutralized by increasing technical efficiency in the use of the most important input – namely coke. Additionally, there was adjustment through raising the domestic sale price of steel from LE 381 per tonne in 1985/86 to LE 611 tonne in 1988/89 – a proportional increase by 60 per cent.

Thanks to trade liberalization measures under ERSAP, HADISOLB was increasingly feeling the pressure of price competition in the Egyptian market for steel products. This effectively puts a limit on the company's ability to pass the cost increase through to customers. The financial position of the company was further aggravated by an increase in the price of natural gas during ERSAP (see Table 6.6).

Electricity As mentioned before, electricity is used at HADISOLB primarily as motive power and secondarily as energy. The issue of reliable and adequate supplies of electricity to the steel complex at Helwan has been the subject of much discussion with EEA. At some point, HADISOLB was seriously considering building its own power generation plant on the premises (Assaf, 1993). Our attention here will be centred on the issue of pricing of electricity and the impact of ERSAP on electricity price and eventually on the prospects of HADISOLB.

EEA has a virtual monopoly of electricity generation in Egypt.[8] The tariff for electricity is set by Cabinet decision, based on submissions by the Ministry of Electricity and Energy which supervises EEA. The latter still influences that price since it actually prepares the submission of the Ministry of Electricity and Energy. As already mentioned, the Government of Egypt (GOE) is committed according to ERSAP to adjust the price of electricity to the level

Table 6.7 *Steel output, costs and prices of electricity, 1987/88–1997/98*

Year	Output 000 tonnes	Average materials cost LE/tonne	Electricity cost 10^6 LE	Av. elect. Price LE/kW/h	Share of elec. cost per tonne %
1987/88	875.0	387.1	18.8	0.0302	5.5
1988/89	879.5	488.1	21.5	0.0302	5.0
1989/90	858.8	618.4	33.3	0.0518	6.3
1990/91	976.8	715.2	56.7	0.0518	8.1
1991/92	894.2	903.7	85.8	0.1100	10.6
1992/93	924.3	990.4[a]	116.7	0.1535*	11.8
1993/94	1067.4	849.4[a]	134.8	0.1535*	14.5
1994/95	1004.9	942.7	90.1	0.1535	9.5
1995/96	893.0	1053.3	84.1	0.1535	8.9
1996/97	1059.5	1053.1	92.6	0.1134	8.3
1997/98	1114.9	1018.4	96.4	0.1134	8.5

Notes:
* Value of intermediate inputs and depreciation.

Source: Data for 1987/88–1991/92, Assaf (1993, p. 2). Data for 1992/93–1997/98 calculated by author from HADISOLB, *Annual Report*, various years.

of long-run marginal cost (LRMC). LRMC depends on various factors, such as technology, scale, fuel cost, interest rate and exchange rate.

Table 6.7 shows the development of output of finished products, total electricity consumption, share of electricity cost and average electricity price to HADISOLB during 1987/88–1997/98.

A number of interesting conclusions may be drawn from this table. The most important are the following. First, the average electricity price increased much faster during the early 1990s, peaking in 1992/93. This is a direct influence of ERSAP. As shown in Table AIV.1, Annex IV, (Development of Domestic Energy Prices under ERSAP) the average electricity price was raised by 38 per cent in May 1990 to exceed the target of 45 per cent of LRMC set according to ERSAP. The price was further increased by 50 per cent in May 1991, bringing it to 60 per cent of LRMC (at the primary-market exchange rate of LE 3.2/US$1). A third increase by 32 per cent went into effect in July 1992, bringing the price to 69 per cent of LRMC of electricity. But after rising to a peak of LE 0.1535 in 1992/93, the electricity price to HADISOLB was frozen for a long time and then it was reduced to LE 0.1134 per kW/h in 1996/97. Second, there was no clear trend in the rate of electricity consumption per tonne of finished products over the period, but it tends to fluctuate around some 822 kW/h per tonne. Third, the average share of electricity in the total cost of materials (including depreciation) has been rising steadily during 1988/89–1993/94. It almost tripled during the period. After accounting for about 15 per cent of total cost of materials in 1993/94, the share of electricity in total cost of materials started falling.

The energy-pricing regime adopted under ERSAP is bound to impact negatively on HADISOLB. But this may be a blessing in disguise: as pointed out above, the integrated steel industry in Egypt consumes much more electricity per unit output than what may be viewed as the norm based on international comparison. There is much room for saving on electricity in this industry. This does not mean that the necessary adjustment to bring electricity requirements per unit output down to reasonable levels is going to be easy. It may also require some capital investment in energy-saving equipment and may call for reorganization of work and tasks at HADISOLB. This is naturally beyond the scope of the present exercise.

But it is relevant to discuss the rationale and method of the energy-pricing regime under ERSAP, which adopts the norm of so-called international prices for petroleum products and natural gas (being tradable) and LRMC for electricity (being a non-tradable). The pricing of electricity is determined at the central level, and is treated as a national parameter. This tends to confuse the function of shadow pricing for the purpose of project evaluation and investment planning with the function of setting actual prices in practice. It also ignores the difference between renewable and depletable resources.

For the purpose of investment planning and project evaluation and selection, it is legitimate to apply a shadow price of energy. But the basis of shadow pricing for a depletable resource is fundamentally different from that for a renewable resource. As we have shown in Annex III, the international price of a depletable energy resource such as oil may not reflect the true scarcity of this resource in Egypt's case because of the big difference in the reserve/output ratio for oil in Egypt and in the world as a whole. According to estimates of proven reserves and most likely rates of annual production, Egypt's oil reserves may last only about 10–11 years, compared to about 30 years at the world level. Hence, world prices of petroleum products, even if they were competitive, would underestimate the true scarcity of these resources in Egypt.[9]

As to the setting of actual prices of electricity, the current method excludes major energy users. It is a common practice in electricity pricing when there is a monopolist producer to involve major users in the process of tariff setting. This provides a better framework to represent the interests of the main parties who are likely to be affected by the decision. We suggest therefore that the current method of setting electricity prices for large energy-intensive industries, such as the steel industry, the aluminium industry, and so on, be changed such that the interests of big consumers of electricity are represented alongside those of the Egypt Electricity Authority (EEA).

It is pertinent at the end of this section to make a case for rethinking the existing framework for pricing in the energy field. Perhaps a restructured Energy Planning Agency (EPA) may fill the gap with regard to the shadow pricing for purposes of investment planning and project evaluation. But the framework for actual price setting needs to be rethought in order to balance the interests of the producer and the major consumers of electricity, and to provide a mechanism for alerting the users with enough lead time to make the necessary adjustment to the price increase.

Liberalizing Input and Output Prices

As part of the structural adjustment component of ERSAP, prices of inputs and outputs in manufacturing were to be liberalized. The main inputs in steel production are sinter and coke. Sinter is obtained by processing iron ore which is produced internally within HADISOLB and hence will not be directly affected by price liberalization. Only coke may be affected by this policy change. As shown in Table 6.6, although the price of coke was adjusted upward almost every year during 1984–91, it has stabilized at LE 380 per tonne during 1991–95. The significant increase in the price of coke actually took place before ERSAP. Contrary to expectation, the price of the most important input in the production of steel (coke) was rather relatively sticky under ERSAP.

Table 6.8 Output quantity, value and price per tonne of steel, 1984/85–1997/98

Year	Output		Price per tonne
	000 tonne	Million LE	000 LE
1984/85	n.a.	n.a.	n.a.
1985/86	730.6	275.0	0.376403
1986/87	688.4	266.7	0.387420
1987/88	875.0	404.9	0.462743
1988/89	879.5	533.1	0.606140
1989/90	858.2	598.5	0.697390
1990/91	976.8	748.8	0.766585
1991/92	894.2	843.8	0.943537
1992/93	924.3	816.2*	0.883047*
1993/94	1067.4	1033.8	0.968522
1994/95	1004.9	1068.6	1.0634
1995/96	893.0	1098.2	1.2298
1996/97	1059.5	1168.7	1.1031
1997/98	1114.9	1228.1	1.1015

Note: * The fall in the average price of finished products in 1992/93 is due to a drastic drop in the price of hot-rolled straps. This is the largest single product, amounting to 232.8 thousand tonnes accounting for 25 per cent of total output of finished products.

Source: HADISOLB, *Annual Report*, various years.

On the other hand, output price was in fact liberalized. As shown in Table 6.8, the average price of finished products rose steadily over the period until 1995/96 (except for 1992/93). The annual rate of increase in the output price was much higher during 1987/88–1991/92. This pattern of output price movement resembles that observed earlier with regard to price movement of the most important input – namely coke (see Table 6.6). An explanation of this apparent relative price stickiness under ERSAP is called for. One reason may perhaps lie in the fact that trade liberalization under ERSAP has created a link between domestic steel product prices and world market prices of steel.

Liberalization of Interest Rates

As already discussed in Chapter 2 of this study, interest rates on pound deposits and loans were liberalized by the Central Bank of Egypt as part of ERSAP starting January 3, 1991. This effectively ended a long period of financial repression; for example, interest on three-month pound deposits was frozen at 8.5 per cent (calculated on an annual basis) since January 1981.

The consequence of interest-rate liberalization was the increase in the interest rate on deposits and hence on loans. The interest rate on 3-month pound deposits peaked at about 17 per cent, calculated on a yearly basis, during the first quarter of 1992. Interest on loans of maturity one year or less was about 20–21 per cent, which is much higher than interest rates on dollar deposits and loans of comparable maturity of 8.5 per cent and 13–15 per cent, respectively (CBE, n.d.).

It should be observed that the interest deregulation resulted in relatively too sudden and sharp rises in interest rates. This actually took place before restructuring public enterprises that suffered from abnormally high leverage ratios. The result was jeopardizing the financial position of public enterprises, especially those in the manufacturing sector.[10] HADISOLB is a glaring case which warrants close examination.

Consider the information in Table 6.3 regarding equity, fixed assets and long-term debt. Until 1986/87, fixed assets were well covered by paid-up capital (equity). Starting in 1987/88, the value of fixed assets increasingly surpassed equity. By 1993/94, the value of fixed assets was more than double equity capital. The leverage ratio (calculated as the ratio of long-term debt to equity) was less than one until the end of the 1980s, but exceeded the benchmark value of one afterwards. Indeed the shaky financial position of HADISOLB becomes clear when overdraft accumulation is considered. The overdraft has 'snowballed' since 1989/90. The 1990s witnessed the skyrocketing of the overdraft from about LE 177 million in 1989/90 to around LE 950 in 1993/94. The overdraft was equivalent of 239 per cent of the company's equity by 1997/98. Here is a bubble that may burst at any time. This is a micro analogue to the over-borrowing syndrome discussed in Chapter 3.

Against this background we consider the effect of interest-rate deregulation. *The interest cost to HADISOLB rose significantly after ERSAP*, affecting operating surplus. Thus according to the data in Table 6.9 interest payments rose steadily between 1988/89 and 1991/92, reflecting a combination of accumulating debt and rising interest rates. Although the debt of HADISOLB continued to grow after 1991/92,[11] interest payments started to decline; perhaps as a result of the decline in interest rates charged by the local banking system during that period. *It is interesting to observe that interest payments exceeded the entire value added for most of the years since 1990/91.*

We may conclude this part by maintaining that the increase in interest rates as a result of deregulation ahead of reform and restructuring of public-sector enterprises endangered the profitability of these enterprises. The case of HADISOLB is a good illustration of this syndrome.

Table 6.9 Interest payments, wages, rent and value added, 1988/98–1997/98 (LE million)

Year	Total wages	Rent	Interest	Operating surplus	Value added
1988/89	102.0	9.5	142.2	–68.9	181.6
1989/90	127.0	18.0	170.9	–135.2	180.1
1990/91	152.0	8.1	250.7	–175.6	247.9
1991/92	158.0	8.5	327.2	–306.7	192.2
1992/93	166.0	8.8	309.5	–347.0	125.9
1993/94	186.0	8.6	288.6	–187.9	296.6
1994/95	202.6	8.8	281.1	–210.0	282.5
1995/96	229.0	9.5	273.9	–111.1	401.4
1996/97	252.6	10.3	263.0	–276.3	185.5
1997/98	279.8	10.2	250.0	–320.0	219.9

Source: HADISOLB, *Annual Report*, various years.

Demand Deflation and Trade Liberalization

As already pointed out in Chapter 2 of this study, ERSAP involved cutting back aggregate expenditure, with the brunt being borne by public spending. This was achieved by cutting food and fertilizer subsidies and, more important from the viewpoint of the impact on the steel industry, by the reduction in public investment outlays. According to the programme, public investment outlays are to be reduced by 5 percentage points during 1989/90–1992/93. Under the first phase of ERSAP (ERSAP I) the public investment programme was actually brought down from 40 per cent to 25 per cent of total central government expenditure between 1989/90 and 1992/93. In relation to GDP, this involved an even more significant drop from 17 per cent to 7.8 per cent. The government programme for reforming public investment included concentrating resources on a smaller number of projects with priority given to three areas: investment that 'crowd in' private investment (infrastructure); investment with large positive externalities (such as health, education and research); and investment not attractive to the private sector (poverty alleviation, correcting regional imbalances and environment). In this context, the demand for the products of the iron and steel industry should be expected to slow down.

With regard to trade liberalization, its macro implications were discussed in Chapter 3 of this study. There, it was suggested that trade liberalization in the Egyptian experience was in effect import liberalization; *the programme did not include significant measures to promote exports*. It was also shown that the Egyptian pound has appreciated under ERSAP. In this context, reducing the protection of import-substituting activities (as shown in Chapter 3 of this study) may lead to shifting resources more to non-tradables than to exports – a typical Dutch disease symptom. We also pointed out the crucial importance of the behaviour of the real exchange rate for the sustainability of trade liberalization.

At the micro level of the iron and steel industry, non-tariff barriers against importation of steel products were removed, and as a compensatory measure the tariff rate was raised from 10 per cent to 20 per cent in July 1994.[12] HADISOLB officials claim that foreign steel products are being dumped on the Egyptian market, particularly products orginating in the countries of the Commonwealth of Independent States (CIS) and channelled through Libya.

Demand deflation concurrently with import liberalization have both contributed to accumulating stocks of finished steel products. This is shown in Table 6.10. According to information from HADISOLB officials through interview, the company was partially able to avoid even greater stock accumulation by adjusting the rate of production to available demand and by offering credit to buyers of steel products. Yet, stocks of finished steel products in 1997/98 amounted to 207.5 thousand tonnes, representing about 20 per cent of annual production.

Table 6.10 Stock of finished steel at HADISOLB, 1990/91–1997/98 (000 tonne)

End of June	Stock
1990/91	103.7
1991/92	168.2
1992/93	99.0
1993/94	129.3
1994/95	100.0
1995/96	120.9
1996/97	188.2
1997/98	207.5

Source: HADISOLB, unpublished data.

Devaluation

It was mentioned in Chapter 3 that the Egyptian pound was nominally devalued as part of ERSAP. The impact of devaluation was to increase the pound equivalent of foreign currency denominated debt (see Table 6.3). However, the impact on profitability may not have been as significant for many reasons. First, HADISOLB produces mainly for the domestic market, and given the world price of steel products, devaluation must in itself increase effective protection for domestic steel production. Second, aside from coke, HADISOLB's inputs are mostly (about 85 per cent) locally produced, and hence devaluation may not be expected to raise production costs substantially. But because the pound has experienced significant real appreciation since the early 1990s, the competitiveness of HADISOLB must have deteriorated. This provides an additional factor to explain accumulating stocks of finished steel products.

To recap, the various elements of ERSAP impact on HADISOLB negatively. The thrust of these measures is to reduce the effective protection of HADISOLB as the only integrated steel complex in Egypt. The implication for industrialization may not be overestimated.

NOTES

1. Information in this part is based on interviews with HADISOLB executives, and Assaf (1993, pp. 12–15); Abou Zeid (1990, pp. 50–61); Ali (1993, pp. 6–12) and Abdel-Rahman (1992, pp. 16–28).
2. Steel is produced mainly (1.2 million tonnes) by handling sinter through oxygen converters (LD process), but a small quantity (0.07 million tonnes) is produced by feeding scrap into electric furnaces (Abou Zeid, 1990, p. 5). Electric steel is thus relatively insignificant.
3. With the notable exception of 1992/93, when total sales exceeded total output for the year because of unusual exports of 93 thousand tonnes to China. See Egyptian Iron and Steel Company, *Annual Report 1993/94, p. 15.*
4. There is also a fifth category, namely workers in capital expansion.
5. In 1997/98 total sales of high-voltage electricity to industry amounted to 3275 million kW/h. See EEA, *Annual Report of Electricity Statistics 1997/98*, p. 49.
6. Interview with the Director of Imports at HADISOLB, who also mentioned that according to Presidential Decree 529/1990 imports of Egypt and Libya from one another shall be exempt of tariffs. This provided an avenue for dumping steel originating in the CIS countries and entering the Egyptian market through Libya. In view of GATT 1994 accords, particularly the market access component, dumping is expected to be an increasingly important factor to reckon with in trade policy design. More on this point later.
7. Since every percentage point increase in coke price results in a 0.25 percentage point increase in total cost (that is, $132 \times (0.25/1.0) = 33$).
8. Some large public-sector industrial companies own and operate their own in-house power plants, notably the Misr-Mehalla Spinning and Weaving Company. But these are only a few exceptions to the general rule of EEA monopoly.
9. There are other problems with the concept of international energy prices as a true indicator of scarcity. Most important is the monopolistic nature of the world oil market, with OPEC on one side and the International Energy Agency on the other.
10. This concern was also expressed by other authors, compare Dilami et al., 'Interest Rate Policy in Egypt', World Bank Working Paper, No. WPS 655, April 1991, especially pp. 27–8.

11. It should be noted that the value of foreign currency debt in Table 6.3 is expressed in local currency. Since the pound was devalued several times as discussed in Chapter 3, the increase in debt is partly due to devaluation, representing an increase in the financial burden to HADISOLB.
12. According to an interview with the Director of Import Department at HADISOLB. It is to be noted that a pyramid of charges and levies is imposed. It may be expressed by the following formula: $[\{x(1 + m)(1 + t)\}(1 + r)](1 + s)$, where x = border price, CIF; m = maritime handling charges = 2 per cent; t = the tariff rate = 20 per cent; r = revenue enhancement charges = 4 per cent; and s = the sales tax = 10 per cent. Thus if $x = 100$, then the final import price becomes 140.

7. ERSAP and industrialization: concluding remarks

Since joining the International Monetary Fund in 1945 as an original founding member, Egypt has signed five stabilization agreements with the Fund. These agreements were: a credit facility in May 1962, which collapsed fairly rapidly; a stand-by arrangement in April 1977; an extended fund facility in July 1978; another stabilization package in May 1987, which was supported by a stand-by credit of SDR 250 million; and finally the stabilization package under the Economic Reform and Structural Adjustment Programme (ERSAP) which has been through various stages since the beginning of the 1990s.

The various packages since the late 1970s and 1980s must be viewed against a dismal background of a stagnant economy, rapidly rising inflation (estimated unofficially at 30 per cent in mid-1987) and a budget deficit which approached 23 per cent of GDP in 1985/86 – and possibly even higher in 1987/88.

The elements of the packages mentioned above reflected with varying degrees the main policy recipe propagated by the IMF. Invariably, they included the following measures; trade liberalization; gradual devaluation-cum-unification of the exchange rate; raising energy prices; decontrol of the prices of agricultural commodities; action to reduce the budget deficit as a proportion of GDP; liberalization of interest rates; setting limits on monetary expansion; privatization; and, lately, a social safety net.

Commitments under a stabilization agreement usually include some strategy-related stipulations in addition to the specific policy measures in different areas. Such commitments, be they of the broad strategic type or the narrow measure type, reflect very clearly the intellectual–theoretical stance of the IMF, where monetarism is the cornerstone for that stance.

Although the Fund always maintains that its strategic and policy prescriptions are detached from any bias on its part, our analysis of thc Egyptian experience under ERSAP reveals that there is clear bias against the public sector and in favour of the private sector. There is also bias against state intervention and in favour of the market as an allocative mechanism. The Fund's strategic stipulations are often couched under the euphemism of 'liberalization' and 'decentralization'. In addition, one may argue that the overall policy prescription of the Fund suffers from basic internal inconsistencies. One such inconsistency is the insistence on both devaluation and trade liberalization as a means to correct the balance-of-trade disequilibrium. Each of these prescribed measures pulls in the opposite direction to the other.

More importantly, measures intended in the Egyptian case to encourage a shift of more resources to the production of tradable goods helped instead to shift more resources to non-tradables (basically to service sectors, and away from commodity-producing sectors). In this respect, we have to distinguish the Egyptian experience of the 1970s and 1980s from that of the 1990s (under ERSAP). While Egypt failed during the first episode to follow the IMF recipe to the full, she implemented it methodically in the second episode. But in both cases, already existing symptoms of Dutch disease persisted. One may even venture the conclusion that under ERSAP, Dutch disease tendencies gained new momentum. This has greatly undermined the country's productive capacity and increased its vulnerability to external shocks.

Our analysis of Egypt's stabilization experience leads to some interesting implication for the theory of devaluation. First, if tradables are subject to administratively set procurement prices while prices of non-tradables are left free, devaluation would fail to re-channel resources from the production of non-tradables to the production of tradables. It would amount to *de facto* imposing a tax on the production of tradables. A good example is wheat *vs. berseem* (Egyptian clover) in the case of winter crops. In this regard, the pricing policy in place during the 1970s and early 1980s appears to have stifled the potential incentive effects of devaluation on production of tradables. Second, if the dollarization of the economy is widespread, devaluation may generate a significant wealth effect. If such a wealth effect was not neutralized (for example, by using a windfall tax), devaluation may lose part of its expenditure-reducing effect; it may even be expenditure-enhancing *if the wealth effect is large enough.* The problem is compounded if dollar (foreign currency) deposits were used as collateral against which loans in local currency may be secured.

The oil-related shocks which the Egyptian economy suffered during the second part of the 1980s impacted rather negatively on the performance of the economy. As a result of such shocks, real GDP growth fell below population growth, resulting in a deterioration of income per capita. Unemployment appeared on the rise, representing more than 10 per cent of the labour force. Domestic inflation did not abate. Both the fiscal deficit and the current account deficit showed no sign of improvement. The economy was increasingly overburdened by debt overhang – external debt outstanding and disbursed (DOD) hit the US$50 billion mark by the end of June 1990, a staggering 144 per cent of GDP. With only half the annual debt service obligations (of around US$6 billion) actually paid, accumulating debt arrears reached US$11 billion in 1989/90. Such indications were symptoms of a severe crisis and contributed to a drop in its creditworthiness. In addition to the sharp decline in the terms of trade since 1982, the country was hit hard by the strongest external shock of its post-Second World War history in the wake of the Gulf crisis of 1990. All that prompted the government to engage in negotiations with the Bank and the Fund which eventually led to ERSAP.

Macroeconomic reform according to ERSAP was tantamount to implementing a development strategy to achieve sustainable economic growth consistent with the country's ability to service its foreign debt. As already mentioned, the stabilization component of ERSAP encompassed measures in the fiscal, monetary and exchange rate areas. The structural adjustment component included measures to deal with public and private sector reform and foreign trade liberalization. In addition, the programme included a social safety-net component.

ERSAP has produced some immediate results, mainly related to the stabilization component of the package. The most important such results are the following. First, domestic inflation subsided, with the inflation rate falling from a double-digit level to single-digit levels starting in 1993/94. Second, the overall fiscal deficit was brought down very drastically, reflecting the tough fiscal stance under ERSAP. Third, the current account deficit was reduced significantly. Finally, ERSAP partly helped in bringing down external debt significantly, with the DOD/GDP ratio falling from 144 per cent in 1989/90 to 47 per cent in 1995/96.

The fiscal adjustment lay at the heart of the stabilization package, and involved trimming off the fiscal deficit, both the overall and the bank financed part. The target was to bring down the ratio of the overall budget deficit to GDP from an estimated high of 20 per cent for 1990/91 to a mere 1.5 per cent by 1995/96. But the deficit was only 1.3 per cent of GDP according to the budget proposal for 1995/96 (although the actual deficit was much higher than that). In effect, this involved a substantial hike in the share of public revenue (from about 25 per cent to about 40 per cent of GDP) and a slight reduction in the ratio of public expenditure. But it is interesting to note that, in relative terms, central government non-tax revenue provided most of the targeted adjustment: namely through price increases, particularly energy prices. The increase in tax revenue was mainly through greater reliance on indirect taxation (a comprehensive sales tax, escalation of stamp tax, and so on) in the face of falling customs revenue because of trade liberalization. The fiscal component of ERSAP did not really embody any effort for tax reform in the true sense of the term.

The structure of total expenditure underwent large shifts over the programme period. Such shifts proved extremely important on both equity and efficiency grounds. The fiscal component of the programme involved an almost tripling of the ratio of interest payments over the period 1989/90–

1992/93. In fact, such payments doubled in just one year (between 1989/90 and 1990/91), corresponding to the liberalization of domestic interest rates and the placement of treasury bills (TBs). During the entire period 1990–97 the government was incurring new domestic debt to refinance interest expenditure accruing on existing debt (Abdel-Khalek, 1998). This is a clear manifestation of an over-borrowing syndrome. At another level, such a tremendous rise in interest payments should have a negative impact on income distribution – a rise in the share of the *rentier* or 'clipping class' and a corresponding fall in the share of labour. Moreover, the hike in interest rates has actually discouraged investment, particularly in the tradables sector, and greatly compounded the problems faced by some public sector enterprises under ERSAP. The case of HADISOLB provides testimony to this, and underscores the important point that public-sector enterprise reform should have preceded interest-rate liberalization. As such, interest rate liberalization is not very helpful for industrialization.

Import substitution polices adopted in Egypt over the years resulted in high intermediate-import content of domestic production. Our calculations indicated that the total (direct plus indirect) import requirements ranged from 55 per cent to 28 per cent in tradables sectors producing either exportables or import substitutes. Sample survey results indicated an even higher import dependence of industry during the 1990s, revealing that imported intermediates account for 65 per cent of total intermediates as an overall average, but reaching 95 per cent in some industries of a pioneering industrial town. Therefore, one of the interesting lessons of the Egyptian devaluation experience of the 1990s is that import-substitution industrialization by itself sets rigid limits to the efficacy of devaluation as an expenditure-switching measure. Import-substitution policy invariably created conditions of low exchange rate elasticity of total imports and, ironically, high import propensity. In this context, the cost-push impact of devaluation cannot be ignored.

Our investigation of the devaluation of the pound under ERSAP (Chapter 3) showed very clearly that nominal devaluation did not translate into lasting real depreciation; *the pound has indeed appreciated significantly under ERSAP despite the maxi devaluation.* Another interesting result of the analysis is related to the effect of devaluation. In the theoretical model underlying IMF prescriptions, devaluation should lead to reduced absorption which in turn helps both the balance of payments and general price stability. In Egypt's experience, it appears that devaluation, at least initially, has led instead to increased absorption. This may be explained by the wealth effect resulting from the revaluation of foreign currency assets in proportion to devaluation, which seems to have outweighed the supposedly low spending propensity of the rich (who are the main holders of foreign currency deposits). This reveals a crucial point – IMF prescriptions lack the general validity which they are believed to have. They should be tailored much more carefully to the specific circumstances of individual countries. To assist this, the use of more policy instruments may be needed.

On the basis of available empirical evidence for Egypt, the familiar Salter ratio (the relative price of tradables *vis-à-vis* non-tradables) has gone down by about 20 per cent over the period 1991–96. Results of recent studies concur with our conclusion, although the order of magnitude may vary (World Bank, 1997, vol. II, pp. 14–15; El-Khawaga, 1996, Ch. 3).

Against this background, one observes that under ERSAP, the share of commodity-producing sectors in value added has continued its trend decline. In 1995/96, this share went down to 50 per cent compared to 52 per cent in 1986/87. On the reasonable assumption that the commodity sectors largely produce tradables, while the service sectors largely produce non-tradables, we conclude that under ERSAP the Egyptian economy continued to be infected with Dutch disease. We also charaterized this as a process of tertiarization – meaning a process of relative expansion of the tertiary sector.

The real appreciation of the Egyptian pound over the period representing ERSAP must have entailed some loss of competitiveness in international exchange. This created a macroeconomic environment which was not the most appropriate either for the trade balance or for the prospects of industrialization. This is particularly so since the main factor for the real appreciation of the pound was the financial liberalization. It is interesting to observe that the appreciation of the pound may have tempted EGYPTALUM to divert more sales to the domestic market.

The complementarity between performance at the micro and macro levels is crucial. For example, adopting the nominal anchor and pegging the pound to the dollar resulted in real appreciation. This sent the wrong signal to producers of tradables: EGYPTALUM found it more lucrative to sell on the domestic market, and HADISOLB's established position in the local market was shaken.

Perhaps the most effective instrument suggested by the IMF, in terms of its narrow objectives, is the interest rate. During the earlier episode (in the 1970s and 1980s), the increase in the domestic interest rates has shifted bank deposits towards longer-maturity deposits and local currency deposits. At the margin, this may be considered a positive development. On the other hand, interest-rate increases under ERSAP, helped by the nominal anchor and the liberalization of capital transactions, triggered interest arbitrage and attracted significant capital inflows. In the process, it fuelled large increases in domestic public debt. A large public debt today means a heavy fiscal burden tomorrow.

With the nominal exchange rate anchor, such capital inflows have led to the accumulation of foreign currency reserves with the monetary authorities.

International reserves of the Central Bank of Egypt (excluding gold) actually reached US$20 billion at some point. This level of foreign international reserves is unprecedented in Egypt's recent economic history – the sterling balances aside. Domestic debt accumulated in parallel, representing the other side of misaligned economic fundamentals: interest rate, inflation rate and nominal exchange rate. Although the ratio of the domestic public debt to GDP has been falling under ERSAP, in per capita terms domestic public debt almost doubled between 1990 and 1997 (Abdel-Khalek, 1998).

It is useful to reflect on the Egyptian economy under ERSAP in the light of the lessons of the Mexican crisis of the mid 1990s. In Egypt's case now, as in Mexico's case then, there is a problem of misaligned economic fundamentals. In the Egyptian case: the pound is appreciating, domestic debt is piling up, the trade gap is increasingly widening, the savings rate is falling and the rate of investment is stagnant. Such a combination of economic fundamentals make up a fragile and unsustainable environment. That raises the important issue of remedial measures. In particular, the exchange regime needs reworking (witness the debate between the Egyptian government and the IMF on devaluation), fiscal retrenchment should be relaxed somewhat, and capital mobility restricted/reconsidered.

We concluded in an earlier part of this study (see Chapter 3) that in certain respects the design of the trade liberalization programme follows the usual pattern borne out by other country experiences. Specifically, emphasis was placed at the outset on dismantling quantitative restrictions, notably import bans. This was accompanied by the tariffication of NTBs, involving an initial increase in the mean tariff rate and a decrease in dispersion (Michaely et al., 1991, p. 3). The pattern depicted in Chapter 3 is the same, implying that, initially, liberalization of the trade regime involved changing the *form* rather than necessarily reducing the *level* of protection. In other words, in the initial phase of trade liberalization, emphasis was placed more on shifting protection to the price mechanism than reducing the absolute level of protection. Whether this has actually encouraged more efficient production remains to be proven, but it has eliminated some rent-seeking behaviour. *Ceteris paribus*, this shift to the price mechanism renders the system more transparent and predictable.

Our analysis of the Egyptian experience of trade liberalization suggests that trade liberalization was in effect import liberalization; *the programme did not include enough measures to promote exports.* One important exception, perhaps, is the correction of the nominal exchange rate bias against exports. The reduction of protection of import-substituting activities brought about by trade reform under ERSAP (see Table 3.10) supported the impact of the real appreciation of the pound in shifting resources more to non-tradables than to exports. This is a typical Dutch disease symptom. We have already presented evidence showing that the share of tradables sectors in GDP has continued its pre-ERSAP decline under the programme.

There is evidence in Chapter 3 that the balance of trade has been actually aggravated by a fall in the real exchange rate, that is, an appreciation of the pound, as concluded. Exports fell in absolute terms during 1991/92 and 1992/93 (despite targeted increases according to ERSAP), while imports rose in 1992/93 (though falling in 1991/92).

One of the cornerstones of structural reform under ERSAP was the adjustment of energy prices in Egypt to the level of world prices. In effect, this amounted to raising energy prices significantly. However, it is curious to observe that the electricity price to HADISOLB, for example, almost tripled between 1990/91 and 1992/93 (from LE 0.0518 to 0.1535 per kW/h), but then was lowered in 1996/97. The adjustment of electricity price to EGYPTALUM was more significant before ERSAP than after. In fact, the price charged for electricity to the aluminium smelter has not changed since July 1992. Although it is well-established that energy prices in Egypt suffered significant distortions, one may not espouse the concept of world prices invoked by the IMF and the World Bank in this case. The heart of the matter is that world prices of energy are only a poor indicator of energy scarcity in Egypt. The logic rests on the fact that petroleum is a depletable resource and is far more scarce in Egypt compared to the world as a whole. On the basis of a two-period model for the optimal rate of oil production, we derive shadow prices for oil which at equilibrium are higher than world prices. But we suggest using these shadow prices for investment decisions rather than for actual pricing of energy.

As expected, the analysis of the effect of stabilization measures on the various socio-economic groups shows that the thrust of the Extended Fund Facility to Egypt for 1979–81 was against 'labour' and in favour of 'capital'. But within each of these two broad categories, there is evidence of differential effects. Labour in the government and public sector has been a clear victim; the effect on private-sector labour was less clear-cut. In total, labour was a clear loser during this earlier episode. Under ERSAP, we believe that the outcome of such factors as privatization, trade liberalization, interest-rate liberalization and cutting the rate of public investment was most probably further deterioration in the share of labour in GDP. Unfortunately, an estimate of this share is not available for the ERSAP period.

In the light of our analysis of the Egyptian case, we may conclude that ERSAP is more likely to have a negative impact on industrial growth and structure in Egypt. We have shown that the exchange rate policy, financial-liberalization and trade-policy components of the programme were at best not conducive to industrial growth. They may eventually prove too obstructive. However, evidence regarding this hypothesis is actually mixed. As already shown in Chapter 4, on the basis of value added generation and exports, the

Egyptian economy was perhaps more industrialized in the 1990s. On the other hand, judging by the share of manufacturing in gross fixed capital formation, it appears that the Egyptian economy has become less industrialized in the 1990s.

Three additional considerations may be invoked here to complete the argument regarding the likely impact of ERSAP on industrial growth and structure.

First, trade liberalization and interest rate liberalization have been pushed too fast, long before the necessary reforms in the real sectors of the economy. For example, pushing trade liberalization before achieving the task of restructuring of public sector enterprises simply forces them to compete from a position of a disadvantage. In fact, it may effectively undermine their financial viability. This carries a real danger of collapse of such enterprises. When non-tariff barriers (such as import bans or quotas) are lifted before putting in place the necessary safeguards, anti-dumping and countervailing duty mechanisms as legitimate defences against unfair trade practices, the competitive position of domestic enterprises may be weakened considerably. Also, when interest-rate liberalization is rushed in before reforming the capital structure of the enterprise, the overdraft may reach dangerous levels. The example of HADISOLB is a case in point on both scores.

Second, ERSAP did not include an industrial policy component in any real sense of the word, for example as in the case of HPAEs. Instead, one is struck by a hands-off stance for the government. This is ill-suited to the conditions of Egypt which is a low-income populous country trying to develop. If development is defined broadly to encompass growth with structural change and equity, then a neutral-incentive regime, which is the essence of trade liberalization under ERSAP, may be the wrong strategy to adopt. As already argued before in this study, there is a real need for a developmental role for the state. Too hasty or premature trade liberalization, in conjunction with other elements of ERSAP, may eventually amount to the de-industrialization of Egypt.

Third, the fiscal and monetary stance adopted under ERSAP reduced aggregate demand and raised real domestic interest rates. The persistence of high real interest rates produced a number of negative effects. It made fiscal adjustment more costly. It resulted in a deterioration of bank portfolios, and hence necessitated subsidized recapitalization of banks. It induced short-term capital inflows, which were mainly sterilized – leading to domestic debt accumulation with mounting debt service burden. And finally it raised the user cost of capital and hence discouraged investment (Abdel-Khalek, 1998).

On the other hand, real appreciation has contributed to a reduction of the saving rate. The World Bank (1995) has reported a fall in rate of national savings (including official transfers) by 7 percentage points during 1990/91–1994/95. This fall in the savings rate may be explained by the tendency of household to substitute present for future consumption (in anticipation of devaluation) and to engage in speculative activities in real estate. The implication of this development for sustainable growth is rather disquieting.

Real appreciation of the pound may be said to have contributed to a consumption binge as well as an import spree. The falling savings rate was the other side of a consumption binge and the trade deficit was partly a reflection of the import spree. It is interesting to observe that the significant rise in interest rates under ERSAP did not boost savings as the exponents of 'financial repression' had expected. The impact of raising the interest rate was felt more at the level of financial variables (de-dollarization, currency substitution) than at the level of the real variables (propensity to save). The contribution of a misaligned exchange rate in producing a consumption binge and an import spree seems to have outweighed the effect of the increased interest rate in bringing about an increase in the saving rate. The consumption-boosting effect of the appreciating pound outweighed the saving-enhancing effect of increased interest rate.

In the Egyptian stabilization and adjustment story, interest rate liberalization was more effective at the level of macro finances (budget deficit) and micro finances (operating surplus of public sector enterprises) than at the level of overall resource balance of the economy.

The effect of ERSAP on industrialization may also be gauged by examining how the programme impacts on the basic industries already existing in Egypt. These are the micro effects of ERSAP. We have conducted case studies of two such industries: iron and steel (HADISOLB) and aluminium smelting (EGYPTALUM). Our conclusion is that the effects of ERSAP may not depend as much on the ownership pattern as it does on the nature of the enterprise – namely: import-substituting *vs.* export-oriented project. The analysis of aluminium smelting in Chapter 5 has demonstrated that the most significant effect is to signal that the era of cheap electricity is over. EGYPTALUM uses up slightly more than 3300 giga W/h of electric energy annually: each percentage point increase in the price of electricity supplied to the company would result in an LE 2 million increase in production cost. Unless certain measures are taken by the aluminium smelter (EGYPTALUM) to raise energy efficiency, calculating electricity cost at world prices of fuel oil would raise the total energy cost of 1 tonne of aluminium to about LE 1178. But this would still imply a total production cost of aluminium which is much below the export prices recorded during 1995–98. But devaluation happened to be particulaly helpful to EGYPTALUM, as it provided a comfortable cushion against the sharp drop in the price of aluminium on the world market after 1988/89.

The tentative conclusion therefore is that the aluminium smelter would not shut down, but would have to adjust particularly to a world of scarce energy resources. Such an adjustment may be achieved through a two-pronged strategy: on the one hand, it would involve cuts in costs, particularly energy costs, and on the other hand it would involve increasing value added (by deepening industrialization *via* product diversification). Our analysis in Chapter 5 indicates that there is great potential in cutting energy costs by reducing specific energy consumption in aluminium smelting. Available evidence does not reveal any significant improvement in energy efficiency at EGYPTALUM (see Table 5.6). Value added may be increased basically through increasing the proportion of fabricated products to total production, and moving further downstream. This is because primary aluminium fetches the basic price determined on the London Metal Exchange, while fabricated aluminiums sell at a premium above the basic price.

The other case study undertaken to examine the micro effects of ERSAP was the iron and steel industry, represented by the largest integrated mills – HADISOLB. ERSAP has actually created far more difficulties for this firm compared to EGYPTALUM. Perhaps the most crucial elements impacting on HADISOLB are interest rate liberalization, trade liberalization, and contractionary measures. The capital structure of HADISOLB, characterized as it was by a very high leverage ratio seriously exposed the company to the dangers involved in interest rate liberalization. The overdraft jumped from a trickle of LE 83 million in 1988/89 to a massive LE 600 million in 1991/92. The thrust of such measures was to reduce effective protection of the steel industry. Unless something is done to help the firm ride through the storm, its prospects are far from being bright indeed.

What prospects are there for industrialization in Egypt – given the various measures under ERSAP?

It is clear that investment in manufacturing, and in tradables sectors in general, has been falling in relative terms under ERSAP. This is consistent with the observation that the Salter ratio (the ratio of the price of tradables to that of non-tradables) has been falling. It means that the system of incentives produced by ERSAP is biased towards non-tradables. One of the problems, it appears, is that trade liberalization was conceived largely by itself and in isolation from other measures as a regime of neutral incentives. But within the broader context of other ERSAP measures, it appears that the outcome was a biased regime of incentives; it strongly favoured non-tradables at the expense of tradables.

Public debate in Egypt currently centres around the increasing role played by the real estate sector. That sector actually epitomizes non-tradable activities. A great deal of concern by policy makers is expressed, especially in the light of the crises in the East-Asian countries, based on the perception that the glut on the real estate markets of those countries contributed to the financial crises which hit their economies in 1997.

We also expressed concern in this volume that a Mexican-type scenario may develop if investors expect correction of the exchange rate. The Egyptian experience under ERSAP may be reminiscent of the experience of Mexico and the debacle that led to the financial crisis of 1994–95 (popularly known as the *Tequila* effect). It may also carry some semblance with the more recent crises in the East-Asian countries. As in both cases, economic fundamentals do not seem to be properly aligned. The pound is appreciating; there is a huge and mounting domestic public debt, and there is a rising trade deficit counterbalanced by short-term capital inflows. In addition, there is a falling savings rate and a stagnant rate of investment. As a result, growth of the economy is sluggish. Such a combination is both extremely volatile and eventually unsustainable.

This actually underscores the fact that globalization imposes rigid limitations on the use of certain policy instruments for stabilization and adjustment. Such globalization is manifested by the increasing integration of financial markets, trade liberalization and capital mobility. In the context of the globalization of financial markets, interest rate differentials may induce massive short-term capital movements and encourages speculative activity. That does not create an enabling environment for industrialization.

Against this background, an alternative package is needed. Such a package would put more emphasis on selective controls *vis-à-vis* market forces. It would also stress the need to increase aggregate supply by adjusting relative prices to provide more incentives for producing staple food crops. The alternative package would also acknowledge the role of the government; in Egypt, government expenditure largely 'crowds in' rather than 'crowds out' private investment. In the technical design of the set of policies, the proposed package underlines the need for a larger number of policy instruments than is usually entertained in Fund-supported packages. But above all, the design of the suggested package is predicated on the vital need to take the international economic environment much more fully into consideration.

Naturally, dissatisfaction with the conventional IMF package calls for the introduction of an alternative. The basic elements of an effective economic reform package should fulfil two requirements: first, to stem and eventually reverse the contraction of the economy; second, to protect the level of living of the poor. It should be realized that equity issues are much harder to face under the strains of contraction. In the light of the analysis in the preceding chapters, we venture some reflections on the nature and content of an alternative package.

1. Overall price stability is crucial both for the balance of payments and resource allocation considerations. It is also important for equity. Egypt's stabilization experience in the 1970s and 1980s has demonstrated the

role of devaluation, the interest rate increase and massive capital inflows as contributing factors to inflation. Instead of increasing the nominal interest rate as a means of raising the real rate of return on financial assets, the stabilization policy should target reducing the rate of inflation. Achieving price stability should be assigned high priority.

2. Remedial measures to counter the adverse effects of external shocks (such as violent commodity price fluctuations, interest rate and exchange rate changes) should be made an integral part of the mechanisms of adjustment. The way forward here has already been shown in an IMF agreement with Mexico in the mid 1980s, which linked IMF support for Mexico to the price of oil. This could naturally be extended to cover interest rate and exchange rate fluctuations.
3. Adopting an appropriate combination of market forces and the price mechanism with planning and direct controls. One of the policy-relevant conclusions of our study (Chapter 4) is that the Egyptian economy has grown increasingly more mixed: thanks to *infitah* and subsequently stabilization and adjustment, the scope of the private sector has widened considerably. There are obviously important policy implications of this development. One notable implication is that economic management will have to take this into account, by relying more on incentives and leverages than on direct control/intervention.

   We have already argued in this study against complete submission to market forces. The exchange rate is just one vital parameter where such submission may prove extremely harmful. In this context the role of the government remains important. The orthodox stabilization package is predicated on a 'crowding-out' assumption. In Egypt, as in LDCs in general, the role of the government is complementary to, rather than competitive with, that of the private sector. Government expenditure, perhaps with some restructuring, should be increased rather than reduced to counteract the contractionary tendencies. The real issue here is not only *what* type of government expenditure, but *how* it is financed. In this context, an adjustment of relative prices to provide adequate incentive for producers of tradables is also vital to the attainment of external balance.
4. Finally, the liberalization of capital transactions in the balance of payments should not be effected indiscriminately. A clear distinction has to be drawn between FDI and FPI. Good stabilization and adjustment packages should encourage the first but not the second. This is the hard lesson of the recurring financial crises.

Annexes

ANNEX I

Table AI.1 Development of the exchange rate system and exchange rates 1945–97

Year	LE/US$	Remarks
1945–49	0.242	Egyptian pound pegged to pound sterling
1949	0.348	Following devaluation of pound sterling by 30.5 per cent in 1949
1962	0.435	1962 devaluation according to stabilization programme
1972	0.391	Following the second devaluation of the American dollar by 10 per cent in 1972. The pound followed the dollar in the first devaluation by 7 per cent in the same year
1973	0.391	Establishment of the parallel market rate
1979	0.700	Devaluation and unification of exchange rate
1981		Return to multiple rates: (a) Central Bank Pool* = LE 0.70/US$; fixed (b) Commercial Banks' Pool** = LE 0.80–0.84/US$; adjustable (c) Accounting exchange rate for clearing accounts and payments agreements with non-IMF members fixed at 0.391 (d) Transactions outside authorized banks (black market)
1991–97		Devaluation and unification of the exchange rate; pegging to the American dollar

Notes:

* Central Bank Pool:
Receipts: Exports of cotton, rice, petroleum plus Suez Canal and Sumed dues.
Payments: Imports of wheat, wheat flour, sugar, tea, edible oil, fertilizers, including shipping and other related charges, plus public debt service and government expenditure abroad.

** Commercial Bank Pool:
All items of receipts and payments other than those under Central Bank Pool.

ANNEX II

Table AII.1 Exchange rates 1973–97 (LE/$)

Date	Official[a]	Parallel market[a]	Authorized Banks' Pool: Declared[b]	Authorized Banks' Pool: Premium	Authorized Banks' Pool: Flexible[b]	Black market	Free banking market	Primary market/ free market	Custom valuation rate
1/9/73	0.391	0.588							0.391
19/2/76	0.391	0.637				0.730			0.391
20/5/76	0.391	0.667				0.741			0.391
28/11/76	0.391	0.700				0.769			0.391
31/12/78	0.391	0.700				0.746			0.391
1/1/79	0.700		0.700			0.746			0.700
Dec. 80	0.700		0.700			0.820			0.700
1/1/81	0.700		0.832			n.a.			0.700
81/82	0.700		0.832			1.010[c]			0.700
82/83	0.700		0.832			1.099[c]			0.700
83/84	0.700		0.832			1.176[c]			0.700
84/85	0.700		0.832	1.288[d]		1.351[c]			0.700
85/86	0.700		0.832	1.329		1.786[c]			0.700
86/87	0.700				1.362	1.889[c]			1.365
87/88	0.700				1.764[e]	2.182[i]	2.299[f]		1.764[j]
88/89	0.700					2.353[i]	2.387		1.890[k]
89/90	1.152[g]					2.637[i]	2.607		2.607[l]
90/91	2.000						2.812	3.199/3.296[h]	2.812

91/92	3.286/3.322
92/93	3.334
1994–97	3.390

Notes:

a. Starting 1/1/1979, the official market was replaced by the central bank foreign exchange pool, and the parallel market was replaced by the authorised banks foreign exchange pool.
b. The declared rate was replaced by the flexible rate on 24/7/1986.
c. The average rate for December of the starting calendar year, that is, Dec. 1981 for 1981/82 and so on.
d. Started on 5/1/1985.
e. Abolished 21/3/1988, when the authorized banks pool was terminated, and transactions therein transferrred to the free banking market.
f. The free banking market was established starting 11/5/1987.
g. The exchange rate in the central bank pool was changed to PT 110 on 15/8/1989, and to PT 200 on 1/7/1990.
h. The primary market was established on 27/2/1991, and abolished 8/10/1991, when transaction were transferred to the free market.
i. Average for the starting calendar year.
j. Tied to the rate in the authorized banks pool
k. Fixed at this rate after abolishing the authorized banks pool.
l. Tied to the rate in the free banking market.

Sources: 1973–81, Abdel-Khalek, 1987, Table 6. Black market rate 1976-85, ibid. 1981/82–1991/92, CBE, *Economic Review*, vol. 32, no. 4, 1991/92. p. 121. Black market rate 1986-89, El-Rifaie, 1992, p. 141. 1992–93 (average for two years) and 1994–1997 from IMF, *IFS Yearbook*. Custom valuation rate, El-Rifaie, 1992, pp. 162–163.

ANNEX III SHADOW PRICING OF DEPLETABLE ENERGY RESOURCES

Assume that society has a given amount of the depletable resource. In the case of petroleum this is given by the level of proven reserves. Let us denote this $\overline{R}$.

Assume that society's time horizon is split into only two time periods; the first being that of the life of the current generation, and the second being that of the life of the next (and last) generation. Society has the choice of producing petroleum in the first or the second period. We assume that it can technically produce any amount (within the $\overline{R}$ limit) in either periods. Let us denote the quantities of petroleum produced in periods 1 and 2, R_1 and R_2, respectively. Assume that in period 1, the price is given at P_1 and the unit cost is technically determined at C_1. P_2 and C_2 are the price and cost in period 2. We assume that: $P_1 = P_1^*$, $P_2 = P_2^*$ (this is the small country assumption) and $C_1 = f_1(R_1)$, $C_2 = f_2(R_2)$, where $f_i = \partial f_i / \partial R_i > 0$ (production cost per unit increases as the rate of production increases).

In this context, the problem of determining the optimal rate of production of a depletable resource (petroleum) is simply that of maximizing the total present value of net revenue from oil production over the two periods, subject to overall resource availability, $\overline{R}$.

Formally, we have:

$$\max\left[\frac{(P_1 - C_1)R_1}{1+\delta} + \frac{(P_2 - C_2)R_2}{(1+\delta)^2}\right] \tag{III.1}$$

subject to

$$R_1 + R_2 \leq \overline{R} \tag{III.2}$$

$$R_1 \geq 0, R_2 \geq 0, \tag{III.3}$$

where δ is the social rate of time discount.

(III.1)–(III.3) may be viewed as the primal of a linear programming problem. The dual of this problem is

$$\min(\lambda\overline{R}) \tag{III.4}$$

subject to

$$\lambda \geq \frac{\partial}{\partial R_1}\left\{\frac{(P_1 - C_1)R_1}{1+\delta}\right\} \tag{III.5}$$

$$\lambda \geq \frac{\partial}{\partial R_2}\left\{\frac{(P_2 - C_2)R_2}{(1+\delta)^2}\right\} \tag{III.6}$$

$$\lambda \geq 0, \tag{III.7}$$

where λ is the Lagrange multiplier.

According to the Kuhn–Tucker theorem (Dorfman et al., 1958), obtaining an optimal production programme which involves production in both periods implies that conditions (III.2), (III.5) and (III.6) be effective, and λ positive. That is

$$R_1 + R_2 = \overline{R} \tag{III.2$'$}$$

$$\lambda = \frac{(P_2 - C_1 - R_1 f_1')}{(1+\delta)} \tag{III.5$'$}$$

$$\lambda = \frac{(P_2 - C_2 - R_2 f_2')}{(1+\delta)^2} \tag{III.6$'$}$$

$$\lambda > 0 \tag{III.7$'$}$$

Note that the RHS of (III.5′) and (III.6′) is the present value of the difference between marginal revenue (MR) and marginal cost (MC). That is

$$\lambda = \text{present value of MR} - \text{present value of MC}$$

or

$$\text{present value of MR} = \text{present value of MC} + \lambda \tag{III.8}$$

Hence condition (III.7′) and the condition for the optimal production programme for a depletable resource shown in (III.8) imply that

$$\text{present value of MR} > \text{present value of MC} \tag{III.9}$$

There is thus a fundamental difference between the equilibrium condition of the production programme of a depletable resource and the corresponding condition for a renewable resource under competition, which is the well-known:

$$\text{present value of MR} = \text{present value of MC} \tag{III.10}$$

Comparing (III.9) and (III.10) enables us to interpret the Lagrange multiplier as the depletion (or scarcity) premium. λ has the limiting value of zero in the case of renewable resources, and increases in proportion to the rate of depletion of non-renewable resources.

It is interesting to note from (III.5′) and (III.6′) above that there is a negative relation between the depletion (or scarcity) premium (λ) and the social rate of time discount (δ). Thus, the more society prefers the present over the future (the higher δ), the smaller will be the depletion (or scarcity) premium (the lower λ) – other things being equal. In this case, society will tend to deplete its resource in the present.

One may illustrate graphically the difference between the equilibrium production point for a depletable resource and that for a renewable resource.

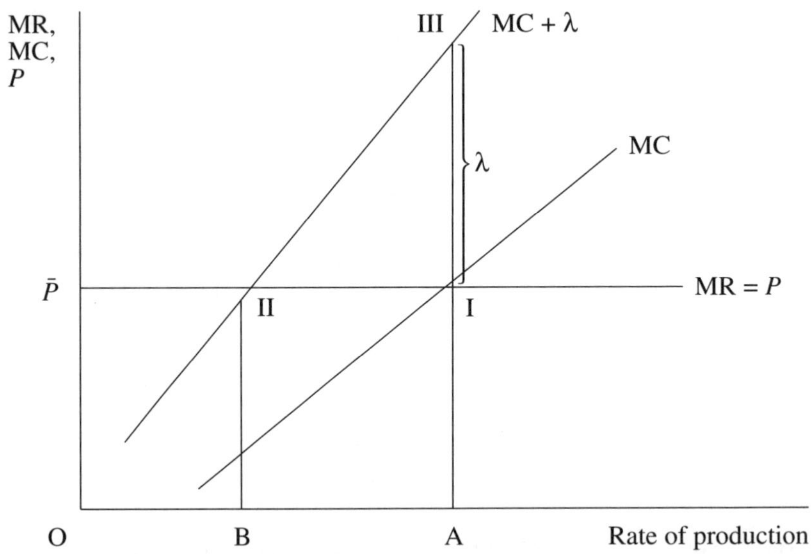

In the above diagram, we illustrate the small country case, where the country's share of world output of the resource is too small to make a difference for the market price of the resource. Point I is the equilibrium point corresponding to the case of a renewable (non-depletable) resource. In such case, $\lambda = 0$, and the rate of production is OA. If we allow for a depletion premium (that is, $\lambda > 0$), we obtain equilibrium point II, where the rate of production is OB < OA. Therefore AB may be a measure of overproduction of the depletable resource. As AB $\Rightarrow$ 0, OA $\Rightarrow$ OB, and point I coincides with point II. OB is the rate of production which balances the welfare of the current and the future generation.

The model developed above has very clear policy implications. *First*, from a sustainable-development perspective, actual output for depletable resource should be adjusted by the coefficient

$$\varepsilon = 1 - \frac{AB}{OA} = \frac{OB}{OA} \qquad \text{(III.11)}$$

This has obvious consequences for GDP estimates and their welfare implications. *Second*, it provides us with a solid theoretical basis for the pricing of hydrocarbon energy – not only petroleum. This has always been a very contentious point between Egypt and the World Bank. The Bank has consistently maintained that energy prices in Egypt are highly distorted in the sense that domestic energy prices are lower than international prices. As part of ERSAP, it was stipulated to correct such distortion.

The problem with such policy prescription becomes obvious in the light of the model developed above. Assuming that international prices of petroleum reflect its true scarcity (a very strong assumption indeed), they may not be the right norm for correcting distortions in Egypt. This is simply because petroleum is more scarce in Egypt than it is for the world as a whole – the depletion rate in Egypt is approximately four times that for the world as a whole (see Table AIII.1). *It follows that international prices may not accurately express the true scarcity of petroleum in Egypt's case.* The fact that petroleum is a tradable does not change this conclusion.

Table AIII.1 Depletion rate of petroleum

			Egypt	World
(1)	Reserves*	(000 bbl)	3 500 000	1 023 668 270
(2)	Production**	(000 bbl/year)	313 900	23 885 819
(3)	Depletion rate (= (2) ÷ (1))		0.09	0.023

Notes:
* 1/2/1999
** 1997

Source: *Oil and Gas Journal*, 29 Dec. 1999.

ANNEX IV ENERGY PRICING UNDER ERSAP: PETROLEUM PRODUCTS AND NATURAL GAS

Measures to adjust energy prices were outlined in the Structural Adjustment Loan known as SAL I (World Bank, 1991, pp. 25–6). According to this agreement, the government indicated its intention to change the weighted average of the domestic prices of petroleum products and natural gas to reflect their internationally traded equivalents and to adjust electricity prices to cover the long-run marginal cost (LRMC), by June 1995. Such adjustments are intended not only to reduce subsidies to the energy sector, but also to reduce cross-subsidies among products.

According to the formula agreed with the World Bank, the conversion of domestic prices to international equivalents will be based on the commercial exchange rate at the time the price increase action is undertaken. With regard to petroleum products, prices of internationally traded equivalents would be based on the most recently published preceding 12-month rolling average of petroleum prices FOB Italy, and when necessary, FOB northwestern Europe as published by Platt's. Considering that ex-refinery products should be priced in such a manner as to reflect indifference between the local and the international markets, transport costs should be subtracted from international equivalents in the case of exports and added in the case of imports.[1] Thus for individual products, the formulae for calculating the international trade equivalents of energy product prices are as follows.

Price Increase Formulation for Petroleum Products and Natural Gas:

1. Premium gasoline = premium gasoline FOB Italy – (premium gasoline FOB NW Europe – regular gasoline NW Europe).[2]
2. Regular gasoline = average of premium gasoline in (1) and naphtha FOB Italy.
3. Liquified petroleum gas (LPG) = LPG FOB Italy.
4. Kerosene = jet kerosene FOB Italy – $5/ton.[3]
5. Gas oil = gas oil FOB Italy.
6. Fuel oil = 3.5 per cent sulphur fuel oil FOB Italy.
7. Diesel fuel = 85 per cent gas oil + 15 per cent fuel oil.
8. Bulk natural gas = fuel oil equivalent (fuel oil + 20 per cent).

The objective is to eliminate the difference between the prices in place at the start of ERSAP in 1990 and target prices (those of internationally-traded equivalents for petroleum products, or LRMC for electricity) by six annual percentage point steps through June 1995. In May 1990 the first step was

Annex Table AIV.1 Development of domestic energy prices under ERSAP

Date	Weighted average domestic petroleum product prices & natural gas prices	Average electricity prices
May 1990	Raised by 43 per cent.	Increase by 38 per cent, exceeding the target of 45 per cent of LRMC set by ERSAP.
May 3 1991		Increase by 50 per cent, bringing them to 60 per cent of LRMC (at the primary-market exchange rate of LE 3.2/US$ 1).
May 1991	Raised to 46 per cent of world prices*.	
Jan 4 1992	Raised to 69 per cent of world prices, exceeding the required 56 per cent.	
June 28 1992	Raised to 80 per cent of world prices, exceeding the required 67 per cent.	
July 1992		Raised by 32 per cent to 69 per cent of LRMC.
Dec 19 1992	Raised to 83 per cent of world prices.	
July 1993		Increased by 10 per cent to exceed agreed target of 80 per cent of the LRMC by June 1993.

Note: * Weighted average of domestic petroleum product prices (WADPPP) had fallen back to a little over one third of world prices in February 1991; thanks to developments in international petroleum market prices and in the exchange rate.

Source: Information collected from various documents: Government of Egypt, 'Memorandum of Economic Policy of the Egyptian Government', Draft No. 1, March 28, 1991, p. 12; IMF, 1993, Appendix V, p. 47, and GOE, 'Economic Reform and Structural Adjustment Program (Phase II)', Letter of Development Policy, September 3, 1993, p. 11.

Memo Items: According to unpublished data obtained from the Egyptian General Petroleum Corporation (EGPC), petroleum product prices stayed at their current levels (December 2000) shown (p. 176) since 1992.

actually taken, when the petroleum product prices were raised by an average of 43 per cent, and electricity prices were raised by 38 per cent. Actual implementation of the energy-price adjustment since 1990 proceeded as shown in Table AIV.1.

The prices stand currently (December 2000) as follows since the dates indicated (PT = piastre = LE 0.01): premium gasoline PT 100 per litre, regular gasoline PT 90 per litre (both since 28/6/1992); kerosene PT 40 per litre, gas oil (regular) PT 40 per litre, gas oil (electricity) PT 45 per litre, diesel oil PT 36 per litre (since 14/7/1993); fuel oil LE 130 metric ton (since 18/12/1992); LPG LE 120 per metric ton (since 3/5/1991); natural gas PT 12.25 per cubic metre since 18/12/1992 (except for companies established under the Foreign Investment Code where the price is PT 28–30 per cubic metre).

ANNEX V ESTIMATING LONG-RUN MARGINAL COST OF ELECTRICITY

Raising electricity prices to the level of long-run marginal cost (LRMC) has been one of the basic components of ERSAP. In this annex, we estimate the LRMC per kW/h of electricity. It is assumed that a significant addition to the nation's electricity supply will have to come only from thermal generation – the scope of hydroelectric generation is rather limited after the construction of the Esna barrage very recently. It is also assumed that nuclear power generation is to be excluded; the programme of setting up nuclear power plants has been shelved. *Our working assumption therefore is that to add significantly to electricity generating capacity in Egypt, new power plants would have to be constructed.* Such plants would have to burn hydrocarbons – mainly natural gas and fuel oil – to produce electricity.

The total cost of producing electricity should include fuel, generation, transmission and distribution, and operation and maintenance (O&M). In addition, the cost should include an allowance for normal system loss.

1. Fuel Cost

Most of the thermal electricity now generated in Egypt uses natural gas and fuel oil known commercially in Egypt as *Mazut.* Other fuels such as diesel oil and gas oil (known commercially in Egypt as *sular)* currently account for a negligible proportion of fuel used to turn power generators. Natural gas accounts for 67 per cent while fuel oil (*Mazut)* accounts for 32.9 per cent. We shall therefore make our calculation of LRMC on the assumption that natural gas will account for 80 per cent and fuel oil will account for 20 per cent, reflecting the current policy of EEA to replace natural gas for fuel oil in power generation. *The calculation will be in terms of units of fuel oil equivalent (foe).*

Our approach is first to make two separate estimates of the LRMC of a kW/h of electricity, one representing economic cost and the other commercial cost. The economic cost of fuel will be based on world prices for fuel oil and natural gas.[4] Since the calculation of domestic prices according to the World Bank formula depends on the exchange rate (see above), given these world prices, the cost in domestic currency (Egyptian pound) *will depend on the exchange rate and hence will rise with the devaluation of the pound.*

The starting point is to determine the quantity of fuel needed to produce one kW/h of electricity. According to data from the Egyptian Electricity Authority (EEA), that quantity was 0.241 kg of foe per kW/h generated in 1992/93. However, we used the value of 0.255 kg foe/kW/h, which seems more consistent with the rate of fuel consumption over the period 1988/89–1991/92.[5] Alternatively, 0.209 kg of natural gas will be needed to produce one kW/h of electricity, since 1.0 kg of LNG is equivalent to 1.22 kg of fuel oil in calorific-value terms.

We therefore have the following data set for 1992/93:

Rate of fuel consumption = 0.255 kg foe/hwh
= 0.209 kg LNG/kW/h

P^m = Domestic market price of fuel oil = LE 130/tonne

P^e = Export price of fuel oil = \$16.38/bb1 = \$107/tonne

P^g = Domestic market price of natural gas = LE.0.1225/m^3 = LE 150/tonne
export price of natural gas = the export price
of fuel-oil equivalent = 1.22 P^e

Calorific value of fuel oil = 18 300 Btu/1b

Calorific value of LNG = 22 300 Btu/1b

1 tonne = 2204.6 1b

1 tonne of natural gas = 1242 m^3

(a) Fuel cost at domestic market prices:

f^m = $[0.2 \times (0.255 \times P^m) + 0.8 \times (0.209 \times P^g)] \times 10^{-3}$
= $[0.2 \times (0.255 \times 130) + 0.8 \times (0.209 \times 150)] \times 10^{-3}$
= $[0.2 \times 33.15 + 0.8 \times 31.351] \times 10^{-3}$ = LE 0.003171 = \$0.000946

(b) Fuel cost at world market prices:

f^e = $[0.2 \times (0.255 \times P^e) + 0.8 \times (0.209 \times (1.22 \times P^e))] \times 10^{-3}$
= $[0.2 \times (0.255 \times 107) + 0.8 \times (0.209 \times (1.22 \times 107))] \times 10^{-3}$
= $[0.2 \times 27.285 + 0.8 \times 27.285] \times 10^{-3}$ = S0.027285 = LE 0.091474

2(a) Capital Cost – Generation:

We assume the capital cost of a reasonable size steam plant is \$600 per kW/h of capacity. We further assume the average load factor = 70 per cent (this is based on data from EEA *Annual Statistical Report 1992/93*, p. 55).

Capital cost per kW/h produced annually:

$$(\$600/365) \times 24 \times 0.7 = \$0.097847$$

We assume a 5-year construction period, with a stream of outlays as follows (based on best practice in this area):

Year	% outlays	Outlay/kW	Present discounted cost (at 10% discount)
1	10	0.009785	0.008895
2	15	0.014677	0.010024
3	30	0.029354	0.022054
4	30	0.029354	0.020049
5	15	0.014677	0.00911
Total	100	0.097847	0.070135

We assume the productive life of a steam power plant is 35 years. Then it is required to recoup this construction cost over the productive years 6 through 40 inclusive. This calls for solving the equation:

$$R / \sum_{6}^{40} (1.1)^{I} = 0.070135$$

where R is the capital cost per kW/h produced. Solution using Lotus 123 gives:

$$R = \$0.007272/\text{kW/h produced.}$$

2(b) Capital Cost – Transmission and Distribution (T&D)

We assume that the cost of transmission and distribution is approximately 15 per cent of capital charges for generation.[6] Thus, transmission and distribution costs will be:[7]

$$= \$\ 0.007272 \times 0.15 = \$\ 0.001091/\text{kW/h.}$$

3. Cost of Operation and Maintenance (O&M)

This is assumed to be 15 per cent of the total capital cost of generation, transmission and distribution. This gives ($0.007272 + $0.001091) × 0.15 = $0.001254.

Let us pull together the various elements of the cost of electricity.

1 (a)	Fuel cost at *domestic market prices*	= $0.000946
1 (b)	Fuel cost at *world market prices*	= $0.027285
2 (a)	Capital cost – generation	= $0.007272
2 (b)	Capital cost – T&D	= $ 0.001091
3	Operation and maintenance	= $0.001254

Total cost: (a) at domestic market prices = $0.010563 = LE 0.035413
(b) at world market prices (economic cost) = $0.036902 = LE 0.123715

It may be interesting to compare the estimates obtained above of the LRMC of electricity to the actual production cost and average selling price of electricity. According to the EEA data for 1992/93:[8]

Total production cost	= LE 2168.119 million
Total electricity generated	= 47096.3 million kW/h
Total electricity sold	= 41988.4 million kW/h
Average cost per kW/h generated	= LE 0.046
Average cost per kW/h sold	= LE 0.052
Average sale price ultra-high voltage	= LE 0.063
Sale price to EGYPTALUM	= LE 0.068

On the basis of these figures, we may conclude that for 1992/93 the sale price of electricity ultra-high voltage is slightly higher than half the economic cost – given the exchange rate and world prices of fuel. However, it appears that EGYPTALUM was already being charged a price for electricity which was almost double the total cost at the domestic market price of fuel.

NOTES

1. The cost is put at $7/tonne to southern Europe for all products except LPG, where the cost is $20/tonne.
2. Egyptian premium gasoline is equivalent to European regular (= 90 per cent octane). Because regular gasoline FOB Italy is not quoted, the price difference between premium and regular gasoline FOB NW Europe is subtracted from the price of premium gasoline FOB Italy.

3. To account for the quality differential between jet kerosene quoted in Italy and regular kerosene produced in Egypt.
4. Natural gas is not yet exported from Egypt. Its world price will then be taken to equal the world price of fuel oil equivalent, i.e. the world price of a quanity of fuel oil having the same calorific value as a given quantity of natural gas.
5. The decline was from 0.269 kg foe/kW/h to 0.259 kg foe/kW/h. The rate of decline was 1.25 per cent per year, which applied on 0.259, the rate of 1991/92. See EEA, *Annual Report of Electricity Statistics* 1992/93, p. 32.
6. Other sources use a higher ratio. For example, a USAID 1979 energy subsidy study uses 25 per cent based on Callahan memo: 'Electric Power Costs in Egypt', dated 15/5/1977. The reason we are using a lower ratio for the cost of T & M relates to the development of the national electricity gird.
7. This may be dropped if EGYPTALUM is given the choice to produce its own electricity needs in-house.
8. EEA, *Annual Report of Electricity Statistics,* 1992/93, p. 47 for production cost and p. 43 for selling price.

Bibliography

Abdalla H., 1995, 'Prospects of Energy in the Arab World, with Special Reference to Egypt', Conference of Egyptian Economists, Cairo, December.

Abdela'tty Wafa', 1990, *Productivity in Manufacturing*, Preliminary Report S13, CAPMAS Labour Information System Project, December.

Abdel-Khalek, Gouda, 1982, 'Growth prospects of the Egyptian economy in the 1980s in the light of the experience of the 1970s', paper presented to the 7th Conference of Egyptian Economists, 6–8 May.

Abdel-Khalek, Gouda, 1987, *Stabilization and Adjustment Policies and Programmes; Country, Study 9 Egypt*, Helsinki, World Institute for Development Economic Research (WIDER).

Abdel-Khalek, Gouda, 1988, 'Income and Price Elasticities of Energy Consumption in Egypt: A Time-Series Analysis', *Energy Economics*, 10(1), January.

Abdel-Khalek, Gouda, 1990, 'Managing Economic Activity in the Context of an Effective Role for the Government', a working paper discussed in Symposium on Developing the Government Role in Economic Activity, Center for Economic and Financial Research and Studies, Faculty of Economics, Cairo University, February, mimeo.

Abdel-Khalek, Gouda, 1991, 'Economic Implications of the Iraqi Invasion of Kuwait: A Strategic Perspective', Center for Economic and Financial Research and Studies, Cairo University, Working Paper No. 10, April.

Abdel-Khalek, Gouda, 1994, 'Egypt's ERSAP: the Orthodox Recipe and the Alternative', in Gouda Abdel-Khalek and Hanaa Kheir-El-Din (eds), *Economic Reform and its Distributive Impact*, Cairo: Dar Al-Mustaqbal Al-Arabi.

Abdel-Khalek, Gouda, 1998, 'Domestic Public Debt: Magnitude Structure and Consequences', background paper to the Egypt Human Development Report 1997–98, published in *Research Paper Series*.

Abdel-Khalek, G. and R. Tignor (eds), 1982, *The Political Economy of Income Distribution in Egypt*, New York: Holmes & Meier.

Abdel-Rahman, M.H., 1992, 'Study of Increasing Steel Production Capacity of HADISOLB to 1.45 Million Tonne Annually', MDCI, October (Arabic), mimeo.

Abou Zeid, M.M., 1990, 'Study and Analysis of HADISOLB Conditions and Feasibility of Shifting from Direct to Continuous Casting of Slabs', MDCI, November (Arabic), mimeo.

Aggag Mahmoud, A.H., 1991, 'Strategy of EGYPTALUM for the Coming Ten Years', MDCI, November (Arabic), mimeo.

Ahmed, Sadiq, Amar Bhattacharya, Wafik Grais and Boris Pleskovic, 1985, 'Macroeconomic Effects of Efficiency Pricing in the Public Sector in Egypt', World Bank Staff Working Papers, No. 726.

Alderman, H. and J. von Braun, 1984, 'The Effects of the Egyptian Food Ration and Subsidy System on Income Distribution and Consumption', *IFPRI Report* 45, July.

Ali, Mohamed M.H., 1993, 'Comparing the Economics of the Current Product Mix with an Alternative Mix for HADISOLB', MDCI, June (Arabic), mimeo.

Amin, Galal, 1987, 'Problems of Economic Adjustment and Development in Egypt', in Said El-Naggar (ed.), *Adjustment and Development in the Arab Countries* (Arabic), Abu Dhabi: Arab Monetary Fund.

Assaf, Mohamed, F.H., 1993, 'Reducing the Cost of Electric Energy at HADISOLB', MDCI, June (Arabic), mimeo.

Banuri, Tariq (ed.), 1991, *Economic Liberalization: No Panacea. The Experience of Latin America and Asia*, Oxford: Clarendon Press.

Bator, Francis M., 1958, 'The anatomy of market failure', *Quarterly Journal of Economics*, August.

Bhagwati, Jagdish, 1986, 'Rethinking Trade Strategy', in John P. Lewis and Valeriana Kallab (eds), *Development Strategies Reconsidered*, New Brunswick, NJ: Transactions Books.

Blejer, Mario I. and Leonardo Leiderman, 1981, 'A monetary approach to the Crawling–Peg system: theory and evidence', *Journal of Political Economy*, 89(1).

Central Agency for Organization and Administration (CAOA), 1985, *Statistical Bulletin*, Cairo: CAOA.

CAPMAS, 1978, *General Census of Population and Housing: Population*, Detailed Results, Country Total, Ref. No. 93/15111/1978, Cairo, September.

CAPMAS, 1983, *Statistical Yearbook–Arab Republic of Egypt, 1952–1982*. Cairo: CAPMAS.

CAPMAS, 1985, *A Study of the Labour Market in Egypt: The Industrial Sector*, Cairo: CAPMAS (Arabic).

CAPMAS, 1990, *General Census* 1986, Final results, vol. 2, Ref. No. 863/90/amt, Cairo.

CAPMAS, 1993, *Measuring Inflation Trends in Egypt*, January, Cairo: CAPMAS (Arabic).

Cardoso, Eliana, 1996, 'Lessons from the Mexican Crisis for Reforming Economies', ECES Distinguished Lecture Series, Cairo.

Central Bank of Egypt (CBE), *Annual Report*, various volumes.

Central Bank of Egypt, n.d., *Report on Monetary and Credit Conditions*, 1991/92, submitted to the People's Assembly.

Cline, William and Sidney Weintraub (eds), 1981, *Economic Stabilization in Developing Countries*, Washington: The Brookings Institution.

Corden, W.M., 1984, 'Booming sector and Dutch disease economics: survey and consolidation', *Oxford Economic Papers*, 36.

Davies, Stephen P., Donald C. Mead and James L. Seale Jr., 1992, 'Small scale manufacturing enterprise in Egypt', *Economic Development and Cultural Change.*

Dervis, K. et al., 1984, 'Policy Analysis of Shadow Pricing. Foreign Borrowing and Resource Extraction in Egypt', WB Staff Working Paper, No. 622, January.

Dorfman, Robert, et al., 1958, *Linear Programming and Economic Analysis*, New York: McGraw Hill.

Dornbusch, Rudiger, 1973, 'Devaluation, money and nontraded goods', *AER*, 63(3), December.

Dornbusch, Rudiger and F. Leslie C. Helmers (eds), 1988, *The Open Economy, Tools for Policymakers in Developing Countries*, New York: Oxford University Press for the World Bank.

El-Edel, Reda, 1982, 'Impact of Taxation on Income Distribution: An Exploratory Attempt to Estimate Tax Incidence in Egypt', in Gouda Abdel-Khalek and Robert Tignor (eds), *The Political Economy of Income Distribution in Egypt*, New York: Holmes & Meier Publishers, Inc.

El-Issawy, Ibrahim H., (ed.) 1988, *Future of the Public Sector in Egypt*, Cairo: Institute of National Planning (Arabic).

El-Khawaga, Abla, 1996, 'External Shocks in Egypt: Application of the Theory of Dutch Disease', unpublished Ph.D. thesis, Faculty of Economics and Political Science, Cairo University.

El-Rifaie, Faika, 1992, 'Inflation Mechanisms and Exchange-rate Policy in Egypt', in Hanaa Kheir-El-Din (ed.), *Inflation Mechanisms in Egypt*, Cairo: Faculty of Economics (Arabic).

El-Shawarby, Sherine, 1997, 'Analysis of the Macroeconomic Effects of the Economic Reform Programme in Egypt Using an Econometric Model', unpublished Ph.D. thesis, Faculty of Economics and Political Science, Cairo University (Arabic).

El-Sheikh, Salah I., 1980, 'An Econometric Model of Egypt', Ph.D. thesis, Queen's University, Kingston, Ontario, Canada.

Fawzi, Samiha, 1993, 'Impact of economic reform policy on investment: case of industrial private sector in 10th of Ramadan City', *l'Egypte Contemporaine*, 84(431) (January).

Fishlow, Albert, 1991, 'Some Reflections on Comparative Latin American Economic Performance and Policy', in Banuri (ed.).

Gelb, Alan and Associates, 1988, *Oil Windfalls: Blessing or Curse?* New York: Oxford University Press for the World Bank.

Girvan, Norman, 1980, 'Swallowing the IMF medicine in the Seventies', *Development Dialogue*, 2.

Grjotheim, K. and B.J. Welch, 1980, *Aluminium Smelter Technology: A Pure and Applied Approach*, Dusseldorf: Aluminium-Verlag.

Handoussa, Heba, 1992, 'The Burden of Public Sector Employment and Remuneration: the Case of Egypt", in Wouter van Ginneken (ed.), *Government and Its Employees: Case Studies for Developing Countries,* published by Avebury for ILO.

Handoussa, Heba, 1991, 'Reform Policies in Egypt's Manufacturing Sector', ch. 4 in Heba Handoussa and J. Potter (eds), *Employment and Structural Adjustment: Egypt in the 1990s*, Cairo: AUC Press.

Hansen, Bent, 1991, *The Political Economy of Poverty, Equity and Growth: Egypt and Turkey*, Oxford: Oxford University Press for the World Bank.

Hansen, Bent and Samir Radwan, 1982, *Employment Opportunities and Equity in Egypt*, Geneva: ILO.

Hassan, Mahmoud Sh., 1992, 'Studying the Feasibility of Reducing Anode Blocs and Paste', MCDI, November.

Helleiner, Gerald K., 1985, 'Stabilization Policies and the Poor', Working Paper No. B.9, Dept. of Economics, University of Toronto, April.

IMF, 1985, 'ARE: Staff Report for 1985 Article IV Consultations', SM/85/17, 24 June.

IMF, 1991, 'Arab Republic of Egypt: Staff Report for the 1991 Article IV Consultation and Request for Stand-by Arrangement', 26 April.

IMF, 1993, 'Arab Republic of Egypt: Staff Report for the 1993 Article IV Consultation and Request for Extended Arrangement', August 24.

IMF, 1997, 'Arab Republic of Egypt: Staff Report for First Review Under the Stand-By Arrangement', 18 March.

Itoh, Motoshige and Karubara Kiyono, 1988, 'Foreign Trade and Direct Investment', in Ryutaro Kominya et al. (eds), *Industrial Policy in Japan*, New York: Academic Press.

Jansen, Karel (ed.), 1983, *Monetarism, Economic Crisis and the Third World,* London: Frank Cass.

Jones, Leroy P., 1981, 'Executive Summary: Improving the Operational Efficiency of Public Industrial Enterprise in Egypt', prepared for USAID, Cairo, September, mimeo.

Katseli, Louka T., 1985, 'Devaluation: a critical appraisal of the IMF's policy prescriptions', *AER*, 73, 2.

Killick, Tony (ed.), 1985, *The Quest for Economic Stabilization: the IMF and the Third World*, London: Gower.

Korayem, Karima, 1982, 'Distributing disposable income and the impact of eliminating food subsidies in Egypt', *Cairo Papers in the Social Sciences*, **5**, Monograph 2 (April 1982).

Korayem, Karima, 1986, *The Impact of Economic Adjustment Policies on the Vulnerable Families and Children in Egypt*, The Third World Forum, Middle East Office and UNICEF (Egypt).

Korayem, Karima, 1993, *Structural Adjustment and Reform Policies in Egypt: Economic and Social Implications*, United Nations, The Economic and Social Commission for Western Asia (ESCWA), 21 October.

Krueger, Anne O., 1978, *Liberalization Attempts and Consequences*, Cambridge, Mass.: Ballinger.

Krueger, Anne O., 1986, 'Problems of Liberalization', in A. Choksi and D. Papageorgiou (eds), *Economic Liberalization in Developing Countries*, Oxford: Basil Blackwell.

Krugman, Paul R., 1986, 'Introduction: New Thinking about Trade Policy', in Krugman (ed.), *Strategic Trade Policy and the New International Economics*, Cambridge, Mass.: MIT Press.

Leibenstein, Harvey, 1978, *General X-Efficiency Theory and Economic Development,* New York: Oxford University Press.

Linder, Staffan B., 1961, *An Essay on Trade and Transformation*, New York: John Wiley & Sons.

Little, Ian M.D., Tibor Scitovsky and Maurice F. Scott, 1970, *Industry and Trade in Some Developing Countries: A Comparative, Study*, New York; Oxford University Press.

Maciejewski, Edwar B., 1983, '"Real" effective exchange rate indices: a re-examination of the major, conceptual and methodological issues', *IMF Staff Papers*, 30(3), 1984, September.

Massad, Carlos and Roberto Zahler, 1984, 'The adjustment process in the eighties: the need for a global approach', *CEPAL Review*, 23.

McKinnon, Ronald I., 1973, *Money and Capital in Economic Development*, Washington, DC: The Brookings Institution.

McKinnon, Ronald I., 1991, *The Order of Economic Liberalization: Financial Control in the Transition to a Market Economy*, Baltimore and London: The Johns Hopkins University Press.

Michaely, M. et al. 1991, *Lessons of Experience in the Developing World*, vol. 7 in Demetris Papageorgiou et al. (eds), *Liberalizing Foreign Trade*, Cambridge, Mass.: Basil Blackwell.

Ministry of Industry, 1986, *Reform of the Price System for Public Enterprises*, Cairo, mimeo.
Ministry of Industry, 1998, *Industry and Industrial Investment Incentives in Egypt*, (prepared by Salwa Soliman et al.), Cairo: The Ministry. (Arabic).
Ministry of Planning (MOP), 1992a, *Preliminary Frame of the Third Five-year Plan for Economic and Social Development (1992/93–1996/97),* Part Two: Sectoral Picture, Cairo, February
Ministry of Planning (MOP), 1992b, *The Third five-year Plan for economic and Social Development* (1992/93–1996/97). Part One: Main Aggregates, Cairo, April.
Ministry of Planning (MOP), 1992c, *Industrial Development in Egypt: Evaluation of the Role of the Five-year Plan 82/83–86/87 and the Five-year Plan 87/88–91/92*, prepared by Abdel-Monsef El-Gayyar, August.
National Bank of Egypt (NBE), 1985, *Economic Bulletin*, XXXVIII(1).
Osman, A.A.-R., 1990, 'Some Controlling Factors of Aluminium Industry and Measures to Deal with the Present and the Future with Application to EGYPTALUM', MCDI, November (Arabic).
Pack, Howard and Larry E. Westphal, 1986, 'Industrial strategy and technological change: theory vs. reality', *Journal of Development Economics*, 22(1).
Papanek, Gustav, 1981, *Industrial Development in Egypt: An Overview*, prepared for USAID, Cairo, August.
Ramos, Joseph, 1985, 'Stabilization and adjustment policies in the Southern cone, 1974–83', *CEPAL Review*, 25.
Sachs, Jeffery, 1996, 'Achieving Rapid Growth: the Road Ahead for Egypt', *Distinguished Lecture Series 3, ECES*, Cairo.
Salvatore, Dominick, 1995, *International Economics*, 5th ed. Engelwood Cliffs, NJ: Prentice Hall.
Scitovsky, Tibor, 1954, 'Two Concepts of External Economies', *Journal of Political Economy*, 62(2).
Shafik, Nemat, 1992, 'Private investment and public policy: the Egyptian case', Ch. 4 in Ajay Chibbar, Mansour Dailami and Nemat Shafik (eds), *Reviving Private Investment in Developing Countries: Empirical Studies and Policy Lessons,* Amsterdam and London: North-Holland.
Shoura Council, 1982, *Report on the Public Sector*. Cairo.
Shoura Council, 1984, *Report on Egyptian Balance of Payments,* Cairo.
Shoura Council, 1985[a], *Investment Policies during the Period 1959/60–1982/83*. June
Shoura Council, 1985[b], *Report on Price Policies*, Cairo.
Shoura Council, 1992, *Wastage in the Egyptian Economy*, Cairo.

Sisson, Charles A., 1986, 'Fund-Supported Programs and Income Distribution in LDEs', *Finance and Development*, vol. 23, no. 1 (March)

Taylor, Lance, 1991, 'Economic Openness: Problems to the Century's End', in Banuri (ed.).

Ten Kate, Adriaan, 1992, 'Trade liberalization and economic stabilization Mexico: lessons of experience', *World Development*, 20(5).

USAID, 1979, 'Food and Energy Subsidies in 1979', Cairo, mimeo.

Williamson, John, 1982, *The Lending Policies of the International Monetary Fund*, Washington, DC: Institute for International Economics.

Williamson, John, 1983, 'On seeking to improve IMF conditionality', *AER*, 73(2), May.

World Bank, 1983 *ARE: Issues of Trade Strategy and Investment Planning*, Report No. 4136 – EGT, 14 Jan.

World Bank, 1984, *Investment Plan Review: Industrialization in Egypt, Performance and Policies,* Washington, DC, October.

World Bank, 1985, *ARE: Current Economic Situation and Medium Term Prospect*, Washington, DC, 18 March.

World Bank, 1987, *Egypt: Review of the Finances of the Decentralized Public Sector,* Report No. 6421 – EGT, 2 volumes, Washington, DC, March.

World Bank, 1990a, *Poverty Alleviation and Adjustment in Egypt*, Washington, DC.

World Bank, 1990b, *The Middle East Crisis: Possible Consequences for the Global Economy*, Washington, DC, mimeo.

World Bank, 1991, *Report and Recommendations of the President of IBRD to the Executive Board on a Proposed SAL in an Amount Equivalent to US$300 Million to the ARE*, Report No. P-5560–EGT.

World Bank, 1992, *Egypt: Financial Policy for Adjustment and Growth,* Report No. 10790/EGT, 3 volumes (30 October).

World Bank, 1993, *The East Asian Miracle: Economic Growth and Public Policy*, Oxford University Press for the World Bank.

World Bank, 1995, *Arab Republic of Egypt, EGYPT – Into the Next Century*, Washington, DC: The World Bank, 2 volumes, 26 May.

World Bank, 1997, *Arab Republic of Egypt, Country Economic Memorandum*, Washington, DC: The World Bank. 4 volumes.

World Bank, 1998, *World Development Indicators 1998*. CD-ROM.

Zaytoun, Mohaya A., 1991, 'Earnings and the Cost of Living: An Analysis of Recent Developments in the Egyptian Economy', in Handoussa and Potter (eds).

Index

Abdel-Khalek, G., 2, 18, 20, 42, 44, 52, 57, 61, 85, 94, 158, 160, 162
Abdel-Rahman, M.H., 137
Abou Zeid, M.M., 133, 134, 143, 144, 145
absorption-reducing effects, devaluation, 28
advance import deposit rate, 82
aggregate demand, 14, 29, 89
agricultural products, pricing of, 6, 19–21, 22, 28, 29, 50
Alderman, H., 15
aluminium industry
  energy prices, impact of increases on, 116–23, 163–4
  impact of devaluation on, 123–5
  microeconomic impact of ERSAP, assessment of, 128–30
  origin and development, 113–15
  output prices, impact of liberalizing on, 125–8
  overview of, 112–13
Amin, G., 42
annual export quotas, 82
anti-dumping measures, 88, 162
appreciation of Egyptian pound
  impact on competitiveness, 159
  impact on savings rate, 89, 162–3
  in relation to aluminium industry, 128
  in relation to devaluation, 68–77, 125, 158
  in relation to industrialization, 160–61
  resulting from inflation, 54
arbitrage, interest, 70–71, 75, 86, 159
Assaf, M.F.H., 133, 145
asset substitution, 2, 9–10
Aswan
  High Dam, 1, 113, 116, 120
  mines, 134
Authorized Banks' Pool, 22, 61

balance of payments, impact of exchange rates liberalization, 62–4
Banuri, T., 87
berseem (clover), 19, 32, 156
Bhagwati, J., 78, 86
bilateral trade-and-payments agreements, termination of, 2, 5, 64
black market, foreign exchange, 8, 34
Blejer, M., 72
broad beans, 19, 36
budget deficit
  1980s crisis, 44
  1987 IMF Stand-by Agreement measures, 27, 28, 29, 30
  impact of devaluation, 6
  impact of ERSAP, 45, 51–2, 53, 58–61, 157
  in relation to interest rate increases, 12
    see also current account deficit; domestic public debt; fiscal deficit
business sector, socio-economic importance impact of pre-1990s stabilization measures, 32, 36
  see also private sector; public sector

Cairo Electricity Distribution Company, 133, 138
capacity utilization, iron and steel industry, 135–6, 140, 141
capital
  capital-goods imports, in relation to cost-push inflation, 66
  capital-intensive industry, 105–8 *see also* iron and steel industry
  capital-intensive technology, 100–101
  capital–labour ratio, 104–9
  capitalization, iron and steel industry, 137

caution needed in liberalizing financial markets, 166
deepening, 98, 107–8
formation, manufacturing industry, 95
market, 9–12, 83–4
mobility, 22–5, 46, 54, 68–77, 84, 85–6, 88–9, 159–60, 162
CAPMAS, Labour Force Sample Survey (LFSS), 31–2
Cardoso, E., 89
cathode current efficiency, 116, 129
cell voltage, 119
Census of Annual Industrial Production (CAIP), 97–109
Central Bank of Egypt
foreign-exchange market intervention, 62, 71–2, 92–3, 97
treasury bills stock, 45–6
centrally controlled prices
in aluminium industry, 125–8
compulsory delivery quota system, 27, 36, 50, 77–8
chemicals industry, 64, 101, 105
'clipping class', 32, 36, 46, 73, 158
clover (*berseem*), 19, 32, 156
coke, price of and impact of increases, 124–5, 133, 138, 140–41, 143–5, 148–9
competitiveness, of Egyptian manufacturing industry, 6, 49, 62–4, 67, 74, 75, 98–100, 141, 145, 159
compradors, 32, 36
compulsory delivery quota system, 27, 36, 50, 77–8
consumption binge, resulting from appreciation of Egyptian pound, 163
Corden, W.M., 52, 95
cost
cost/price distortions, 17–22, 28–9
see also 'international' energy prices
cost-push inflation, 15, 28, 34, 66, 158
of living, impact of devaluation on, 64, 67
of production *see* production costs
see also 'international' energy prices
cotton industry, 1, 19–20, 50, 101
countervailing duty mechanisms, 88, 162
credit
ceilings, 2, 13–14, 29, 34, 35–6, 70
letters of, 82
'crowding in' hypothesis, 53, 103, 151, 165
'crowding out' hypothesis, 53, 85, 103, 165, 166
currency
speculation, 8, 71, 89
substitution, 75, 163
current account deficit, 43, 53, 58–61, 156, 157
see also budget deficit; domestic public debt; fiscal deficit
current efficiency ratio (CER), 118, 119
customs
duties, 2
exchange rate, revaluation, 81

declared parallel-market exchange rate, 3, 8–9
de-dollarization, 9, 71, 75, 163
deepening industrialization, 129
deflationary measures, 36, 140, 151–2
de-industrialization, 22, 37, 53, 88, 95, 96, 162
see also tertiarization of economy
demand
deflation, 36, 140, 151–2
demand-pull inflation, 15
pre-1990s stabilization measures, effects of, 33–7
Dervis, K., 18
devaluation
1970s measures, macroeconomic effects of, 3–9, 15, 17, 18, 20
1980s measures, approach and impact, 22–5, 26, 28–9
effect on domestic production costs and cost of living, 64–7
ERSAP measures, overview of, 46–7
inflationary pressures associated with, 15, 28–9
impact on wages, 34–5
nominal, as against real, 67–77
in relation to Egyptian manufacturing industry, 92, 97, 123–5, 140, 141, 152–3, 158–9, 163

in relation to trade liberalization, 83, 156
see also exchange rate liberalization
devaluation-cum-unification *see* devaluation
direct energy requirements
aluminium production, 122
steel production, 133–4
dirty float, Egyptian pound, 46
dollar peg, 64, 159
dollarization, 6, 28, 42, 46, 156
domestic energy prices *see* energy prices
domestic interest rates *see* interest rate liberalization
domestic public debt, 2, 51–2, 72, 85–6, 159–61, 162
see also budget deficit; current account deficit; fiscal deficit
domestic price liberalization *see* price
domestic production costs *see* production costs
Dornbusch, R., 6, 52
drinks industry, 101
dumping, due to import liberalization, 140
see also anti-dumping measures
Dutch disease, 57, 83, 94, 95, 152, 156, 159, 160

East Asia, financial crisis, 164
economic growth, in relation to 1987 IMF Stand-by Agreement, 27–30
see also GDP
economic reform strategy
in the 1990s, 42–54, 55–6
pre-1990 changes in, 33, 37
see also ERSAP (Economic Reform and Structural Adjustment Programme)
economies of scale, 87
EFF (Extended Fund Facility), IMF (1978), 2, 14–17, 20–21, 155, 161
efficiency
considerations relating to impact of ERSAP measures, 14, 45, 157–8
in relation to electricity industry, 116–23
in relation to energy use in iron and steel industry, 141–8
Egypt Electricity Authority (EEA), 148
EGYPTALUM (The Aluminium Company of Egypt) *see* aluminium industry
Egyptian pound *see* appreciation, of Egyptian pound; devaluation
electric foundries, Nag's Hamady, 114
electric steel, 143
electricity
prices, 49, 112, 116–23, 124–5, 133, 138–41, 145–8, 161, 163, 176–9
requirements, manufacturing industry, 113–15, 128–9, 133–4, 138–9, 141–3
see also energy prices
El-Edel, R., 15
El-Issawy, 97
El-Khawaga, A., 57, 74, 95, 159
El-Rifaie, F., 61
El-Sheikh, S.I., 5
employment generation, manufacturing industry, 92, 95, 96, 97, 100, 103, 105, 107, 136–7
see also unemployment
energy-intensive industry *see* aluminium industry; iron and steel industry
energy prices
distortion of, 17–19, 26, 49, 92–3, 108–9, 116–23, 124, 147–8, 161, 174–6
impact on manufacturing industry, 53, 112–25, 128–30, 138–48, 163–4
see also coke; electricity; natural gas; oil
energy requirements *see* energy prices: impact on manufacturing industry
equity, considerations relating to impact of stabilization measures, 14, 15, 19, 45, 85–6, 157–8
ERSAP (Economic Reform and Structural Adjustment Programme)
aluminium industry, microeconomic effects on, 115–30
foreign exchange reform, macroeconomic effects, 61–77
iron and steel industry, microeconomic effects on, 139–53
main elements of, 44–51
nature and effects, assessment, 51–4, 88–9

prelude to, 42–4, 57–61
in relation to future industrialization of Egypt, 155–66
trade liberalization, macroeconomic effects, 77–88
exchange rate liberalization
1973–97 regime and changes, 46–7, 161–4
impact on aluminium industry, 123, 128
nominal exchange rate anchor, 83, 159–60
post-ERSAP, real effective exchange rate (REER), 67–77
precedence given to reform of over economic reform, 42
pre-ERSAP, stabilization measures, 2–9
see also devaluation
exchange risk, 85, 88
'excise tax' effect, 18, 141
exports
annual export quotas, 82
export bans, elimination of, 78
impact of exchange rate liberalization, 62–4, 66, 161
import liberalization at expense of, 83, 151–2
of oil, 4–5, 58
in relation to Egyptian manufacturing industry, 6, 91, 92, 95, 96, 125, 126, 134
Extended Fund Facility (EFF), IMF (1978), 2, 14–17, 20–21, 155, 161
external shocks, impact of, 29–30, 57–61, 156–7, 166
external trade, component of 1970s reforms, 2

factor proportions/intensity, 104–9, 136–7
Fawzi, S., 66
fertilizer subsidies, 46, 151
financial deepening, resulting from interest rate increases, 9
first five-year-plan (1982/83–1986/87), 92–7, 114
fiscal deficit
post-ERSAP, 58–61, 157
pre-ERSAP, 2–5, 12, 14–15, 43, 156
socio-economic impact of reducing, 34, 35–6
see also budget deficit; current account deficit; domestic public debt
fiscal policy
in 1970s reforms, 2, 14–17
in relation to ERSAP, 44–5, 73, 162–3
see also monetary policy
Fishlow, A., 52, 87
fix-price rule, tradable commodities, 5–6, 34
floating exchange rates, 46, 67
food
and food-processing industry, 101, 103, 104, 105, 108
imports, in relation to cost-push inflation, 66
subsidies, 15, 17, 46, 151
foreign currency reserves, 159–60
foreign exchange market, liberalization of *see* exchange rate liberalization
foreign trade liberalization *see* trade liberalization
fossil fuels, use of in production of electricity, 121
fuel oil, price of, 26
full employment, 86
see also unemployment

GATT (General Agreement on Tariffs and Trade), 54
GDP
decline following oil-related shocks, 156
ERSAP goals, 45
over early years of ERSAP, 58
pre-ERSAP, overview, 2–5, 27, 42–3
in relation to labour, 161
share of agriculture in, 20–21
share of Egyptian manufacturing industry in, 22, 92–6
share of imports in, 66
see also economic growth
Gelb, A., 95
government
bonds, 12 *see also* treasury bills
expenditure, importance of for sustainable reform, 165–6
procurement, 6, 20, 27, 52–3

sector, impact of stabilization measures, 31, 34, 52–3, 100, 161
see also public sector
Grjotheim, K., 119
Guidida mines, Bahariya oases, 103, 104
Gulf crisis (1990), 44, 157
Gulf Organization for Development in Egypt (GODE), 2, 25, 29

HADISOLB *see* iron and steel industry
Handoussa, H., 31, 32, 34, 42, 97, 100
Hansen, B., 34, 36, 57, 95
Harmonized System of Commodity Classification, 78
Hassan, M.Sh., 122
Hecksher-Ohlin model, 86
High Aswan Dam, 1, 113, 116, 120
high performing Asian economies (HPEs), 87–8
Household Budget Survey, 15
hydroelectric power, 113–14, 120

idle capacity, 42, 53, 140, 141, 135–6, 137–8
IMF stabilization packages, Egypt
1962 credit facility agreement, 1, 155, 156
1977 Stand-by Agreement, 2, 155, 156
1978 Extended Fund Facility (EFF), 2, 14–17, 20–21, 155, 161
1987 Stand-by Agreement, 22–30, 155
ERSAP *see* ERSAP (Economic Reform and Structural Adjustment Programme)
'implicit' exchange rates, 62–4
imports
impact of exchange rate liberalization, 62–4
import bans, reduction of under ERSAP, 50, 78, 81–4, 162
liberalization, 2, 5, 12, 22, 36, 49, 83, 98, 140, 151–2, 160
manufacturing industry inputs, impact of devaluation on, 123, 124–5
requirements, domestic industry, 64–6
strangulation of, 27, 93
substituting activities, 158, 160
see also iron and steel industry
income generation, manufacturing industry, 107
indirect energy requirements, aluminium production, 122
indirect taxation, 45
industrial output, 91–2
industrial products, domestic price liberalization under ERSAP, 49
industrial structure *see* structure, of Egyptian manufacturing industry
industrialization, sustainability of, 42, 84–8, 129
infitah (open-door policy), 1, 32, 42, 95, 96, 98, 100, 166
see also market
inflation
impact of ERSAP, 53, 54, 58, 73–4, 86, 157
importance of controlling for sustainable reform, 165–6
pre-ERSAP, 2, 3, 6, 12, 14, 15, 43, 156
in relation to devaluation, 28–9, 66
input
imports by manufacturing industry, impact of devaluation, 123, 124–5
prices, effect of liberalizing on Egyptian iron and steel industry, 148–9
subsidies, industrial products, 49
interest rate liberalization
impact on fiscal and monetary policy, 45–6, 162–3
impact of increases on manufacturing industry, 22, 53, 128, 132, 137, 140, 149–51, 158
leading to appreciation of Egyptian pound, 68–77
pre-ERSAP measures, 2, 9–13, 27, 30
precedence given to reform of over economic reform, 42
in relation to capital mobility, 75–7, 84, 159–60
in relation to trade liberalization, 86
socio-economic impact of increases in, 34

'international' energy prices, 17–19, 26, 49, 92–3, 108–9, 116–23, 124, 147–8, 161, 174–6
  see also cost/price distortions
investment
  'crowding in'/'crowding out' theses, 53, 85, 103, 151, 165, 166
  disincentive effects of domestic debt, 85–6
  impact on of interest rate liberalization, 158, 162
  public sector, decline in, 46, 151, 161
  in relation to Egyptian manufacturing industry, 92, 95, 96
  in relation to structural reform, 17
iron and steel industry
  effect of devaluation on, 152–3
  effect of interest rate liberalization on, 149–51
  effect of trade liberalization on, 151–2
  effect of input/output price liberalization on, 148–9
  energy requirements and impact of price increases, 138–48, 163
  overview of, 132, 164
Itoh, M., 87

Jansen, K., 17
Japan, trade liberalization, 87
Jones, L.P., 91

kerosene, price of, 26
Killick, T., 2
Kiyono, K., 87
Korayem, K., 15, 20, 25, 42, 57, 64, 73
Krueger, A.O., 78, 86
Krugman, P.R., 87

labour
  absorption *see* employment generation, manufacturing industry
  Labour Force Sample Survey (LFSS), CAPMAS, 31–2
  market, in relation to stabilization programmes, 98–100, 161
  migration, from agricultural sector, 21, 34–6, 98, 100
  training, importance of in aluminium industry, 129–30
    see also wages
'law of one price', 8
leather industry, impact of devaluation, 64
Leiderman, L., 72
letters of credit, 82
Linder, S.B., 37, 87
Little, I.M.D., 86
London Metal Exchange, 115, 123, 125, 130, 164
long-run effects of ERSAP measures, aluminium industry, 112–13

machinery industry, impact of devaluation, 64
macroeconomics
  1970s reforms, effects of, 3–22
  ERSAP, thrust and effect of, 44–7, 57–89
  macro indicators of health of manufacturing industry, 92–7
maize production, 19
manufacturing industry
  1980s decline in, 27
  competitiveness of, 6, 49, 62–4, 67, 74, 75, 98–100, 141, 145, 159
  cost/price distortions, 21–2 *see also* 'international' energy prices
  impact on wages of pre-1990s stabilization measures, 34
  macro indicators, 92–7
  overview of, 91–2
  structure of, 97–109
    see also aluminium industry; industrialization; iron and steel industry
market
  failure, 87
  mechanism, deference to, 1, 37, 52–3, 155, 166 *see also infitah*
maxi-devaluation *see* devaluation
McKinnon, R.I., 9, 12, 13, 83, 84, 85
mechanization, 108
metal and metal products industry, 100, 101–3, 105, 107, 108
Mexico, debt crisis, 54, 71, 84, 88–9, 160, 165, 166
Michaely, M., 82, 83, 84, 86, 160
microeconomic effects of ERSAP
  in relation to aluminium industry, 112–30

in relation to iron and steel industry, 132–53
monetarism, as basis for credit ceilings, 13–14
monetary policy, 2, 45–6, 73, 162–3
see also fiscal policy
monopolies, public – phasing out under ERSAP, 51

Nag'a Hamady *see* aluminium industry
national savings, fall in resulting from real appreciation, 89, 162–3
natural gas, price of, 26, 49, 116, 124, 133, 138, 147, 174–6
neoclassical view of trade liberalization, 86–7
'noise', in capital stock data, 104
nominal devaluation as against real, 67–77
see also devaluation
nominal effective exchange rate (NEER), 66–77, 83, 159–60
nominal interest rates, 9, 13
see also interest rate liberalization
non-demand deposits, impact of interest rate increases, 9
non-metallic and mineral product industry, 101, 103, 104–7
non-tariff barriers, 50, 77–8, 80, 81–4, 128, 152, 160, 162
non-tax revenue, 157
non-tradable products
cost/price distortions, 19–21
move towards investment in, 57, 74, 77, 95, 156, 159, 160, 164

oil
boom (1979–81), 22, 96
depletion, 18, 19, 141, 148, 160
exports, 4–5, 58
price distortions, 17–19, 92–3, 108–9, 116, 147–8, 174–6
related shocks, 25, 57–8, 96, 156
open-door policy, 1, 32, 42, 95, 96, 98, 100, 166
Osman, A.A.-R., 113
output prices, impact of liberalization on manufacturing industry, 125–8, 148–9
'overborrowing syndrome', 84, 85–6, 158
overdraft, iron and steel industry, 134, 137, 150, 162, 164
oxygen steel, 143

Pack, H., 87
Papanek, G., 91
paper industry, 64, 107
parallel-market exchange rate, 3, 8–9, 46
Paris Club, 29, 51–2
peasantry, nature of and socio-economic impact of early stabilization measures, 32, 36
petroleum products, 'world price', 108–9, 116, 124, 147–8, 161, 174–6
Ponzi finance scenario, 85
pre-baked cells, 119–20, 121, 122
price
distortion, energy, 17–19, 26, 49, 92–3, 108–9, 116–23, 124, 147–8, 161
of energy *see* energy prices
leverage, in relation to energy use in iron and steel industry, 142, 143–8, 163
liberalization, impact of, 49–50, 73–4, 125–8
see also cost/price distortions
printing and publishing industry, 64, 100, 105, 107
prior approvals, exports, 82
private sector
ownership, pattern of in Egyptian manufacturing industry, 98–101
reform, as part of ERSAP, 50–51, 155
socio-economic impact of pre-1990s stabilization measures, 34–6
wage labour in, 31–2 *see also* wages
privatization, 101, 103, 161
procurement, government, 6, 20, 27, 52–3
product
diversification, 129, 163, 164
mix, 51, 114–15
production costs
aluminium industry, impact of devaluation on, 123–5, 129–30
effect of devaluation on, 64–7
impact of interest rate increases, 12

profitability of steel industry, impact of interest-rate liberalization, 149–51, 153
protectionism, high performing Asian economies (HPAEs), 87–8
see also non-tariff barriers; tariffs
public-sector
business, overview of, 32
cost/price distortions, 21–2
ERSAP bias against, 52–3, 155
investment in, impact of ERSAP, 46, 151, 161
ownership, pattern of in Egyptian manufacturing industry, 98–101
Public Business Sector Law, 47–9
reform, 47–9, 96–7
in relation to fiscal deficit, 15
wage labour in, 31, 34, 36

quantitative restrictions, dismantling, 160
see also non-tariff barriers; tariff barriers
questionnaire results, HADISOLB officials, 139–41
quotas, 27, 36, 50, 77–8, 128, 162

Radwan, S., 34, 36
real devaluation, as against nominal, 66–77
see also devaluation
real effective exchange rate (REER), 3–9, 67–77, 83, 88–9, 161
see also exchange rate liberalization
real estate, 95, 164
real exchange rate, 3–9, 67–77, 83, 88–9, 161
see also exchange rate liberalization
real interest rates, 9, 162
see also interest rate liberalization
real wages, 67, 75, 98
see also wages
recession, danger of in relation to 1987 IMF Stand-by Agreement, 29
recycling, aluminium scrap, 120
rentiers, 32, 36, 46, 73, 158
rent-seeking behaviour, 82
rescheduling of debt, under ERSAP, 51–2
resource depletion, 18, 19, 141, 148, 160, 170–73
revenue
aluminium industry, impact of devaluation on, 125
tax, 45, 157
rice production, 19–20, 36

sales tax, 53, 80–81, 140, 141, 157
Salvatore, D., 70
Scitovsky, T., 87
second five-year-plan (1982/83–1986/87), 92–7
sequencing and stability, in relation to ERSAP, 84–8
service
employment, iron and steel industry, 137
sector, share in GDP, 94
shadow price, 170–73
see also aluminium industry
Shafik, N., 53, 103
shocks, 29–30, 57–61, 156–7, 166
short-run effects of ERSAP measures, aluminium industry, 112–30
sinter, 133, 148
Social Fund for Development (SFD), 44, 50–51
socio-economic analysis of pre-1990s stabilization packages
impact on social groups, 33–7, 161
social matrix, overview of, 30–33
Soderberg cells, 119, 121
South Korea, stabilization-liberalization programme, 84, 87
Southern Cone countries, stabilization-liberalization programme, 54, 84, 88
speculators, 8, 71, 89
stabilization experience before 1990s, 1–37, 40–41
steel industry *see* iron and steel industry
sterilization, of capital inflows, 72, 73, 85, 162
stock
accumulation, in iron and steel industry, 136, 152, 153
capital, 104–5
structural adjustment *see* ERSAP (Economic Reform and Structural Adjustment Programme)
structural reform *see* IMF stabilization packages, Egypt

structural rigidities, 52–3
structure, of Egyptian manufacturing industry
  factor proportions/intensity, 104–9, 136–7
  impact on of trade liberalization, 86
  overview, 97
  public and private sector ownership, pattern of, 98–101
  types of industry, 101–4
subsidies, 2, 15, 17, 19–20, 34, 36, 37, 46, 151
Suez Canal dues, 25, 58
sugar cane production, 19–20
supply-side measures, pre-1990s – effects of, 33–4
sustainability of liberalization programme, 83, 84–8, 89, 160–66

tariff reform, as part of ERSAP, 47, 50, 78–81, 82, 128, 152
taxation
  modifications to included in Extended Fund Facility, 14
  revenues, 45, 157
technically unattainable capacity, iron and steel industry, 137–8
technology
  capital-intensive, 100–101
  non-tradability of, 87
  technological change, pace of, 108
Tequila effect, 165
tertiarization of economy, 94, 159
  see also de-industrialization
textile industry, 81, 100, 101, 103, 104, 105, 107–8
Tignor, R., 20
time deposits, impact of interest rate increases, 9
tobacco industry, 101–3
tourism, 58, 95
tradable products
  cost/price distortions, 19–21
  declining investment in, 5–6, 74, 83–4, 95, 156, 159, 164
  import requirement, 64–6
trade liberalization
  effect on Egyptian iron and steel industry, 132, 145, 151–2
  impact of ERSAP measures on aluminium industry, 128
  non-tariff barriers, 81–4
  overview, 37, 77–8
  in relation to devaluation, 3, 156
  in relation to import liberalization, 2, 5, 12, 22, 36, 49, 83, 98, 140, 151–2, 160
  sequencing and stability, 42, 53–4, 84–8, 162
  tariff reform, 47, 50, 78–81, 82, 128, 152
transition costs, trade liberalization, 86, 87
transport equipment industry, impact of devaluation, 64
treasury bills (TBs), 45–6, 68–70, 72, 73, 85, 158
types, of manufacturing industry, 101–4

unemployment, 42–3, 86, 156
  see also employment generation, manufacturing industry
unification of exchange rate *see* exchange rates
unions, in relation to public and private sector workers, 31, 32
USAID, report on manufacturing industry efficiency, 108, 116
utilities, public, 95

value added, in relation to viability of manufacturing industry, 92, 95, 96, 98, 101–3, 129, 130, 161, 164
viability, of aluminium industry, 129, 163, 163–4
von Braun, J., 15

wage labour *see* labour
wages, 25, 31–2, 34–5, 37, 58, 67, 75, 98
wealth effect, of devaluation, 6, 28, 29, 156, 158
Welch, B.J., 119
Westphal, L.E., 87
wheat production, 19–21, 36, 52–3, 156
Williamson, J., 2
wood and furniture industry, 64, 105, 107
World Bank, 1, 17, 18–19, 52, 78, 87–8, 91, 108, 116, 137

see also ERSAP (Economic Reform and Structural Adjustment Programme)

X-efficiency, 108, 129, 140, 142–3

Zaytoun, M., 34